Invading Iwo Jima on February 19, 1945, U.S. Marines of the 5th Division inch their way up a steep beach front of soft volcanic sand in the shadow of Mount Suribachi. The invasion of Iwo, bringing the Americans to within 660 miles of Tokyo, signaled the beginning of final preparations for the invasion of Japan itself.

THE ROAD TO TOKYO

Other Publications:
THE ENCHANTED WORLD
THE KODAK LIBRARY OF CREATIVE PHOTOGRAPHY
GREAT MEALS IN MINUTES
THE CIVIL WAR
PLANET EARTH
COLLECTOR'S LIBRARY OF THE CIVIL WAR
LIBRARY OF HEALTH
CLASSICS OF THE OLD WEST
THE EPIC OF FLIGHT
THE GOOD COOK
THE SEAFARERS
HOME REPAIR AND IMPROVEMENT
THE OLD WEST
LIFE LIBRARY OF PHOTOGRAPHY (revised)
LIFE SCIENCE LIBRARY (revised)

For information on and a full description of
any of the Time-Life Books series listed above,
please write:
Reader Information
Time-Life Books
541 North Fairbanks Court
Chicago, Illinois 60611

This volume is one of a series that chronicles in
full the events of the Second World War.

WORLD WAR II · TIME-LIFE BOOKS · ALEXANDRIA, VIRGINIA

BY KEITH WHEELER
AND THE EDITORS OF TIME-LIFE BOOKS

THE ROAD TO TOKYO

WORLD WAR II

Editorial Staff for *The Road to Tokyo*
Editor: Gerald Simons
Designer: Thomas S. Huestis
Text Editors: Brian McGinn, Henry Woodhead
Staff Writers: Susan Bryan, Dalton Delan,
Kumait Jawdat, Robert Menaker, John Newton,
Teresa M.C.R. Pruden
Chief Researcher: Oobie Gleysteen
Researchers: Loretta Y. Britten, Charlie Clark,
Frances R. Glennon
Copy Coordinators: Eleanore W. Karsten,
Peter Kaufman, Victoria Lee
Art Assistant: Elizabeth Reed
Picture Coordinator: Alvin L. Ferrell
Editorial Assistant: Connie Strawbridge

Special Contributor
Robin Richman (pictures)

Editorial Operations
Design: Ellen Robling (assistant director)
Copy Room: Diane Ullius
Production: Anne B. Landry (director), Celia Beattie
Quality Control: James J. Cox (director), Sally Collins
Library: Louise D. Forstall

Correspondents: Elisabeth Kraemer-Singh (Bonn);
Margot Hapgood, Dorothy Bacon (London); Miriam
Hsia, Susan Jonas, Lucy T. Voulgaris (New York);
Maria Vincenza Aloisi, Josephine du Brusle (Paris);
Ann Natanson (Rome); Susumu Naoi, Katsuko
Yamazaki (Tokyo). Valuable assistance was provided
by: Jay Brennan and Nakanori Tashiro, Tokyo. The
editors also wish to thank: Judy Aspinall, Lesley
Coleman, Karin B. Pearce, Pat Stimpson (London);
Carolyn T. Chubet, Christina Lieberman (New
York); Mimi Murphy (Rome); Miwa Natori, Eiko
Fukuda (Tokyo).

The Author: KEITH WHEELER was a reporter for a South
Dakota newspaper, a war correspondent for the Chicago *Daily Times* and on the staff of *Life*. While covering the war in the Pacific for the *Daily Times*, he was
critically wounded at Iwo Jima. He has published a
number of novels and nonfiction volumes, among
them *The Pacific Is My Beat* and *We Are the Wounded*. He is the author of five books in Time-Life Books'
Old West series: *The Railroaders*, *The Townsmen*,
The Chroniclers, *The Alaskans* and *The Scouts*.

The Consultants: COLONEL JOHN R. ELTING, USA (Ret.),
is a military historian and author of *The Battle of
Bunker's Hill*, *The Battles of Saratoga* and *Military
History and Atlas of the Napoleonic Wars*. He edited
*Military Uniforms in America: The Era of the Ameri-
can Revolution, 1755-1795* and *Military Uniforms of
America: Years of Growth, 1796-1851*, and was asso-
ciate editor of *The West Point Atlas of American Wars*.

HENRY H. ADAMS is a retired Navy captain who served
aboard the destroyer U.S.S. *Owen* in the major campaigns of the central Pacific. A native of Ann Arbor,
Michigan, he graduated from the University of Michigan and received his M.A. and Ph.D. degrees from
Columbia University. After his service in World War II
he was a professor at the U.S. Naval Academy in Annapolis, Maryland, and was later head of the English
Department at Illinois State University. His books in-
clude *1942: The Year That Doomed the Axis*, *Years of
Deadly Peril*, *Years of Expectation*, *Years to Victory*
and *Harry Hopkins: A Biography*.

ROBERT SHERROD, author of several books about
World War II, covered the War from its beginning
for *Time* and *Life*. His experience was tied closely
to the events described in this volume: He landed
on Iwo Jima with the 4th Marine Division and on
Okinawa with the 6th, flew combat missions from
carriers in dive bombers and torpedo bombers and
endured some "frankly frightening" experiences
while dodging Kamikazes.

Library of Congress Cataloguing in Publication Data

Wheeler, Keith.
   The road to Tokyo.

   (World War II; v. 19)
   Bibliography: p.
   Includes index.
   1. World War, 1939-1945—Pacific Ocean.
2. World War, 1939-1945—Naval operations, American.
3. World War, 1939-1945—Naval operations, British.
4. World War, 1939-1945—Aerial operations, Japanese.
I. Time-Life Books.   II. Title.   III. Series.
D767.W46   940.54'26   79-8508
ISBN 0-8094-2540-8
ISBN 0-8094-2539-4 lib. bdg.
ISBN 0-8094-2538-6 retail ed.

CONTENTS

THE FLEET'S ATTACK BASE

Advancing U.S. power toward Japan, aircraft carriers, battleships and cruisers sweep in line into the Ulithi atoll, a new naval base 3,700 miles west of Hawaii.

ULITHI ATOLL: "THE NAVY'S SECRET WEAPON"

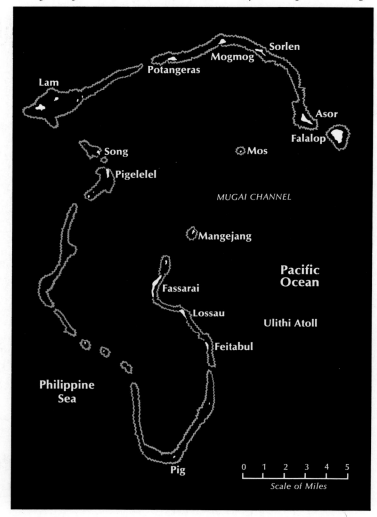

Ulithi's lagoon, 20 miles long and 10 miles wide, was entered from the east through Mugai Channel. Patrol boats led warships to assigned moorings.

On September 22, 1944, only one month after U.S. Marines had wrested the Mariana Islands from Japanese defenders at a terrible cost, a small American invasion force took the next giant step on the road toward the Japanese homeland at no cost whatsoever. A regiment of soldiers slid ashore in rubber boats on a tiny palm-dotted island in the Ulithi atoll in the western Caroline Islands. There they learned from friendly inhabitants that the Japanese garrison had departed weeks before.

Ulithi was not much to look at. It consisted of 30-odd islets, all of them low, flat and—at a casual glance—useless. But together with fringing coral reefs, the islets formed a huge rough oval that enclosed and sheltered a deep lagoon. Here was a natural anchorage that could accommodate hundreds of ships at one time. And the best of it was that Ulithi lay only 1,500 miles from Japan, 900 miles from Iwo Jima, 1,200 miles from Okinawa.

With work, the atoll would make an ideal forward base for future naval operations. Indeed, Admiral Chester W. Nimitz, the commanding officer of all Allied forces in that part of the Pacific, would call that base "the Navy's secret weapon," and his censors would make sure that no reporter divulged the secret.

By October 1, the atoll was the scene of massive activity. Working at fever pitch, Seabee battalions enlarged one islet with sand fill and built causeways on sunken gravel-filled pontoons. The construction teams then covered three islets with roads, piers, workshops, a headquarters complex, airstrips and living quarters for a peak staff of 7,000 men. Service ships of all kinds poured in from Pearl Harbor and the Eniwetok atoll in the Marshall Islands to repair and maintain the fighting Navy. Seabees unloaded up to 300 tons a day of the "beans, boots and bombs" that funneled in from Hawaii and ports in California and Washington.

The basic work was completed ahead of schedule in November, and by then a large flotilla of battleships, carriers and destroyers was in the harbor seeking supplies. Ulithi was ready to join the War.

In a small portion of the vast Ulithi lagoon, busy service ships ply among scores of anchored warships, scattered freighters and a squadron of flying boats.

American planes of all types line a 3,500-foot airstrip on Falalop, one of Ulithi's biggest islets. The Seabees enlarged a crude airstrip built by the Japanese.

Shirtless Marine mechanics labor over the engine of a Corsair fighter.

Ground crewmen admire a row of Helldiver bombers parked on Ulithi.

Towing a long train of 500-pound bombs, a truck moves gingerly over Falalop's rough roads to the airstrip where planes were armed for combat missions.

Propped on sawhorses, plywood infantry landing craft (below) are repaired by the Navy shipwrights on Ulithi. The craft, often damaged in landings on coral reefs, were in constant need of reinforcement and caulking.

Crewmen (above) bring hoses ashore from a small, self-propelled fuel barge that moved along pontoon piers to gas up trucks and bulldozers. Much larger barges were dispatched into the lagoon to fuel the ships not serviced directly by oceangoing tankers and oilers.

Newly completed installations crowd the islet of Sorlen (right), among them repair shops, Quonset hut offices, mess halls, barracks, power generators, communications facilities, a hospital, a chapel and even a theater.

Nesting destroyers, linked by ramps, are serviced by technicians from the large tender on the left—a floating workshop crammed with tools and supplies.

Cranes on a big Navy repair ship take aboard supplies from a smaller vessel in Ulithi's lagoon.

Dangling sailors repaint the bow of an escort carrier while their mates offer unsolicited advice.

Camouflaged aircraft carriers, riding at anchor in the lagoon, form what their crewmen proudly called Murderer's Row. The camouflage was designed to mislead the Japanese as to a ship's true size, type and direction of movement.

Cases of foodstuffs and ammunition are unloaded on the hangar deck of a carrier being stocked for combat duty by Navy stevedores. The ship was scheduled to join up shortly afterward with another carrier and a destroyer, seen moving out in the background.

1

In September of 1944, when Franklin Roosevelt and Winston Churchill met in Quebec for their seventh major conference since the start of World War II, the stress of their responsibilities showed plainly on both men. The Prime Minister was just over his third bout with pneumonia, and the voyage to Canada aboard the *Queen Mary* had failed to restore the color to his face. The President's once-robust frame looked shrunken; the clinical eye of Lord Moran, Churchill's personal physician, judged that Roosevelt had lost about 30 pounds. "You could have put a fist between his neck and his collar," Moran confided to his diary.

Still, the Allied leaders were in excellent spirits. For the first time in their long association, they could say with confidence that they were winning the War and, by straining a bit, could even catch glimpses of the dark road's end.

As Churchill, in jubilation, put it: "Everything we have touched has turned to gold." The Allies had broken out in Normandy and were on their way to the Rhine. Optimists were predicting the collapse of Adolf Hitler's Reich before the year was out. In the Pacific, the inner wall of Japan's defenses had been breached with the taking of the Mariana Islands; the weight of the loss of the key island, Saipan, had toppled the Empire's original war cabinet and its firebrand Prime Minister, Hideki Tojo.

At Quebec's historic castle-fortress, the Citadel, where Roosevelt and Churchill occupied suites, the relaxed atmosphere was underscored by the presence of both leaders' wives. Watching the two couples exchange greetings, one observer was reminded of a happy family reunion.

Somewhat less than perfect harmony prevailed at the nearby Château Frontenac, where the Combined Chiefs of Staff of Great Britain and the United States were quartered. In daily sessions at the hotel, the Chiefs tackled the task of setting the course that the Allied war effort would take from then on, meanwhile trying to resolve their own differences and preparing recommendations to present to Roosevelt and Churchill for their approval. The men who directed the land, sea and air forces of their respective countries were discovering that the prospect of victory in no way simplified the problems of the planning and the strategy required to bring the War to a close.

The final conquest of Japan posed its own special complications. In carrying the War ever closer to the Japanese

MASTER PLAN FOR INVASION

homeland, the attackers would be steadily lengthening their lines of supply from the U.S. West Coast and Pearl Harbor; the burden of moving great masses of matériel would be magnified in direct ratio to the distances involved. Moreover, Japan's remaining strength, and its will to resist, could not be accurately gauged. Finally, among those few American conferees who were privy to the knowledge that their country had nearly completed development of an atomic bomb, there was a haunting sense that conventional ideas about the very nature of warfare might soon be obsolete.

Beyond all these considerations, new political factors had to be taken into account. Thus far, the war in the Pacific had been a largely American affair; now it became necessary to accommodate Britain's sudden desire for a piece of the action. "The time had now come for the liberation of Asia," Churchill later explained, "and I was determined that we should play our full and equal part in it. What I feared most at this stage of the War was that the United States would say in after-years: 'We came to your help in Europe and you left us alone to finish off Japan.' We had to regain on the field of battle our rightful possessions in the Far East, and not have them handed back to us at the peace table."

During a plenary session of the conference, Churchill proposed sending a part of the British fleet to the Pacific to serve under American command. Roosevelt replied magnanimously, "I should like to see the British fleet whenever and wherever possible." But one American present at the meeting was bitterly opposed to the idea of British involvement in the Pacific theater: lean, unsmiling Admiral Ernest J. King, Chief of Naval Operations and Commander in Chief, U.S. Fleet. King was widely held to be the toughest graduate ever turned out by Annapolis. Even Roosevelt held him in some awe, and had been heard to observe that his top-ranking admiral "could chew spikes for breakfast."

King was appalled by the President's ready answer to Churchill, and he tried to fend off a firm decision by noting that the proposition was under study. Stung by this tepid response, Churchill growled, "The offer of the British fleet has been made. Is it accepted?" Roosevelt quickly said, "Yes." One of the British witnesses to the scene later joked that the minutes of the meeting should have read: "At this point Admiral King was carried out."

To King, the idea of a British task force tagging along with the U.S. Pacific Fleet represented a last-minute effort to cash in on a war the American Navy had been fighting for three years. Moreover, he believed that the British ships would be a nuisance and a burden; built and manned to operate close to base, they were unable to stay at sea for the long stretches required in the Pacific. King, in fact, had held the Royal Navy in low esteem ever since an incident in the summer of 1942. Under orders from the Admiralty in London, British commanders charged with escorting an Anglo-American convoy to Russia had withdrawn the protective force, including two American warships under their command, because of a presumed threat by the German battleship *Tirpitz*. As a result, 22 of the 25 merchant ships of the convoy had been sunk, easy prey to prowling German planes and U-boats.

In any event, King knew that the United States already had more than enough navy in the Pacific to take care of what remained of the Japanese fleet, and the last thing that he wanted was a lot of strangers around to clutter up sea room and the structure of command. But all that he could salvage from the conference was a commitment that the British would supply themselves rather than depend on the Americans for sustenance.

King's frustration at Quebec was compounded by an issue that involved only the Americans. For months, at their regular Washington meetings, the U.S. Joint Chiefs of Staff had weighed the question of whether the Philippines were a necessary steppingstone on the road to Tokyo. King had strongly argued that they should be bypassed and that the island of Formosa, 200 miles closer to Japan, should be taken instead, along with a beachhead on the China coast.

The idea of skipping the Philippines outraged General Douglas MacArthur, whose well-publicized pledge to retake the islands was based both on a belief in their strategic value and on a deeply felt commitment to the Filipinos. MacArthur was further incensed when word reached his Southwest Pacific Area Command that King had dismissed his ardent desire to liberate the islands as irrelevant to the efficient winning of the War. In the general's view, the Americans' return to the Philippines was imperative—not only to redeem U.S. prestige in that part of the world, but also to sever Japan's lines of communication with its conquered territories in Southeast Asia. Moreover, MacArthur saw another advantage in retaking Luzon, the Philippines' northernmost island and site of the capital city, Manila. From Luzon, he believed, the Americans could strike directly at Japan, thus speeding up the timetable of the war against the enemy's homeland and eliminating the need for a costly invasion of Formosa.

Undeterred by his remoteness from Washington, the general had waged a skillful campaign to persuade the Joint Chiefs and President Roosevelt that the Philippines were a must. Over the months, to King's annoyance, MacArthur's efforts had gradually borne fruit. In early September, on the eve of their departure for the summit conference at Quebec, the Joint Chiefs had confirmed their go-ahead to MacArthur for an invasion of the Philippines' southernmost island, Mindanao, and had directed him to follow it up with an invasion of the large central island of Leyte.

The Chiefs were at Quebec just two days when, totally unexpectedly, they had more good news to send to MacArthur. While at a formal dinner tendered them by their Canadian hosts, they received a top-secret message saying that carrier-based U.S. Navy pilots probing the skies over Leyte had reported little Japanese opposition, and that Ad-

miral William F. "Bull" Halsey, commander of the Third Fleet, was recommending that the Mindanao invasion be scrubbed in favor of a direct assault on Leyte. The Chiefs—Admiral King among them—left the table for a private parley. The upshot was a directive to MacArthur to launch his Philippines campaign at Leyte and, moreover, to move up the projected date from December 20 to October 20.

A decision was yet to be made as to whether to allow MacArthur to move on from Leyte to his most cherished objective, Luzon. But an exuberant promise by the general to take the island in six weeks was beginning to impress King's colleagues on the Joint Chiefs, and King knew it.

Although his case against the Philippines was clearly lost, he was still determined to press the case for Formosa. As he saw it, and as he had argued again and again in Washington, Americans planted on Formosa and in the port of Amoy on the Chinese mainland would stand astride the South China Sea, Japan's main lifeline to the oil, rubber and other essential resources of Southeast Asia. From Formosa, moreover, the Americans' new B-29s would be able to carry heavier bombloads to Japan than would be possible from the more distant airfields of Luzon. Philippines or no, King remained certain that Formosa and Amoy were the most decisive

positions from which to bring the Empire to its knees.

But he was soon to find that he was now virtually alone in this view. On September 29, two weeks after the Quebec Conference disbanded, he met in San Francisco with the five men directly charged with American land, sea and air operations in the Pacific theater: Admiral Chester W. Nimitz, the overall boss of the theater as Commander in Chief, Pacific Ocean Areas; Rear Admiral Forrest P. Sherman, his plans officer; Admiral Raymond A. Spruance, commander of the Fifth Fleet; Lieut. General Millard F. Harmon, commander of the Army's air forces in Nimitz' zone, and Lieut. General Simon Bolivar Buckner Jr., recently named to command the newly formed Tenth Army.

The meeting, which was held in a secluded conference room at the Federal Building, was marked by an undercurrent of tension. The primary item on the agenda was Formosa, and the men with King had a delicate task to perform. Their goal was to talk him out of the idea of invading the island and to propose an entirely different course of action instead—the invasion of the western Pacific islands of Iwo Jima and Okinawa.

Until recently Nimitz, along with most of the Navy brass, had concurred in King's strenuous espousal of Formosa. Nimitz was no admirer of the majestic MacArthur; in fact, he kept a picture of the general on his desk at Pearl Harbor to remind himself "not to make Jovian pronouncements complete with thunderbolts." But he had gradually swung round to the view that Formosa was neither the best nor cheapest way to get at Japan's belly, and to that extent he was now MacArthur's ally. Nimitz had not come to the meeting empty-handed. He gave King a single sheet of paper setting forth, in tightly drawn summary, the arguments against Formosa and for Iwo Jima and Okinawa.

King studied the document, frowning with obvious dissatisfaction. He turned to Buckner; what didn't he like about Formosa? Buckner cited intelligence reports indicating that Japan's elite Kwantung Army, formerly based in Manchuria, was now garrisoned on Formosa. In his judgment the U.S. would need nine divisions, and might suffer up to 50,000 casualties, to gain a solid foothold on the island.

Nimitz asked Harmon to present the airman's view. As a B-29 base, Harmon said, Formosa posed a serious hazard.

The plan for capturing it—if the United States had to take it now—included only the southwestern part of the island. Bases there would leave the big bombers about as far from Japan as they would be if they were based in the recently seized Marianas; furthermore, in operating from airfields in the lower half of Formosa, the B-29s would have to risk fighter attack from the Japanese-held upper half on their way to and from Tokyo.

King turned to Nimitz. How useful were the two alternative objectives he proposed? The first, Iwo Jima, was a mere smidgen of an island, eight square miles of rock and ash in the Volcano group of the Bonin island chain. Iwo lay only about 660 miles southeast of Tokyo and on the direct route from the Marianas to the Japanese capital. In Japanese hands the island represented a peril to the B-29s that would soon begin flying out of Saipan, Tinian and Guam. But in U.S. possession, Iwo could serve both as a fighter base to support the big bombers en route to Japan and as a haven for any that were damaged during an attack.

Nimitz' second proposed objective, the much larger island of Okinawa, lay in the great arc of half-submerged mountain peaks that make up the Ryukyu island group, southwest of the southernmost Japanese home island of Kyushu. Okinawa—only about 350 miles from Kyushu and less than 1,000 miles from Tokyo—could be a nearly ideal bomber base. Moreover, it had plenty of room. Okinawa and a satellite island, Ie Shima, could support enough airfields to handle about 800 bombers and the necessary fighter escorts.

Okinawa might also accommodate the mountains of supplies, the acres of fuel tanks and the armies of men that would have to be staged forward should the Allies launch an invasion of Japan itself. Nimitz himself did not believe that an invasion of the enemy's own soil would ever become necessary, and he knew that King shared his view; U.S. Navy doctrine held that Japan could be starved into submission without any need to set foot on the home islands. But the Army, Nimitz also knew, held that Japan would never surrender until the homeland was occupied.

After Nimitz had expounded his views, King turned to Admiral Spruance. "Haven't you something to say?" he demanded. "I understand Okinawa is your baby." In fact Spruance had for months been urging both Iwo and Okina-

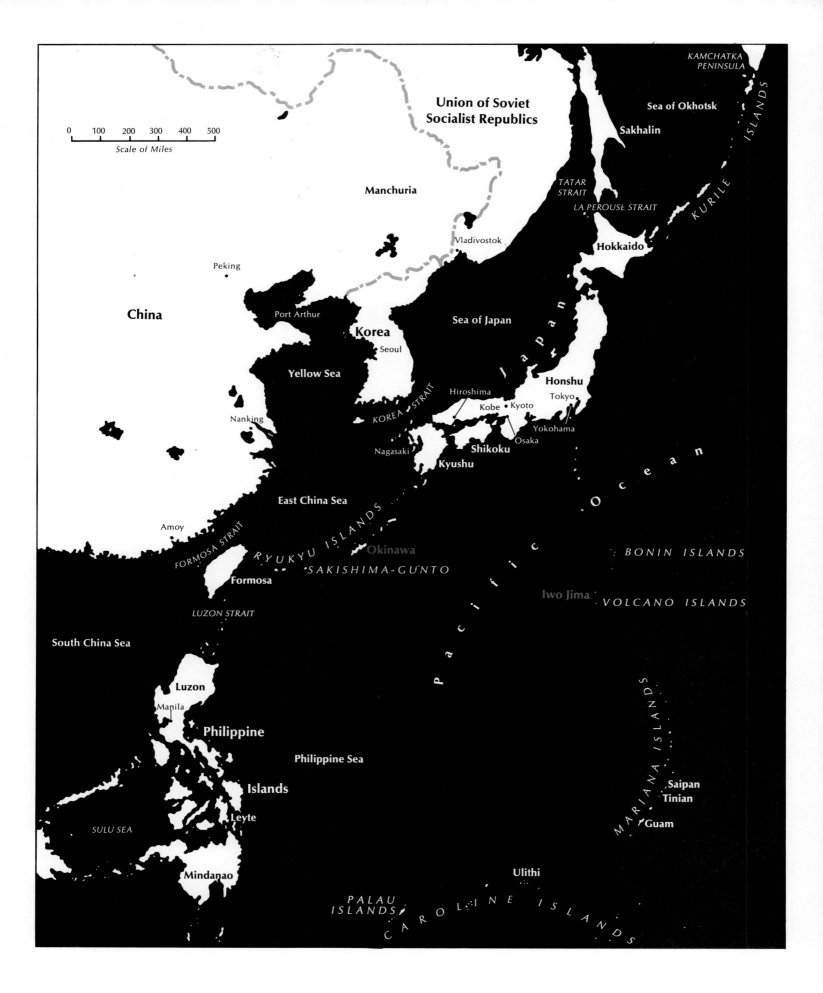

wa. But he was a notoriously diffident man who did not like to raise his voice. At King's question, the commander of the Fifth Fleet smiled and shook his head. Nimitz, he said, was doing fine.

In the end King yielded, at least in part. He would not agree to wipe Formosa off the agenda entirely, but he would consent to taking Iwo and Okinawa first. He would carry the judgment of the conferees to the Joint Chiefs and let them know. None of the six men gathered in San Francisco could have guessed that they had just chosen the sites of the last two major land battles of World War II.

On October 3 the Joint Chiefs of Staff issued a new set of directives. MacArthur, now poised for the assault on Leyte, was instructed to go on to invade Luzon on December 20. Nimitz was instructed to invade Iwo Jima on January 20 and Okinawa on March 1. Before long, however, the timetable proved to be unrealistic. The Luzon invasion had to be put off to January 9, Iwo to February 19 and Okinawa to April 1.

The postponements were forced not only by stiff Japanese resistance on Leyte, but also by a shortage of shipping. With two major campaigns about to open, and with the continuing demands of the war in Europe, the search for cargo space had turned into a fiercely competitive scramble. Even when the bottoms were available, the sheer distances involved in hauling enormous quantities of matériel across the Pacific were a shipper's nightmare. Okinawa, for example—the closest to Japan of the U.S. objectives—lay 6,200 nautical miles from San Francisco; a cargo vessel steaming at 10 knots would take 26 days to make the trip.

Another problem loomed at the delivery end. Past experience had shown that once a theater commander got his hands on a ship he was reluctant to send it back, preferring instead to use it as a local supply shuttle or as a floating warehouse. Such tie-ups could mean paralysis for another operation. The planners of Iwo and Okinawa had a taste of this prospect after MacArthur's forces landed on Leyte on the 20th of October; at one time the general had 221 ships immobilized offshore.

The preparations for Iwo and Okinawa required dealing with some formidable natural obstacles as well. Among the islands of the Pacific there were few harbors worth the name. About the best an off-loading skipper could hope for

was an open roadstead exposed to wind and tide. He was more likely to find a fanged coral reef ready to tear the bottom out of landing craft. Moreover, a swamp, a jungle or a cliff was likely to line the water's edge. To put cargo ashore at all necessitated the use of shallow-draft, flat-bottomed, ramp-bowed landing vessels. Among the various types of craft used for this purpose, the LSTs and LSMs, which had long since become the premium work horses of the War, were now in short supply.

The problem was further complicated by the fact that the Pacific islands did not of themselves furnish much that would be useful to an invading force, nor was there much that could be confiscated from the enemy. The attackers would have to bring with them just about everything they needed to capitalize on their conquests: portable docks, steel matting for runways, sawmill equipment, concrete mixers, cranes, asphalt plants, jeeps, radios, telephones, fuel, food, beer, cigarettes, toilet paper.

And, always and foremost, there had to be bulldozers—to lay the groundwork for all the things that had to be built from scratch: airfields, roads, communications networks, warehouses, oil-storage depots, hospitals, barracks, headquarters. The unremitting demand for fabrication brought into painful focus another perennial shortage of the Pacific war. There were never anywhere near enough carpenters, electricians, machinists, plumbers, stevedores, truck drivers, bulldozer skinners, crane operators or men to run a sheepsfoot roller—the giant machine with hooflike studs that was used to tamp the crushed coral surface of a new runway.

The nuts-and-bolts labor of preparing for Iwo and Okinawa, assigned by Nimitz to his Pacific Ocean Areas staff, was under way within days of his directive from the Joint Chiefs. To amass as much data as possible on what the attackers might encounter, the planners interrogated Japanese soldiers taken prisoner during previous invasions in the Pacific and pored over Japanese documents picked up in the course of those campaigns; they also sifted old issues of Japanese publications that were in hand—examining everything from military analyses to manufacturers' advertisements. From these sources they were able to arrive at some tentative intelligence estimates, but it was clear that more up-to-date information, in a continuing flow, was essential.

Two submarines furnished with special cameras were sent

forth from Pearl Harbor to photograph the beaches and coastal defenses of Iwo Jima and Okinawa. The *Swordfish,* dispatched to Okinawa, never returned from her mission. The *Spearfish* had better luck at Iwo. Photographs taken through her periscope provided a useful estimate of Iwo's coastal defenses and a good enough view of the beaches to permit American scientists to determine the nature of the volcanic soil on which the invaders and their equipment would have to land.

But the main attempt to probe the secrets of the two islands was made from the air. Although this approach had obvious drawbacks—the Japanese were well known for their skill at concealing their defenses in caves and underground tunnels—intensified aerial reconnaissance of Iwo was begun by planes based in the Marianas, while photography of Okinawa was left to planes from U.S. fast carriers.

The U.S. planners already knew a bit about Okinawa's history and a good deal about its approximate size, shape and topography. The Japanese had occupied the island since 1879 and had signaled its importance by making it a prefecture of Greater Tokyo—in effect, an integral part of the homeland. Okinawa appeared to be a natural stronghold. About 60 miles long, it was mountainous in the north, ruggedly hilly in the south and squeezed at the waist to a width of only two miles. Its coastline was a tortured succession of bays, inlets, stream mouths, promontories and peninsulas, so that the whole island suggested a rampant Oriental dragon.

Aside from these facts, current information about Okinawa was scant. Few Americans had set foot on the island since Commodore Matthew C. Perry and his Naval squadron paused there en route to Japan in 1853. After a search, Navy intelligence officers managed to track down, back in the United States, one American civilian who had spent a few years on Okinawa and who furnished some valuable data. But much remained guesswork. Okinawa's civilian population—thought to be about 450,000, mostly farmers—might or might not be a major hindrance when the invasion came. Nimitz' staff could only guess at the size of the military force stationed on the island, and the Americans knew almost nothing about the disposition of the defenses.

When the camera-bearing U.S. carrier planes appeared over Okinawa on the morning of October 10, they were on a bombing mission as well—to blast any Japanese planes and ships that might attempt to disrupt MacArthur's invasion of Leyte 10 days hence. By the time the raid ended at sunset, 1,000 Hellcats, Helldivers and Avengers had sunk at least 15 ships; according to a Japanese report captured later, they had exploded five million rounds of small-arms ammunition, killed a Japanese general and set 300,000 sacks of rice ablaze.

Though the photographic part of the mission produced thousands of pictures, clouds concealed the precise details that the Americans were seeking. They were soon to discover that Okinawa was more often cloud-covered than clear. But after subsequent photographic flights by B-29s from the Marianas, the planners were able to come up with a fairly accurate map of the island.

Aerial reconnaissance of tiny Iwo Jima proved revealing enough to cause considerable concern to the commander of the powerful Fifth Fleet, Admiral Spruance. As repeated flights brought back evidence of steadily expanding defense installations, Spruance began to question the wisdom of assault. A prediction by Marine Lieut. General Holland M. "Howlin' Mad" Smith that the island would cost 15,000 casualties increased the admiral's misgivings; Smith, who was slated to be in charge of the Marine expeditionary force en route to the invasion, loved a fight and rarely aired his worries about possible casualties to come. Spruance also raised the question of the operation's necessity when Major General Curtis E. LeMay, in command of B-29s in the Marianas, visited him on his flagship, the *Indianapolis.* Spruance wanted to know how badly LeMay's bomber command needed the island.

"Without Iwo," LeMay told him, "I couldn't bomb Japan effectively."

"This took a load off my mind," Spruance said later.

In late November, the tempo of preparations for both U.S. assaults began to accelerate. As the earlier of the two objectives, Iwo was first to undergo the preliminary softening-up process. B-29s and B-24s from the Marianas, later joined by carrier planes, hit the island for what was to turn out to be a record of 74 straight days of bombing. Naval bombardment forces also arrived offshore, pouring in a hail of fire from the 16- and 14-inch main batteries of battleships, the 8- and

6-inch guns of cruisers, and the 5-inch guns of destroyers. No island had ever before suffered such methodical punishment as a prelude to invasion.

On December 16, while Iwo was being thus pounded, Admiral Nimitz received a visit at his Pearl Harbor headquarters that he had expected but did not especially welcome. The visitor was Admiral Sir Bruce Fraser, newly dispatched by London to serve as commander in chief of the British Pacific Fleet. Headquartered in Sydney, Australia, Fraser had administrative responsibility for four carriers, two battleships, five cruisers and 15 destroyers—about the strength of one group of the U.S. fast-carrier task force.

The visit of Fraser and his staff was preceded by such a barrage of messages from London and Sydney heralding their arrival that Nimitz dryly observed in a note to Admiral King in Washington: "I do not need Paul Revere (with his three lanterns) to tell me that the British are coming." When the delegation arrived, Nimitz was as usual the soul of courtesy. He had met Fraser 10 years earlier, while both were Naval captains on Far East duty, and now invited him to be his houseguest.

As soon as the two men got down to cases on the purpose of Fraser's visit—settling the matter of how best the British fleet might be deployed in the Pacific—Nimitz was all candor. A question of primary concern had to be answered if Fraser's fleet was to operate with the far-ranging American task forces: how long could the British ships stay at sea without returning to base? Fraser hedged. His fleet now had its own supply train with tankers for refueling at sea, he

said. However, the tankers had limited pumping capacity and used a time-consuming over-the-stern method of refueling that prevented more than one ship from being serviced at a time. British seamen had not yet mastered the American technique of swift, side-by-side refueling, which permitted a tanker to supply, simultaneously, a ship on each side of it. When Nimitz pressed for specifics, Fraser estimated that he could remain at sea "on station"—combat-ready—for eight days a month. Nimitz pressed harder. "We compromised on twenty," he later laconically reported.

Nimitz suggested that, all things considered, the British might most profitably occupy themselves deep in the southwest Pacific, raiding Japanese oil installations on Sumatra. That was far short of what the British had in mind. They wanted a role in the main show—not just to satisfy Churchill's geopolitical reasons but also to exact revenge for the humiliating loss of the battle cruiser *Repulse* and the battleship *Prince of Wales* to Japanese bombers off Malaya in December of 1941. Relenting somewhat, Nimitz allowed that perhaps a useful role could be found for the newcomers in the Okinawa operation, which was then in a somewhat less advanced planning stage than the assault on Iwo. He turned the British over to Admiral Spruance to see if something could be worked out along that line.

Spruance was hesitant about attempting to incorporate the British, with their differing operational methods, into American fleet formations; but he soon came up with a way to oblige them with useful collateral work. Southwest of Okinawa, down toward Formosa, lay Sakishima-gunto, a group of islands where the Japanese were known to maintain sizable air groups. He suggested to Vice-Admiral Sir Bernard H. Rawlings, the tactical commander of the British fleet, that it would be helpful if his task force kept Sakishima quiet. Rawlings gracefully accepted.

The planners of the assaults on Iwo and Okinawa had no doubt that the operations would be costly. Each island was close enough to the heart of the Japanese Empire to guarantee a last-ditch fight by the defenders. Iwo was believed to hold about 15,000 troops, and the size of Okinawa's garrison was certain to be far larger. In both cases, as the Americans saw it, it would be necessary to overwhelm the defenders by sheer mass—bringing to bear more men, more

Admiral Ernest J. King, Chief of Naval Operations (center), meets with Admiral Chester W. Nimitz, commander of the Pacific Ocean Areas (left), and Admiral Raymond A. Spruance, Fifth Fleet commander, aboard Spruance's flagship in July 1944, soon after the conquest of Saipan. King, who was responsible for the Navy's long-range planning, was six feet two inches tall, stiff as a ramrod and given to tough-guy aphorisms, such as, "Difficulties is the name given to things it is our business to overcome."

THE FIRST AMERICAN LANDING ON OKINAWA

The first American landing on Okinawa took place in 1853, almost a century before the Tenth Army stormed ashore under the guns of the Pacific Fleet. The landing was led by Commodore Matthew C. Perry, on his historic mission to open trade relations with Japan, and like later naval strategists he wanted to establish a base on the island before pushing on to Japan proper. "The very door of the empire," was what he called Okinawa.

Quickly, Perry negotiated a short-term lease for a coaling station with Okinawa's local ruler. And the American had more ambitious ideas still. On his return from Japan in 1855, Perry recommended that the U.S. establish a permanent western Pacific Navy base on Okinawa. But his idea fell on deaf ears. Some 24 years later, Japan annexed the strategic island and turned it into a bastion of its ever-growing empire.

Perry stands for a hero's portrait following his return.

Backed by U.S. Marines, Perry and his officers (right) prepare to enter the gates of Shuri Castle, home of Okinawa's ruling family, in 1853.

arms and more firepower than ever before employed in the Pacific war. And most of the invading troops were to be drawn from those already combat tested in the arena, from Guadalcanal to Guam.

For the taking of Okinawa, seven divisions, four Army and three Marine, were to be committed—more manpower than had been involved in the entire North African invasion in 1942. The amphibious operation would require more than 1,300 ships. And U.S. fast carriers would be somewhere near at hand, keeping meddlers at bay with their planes. The assault force alone was calculated to be 182,821 men and 746,850 tons of cargo. It was to arrive in 433 ships, converging on precisely timed schedules from 11 ports all across the Pacific, from Seattle on the West Coast of the United States to Leyte in the Philippines and Guadalcanal in the Solomons. Behind the assault force, scores of thousands of service and garrison troops and millions more tons of cargo were scheduled to arrive at intervals 10 days apart, continuing for 210 days.

Until the assault waves reached the beach at Okinawa, they would be under the charge of Vice Admiral Richmond Kelly Turner, commander of the amphibious force. By now Turner was a virtuoso of amphibious landings; he had been honing the technique ever since the landing at Guadalcanal in 1942. Once the troops were established on land, they would come under the new Tenth Army, commanded by General Buckner. Son and namesake of Lieut. General Simon Bolivar Buckner, a Confederate hero of the Civil War, the 57-year-old general had spent most of the War up to now in charge of the Alaska Defense Command.

Buckner was a career soldier and a stern disciplinarian. As commandant of cadets at West Point in the 1930s, he had wearied his charges by leading them on 35-mile hikes; he had also denied them the use of underarm deodorants on the grounds that a man should smell like a man. More recently, in Alaska, he had earned an awesome reputation for his practice of sleeping under a single sheet whatever the temperature, and for his off-duty hobby of stalking the savage Kodiak bear. Buckner was believed to be a sound infantry technician, but this remained to be demonstrated in the field.

The Iwo Jima operation, scheduled to begin some six weeks before Okinawa, was also to draw on Admiral Turner's expertise in delivering the assault force. The muscle work, the lion's share of the killing and dying, was assigned to 70,647 Marines of two assault divisions, the 4th and the 5th, and one reserve division, the 3rd. Transporting the men would be relatively simple because both assault divisions were in the Hawaiian Islands, while the reserve was even closer by on Guam. Once ashore, the Marines would become the V Amphibious Corps, commanded by Marine Major General Harry Schmidt, who had led the 4th Division in the assault on Saipan.

The invasion of Iwo was to be the largest Navy-Marine operation ever assembled. Admiral Turner's command comprised 485 vessels. To hammer the target, he had eight old battleships, a dozen escort carriers, 19 cruisers and 44 destroyers. To carry the men and their tools, there were 43 transports, 63 LSTs and 31 LSMs. Including the fast carriers, the entire armada would total more than 800 ships. Counting the crews of Turner's ships, those of the fast carriers, and the Army and Navy garrison troops assigned to follow the assault, the Iwo expedition would engage the efforts of more than a quarter of a million men.

In early February, the Iwo Jima attack force was on the verge of moving out when a new and potentially sensitive element was introduced into the complex equation of the war in the Pacific. On the 4th of the month, Roosevelt and Churchill met Josef Stalin on the Soviet dictator's own soil —the resort of Yalta in the Crimea—for a week-long conference intended primarily to settle the shape of postwar Europe, but also to discuss the part Russia would play in the war on Japan.

For months the Americans had been pressing the Russians to join the fight against the Japanese once Hitler was out of the way. Any prospect of the Reich's collapse by the end of 1944 had faded with the Germans' surprise counteroffensive in the Ardennes, but now the Allies were on the move again and Germany's defeat was expected no later than July 1. At Yalta, Stalin finally revealed what he wanted as compensation for striking at the Japanese within three months of the fall of the Reich. The price he quoted was steep. It included, among other items, the return to Russia of the Kurile Islands, held by Japan since 1875, as well as the southern half of Sakhalin and the naval base of Port Ar-

This reconnaissance photograph taken on the 10th of October, 1944, during the first U.S. air raid on Okinawa, gave American strategists a close-up look at the island: the Yontan airfield, which is being bombed by carrier-based planes; the Kadena airfield (left); the Hagushi beaches (upper left); and a neat mosaic of farmers' fields.

thur—both acquired by Japan in its victory over czarist Russia in the war of 1905.

In addition, Stalin implied that if and when the Russians came into the war against Japan they would certainly require a new flow of American Lend-Lease matériel, by way of the Far East. And that requirement, inevitably, would place an extra burden on the shipping capacity of the United States even as American logisticians were struggling to find enough cargo space for the climactic American operation in the Pacific—the actual invasion, by foot soldiers, of the home islands of Japan.

Still, the discussions of the Big Three at Yalta had brought that finale into closer view, and the U.S. Joint Chiefs now had to take a new look at what had thus far been no more than a tentative plan. It envisioned two assaults, respectively code-named *Olympic* and *Coronet,* spaced four months apart. The first projected a landing on Japan's southernmost island, Kyushu. The other called for the subsequent invasion of the main island of Honshu, striking directly across the Kanto Plain toward Tokyo itself.

But Iwo and Okinawa had to be conquered first. On February 16—D-day-minus-3 for Iwo—a task force of U.S. warships commanded by Rear Admiral William H. P. Blandy moved in for the final preinvasion bombardment of the island. The force included six battleships, four heavy cruisers, a light cruiser and 16 destroyers; among the battleships were the *Nevada,* the *Texas* and the *Arkansas,* all veterans of the Normandy invasion, and the 30-year-old *New York,* which had helped cover the North African landings.

Previous assaults on the islands of the Pacific had taught the Navy a vital lesson: area bombardment—the indiscriminate blanketing of an objective—did little good. Instead, Blandy's plan called for the utmost precision. Iwo had been divided into numbered squares, with each square assigned to a specific bombardment ship; in addition, all the known targets, which included blockhouses, pillboxes and "covered structures," were also numbered. As each target was destroyed, it was to be checked off on a master list kept aboard Blandy's command ship.

Of the nearly 700 targets on Iwo, no more than 17 had been ticked off the list by the time the fleet stopped bombarding the island that first day and moved out to sea for the night. Low-hanging clouds had obscured the targets;

pilots from the carrier *Wake Island,* serving as gunfire spotters, had been unable to track the fall of the incoming shells through the overcast.

When Blandy's force returned the next morning, the sky was clearer—and so were the tactics of Iwo's defenders. On the previous day, U.S. minesweepers moving in close to shore in advance of the bombardment had encountered only scattered enemy fire from rifles and light machine guns; now, however, Japanese coastal batteries opened up on them from Iwo's beachside cliffs. A single 150mm gun zeroed in on the cruiser *Pensacola* as she moved in to cover the minesweepers. She was hit six times in three minutes, set ablaze and flooded; the executive officer and 16 men were killed, and 119 were wounded. Several hours later, 13 gunboats covering the approach to shore of Navy demolition teams took a savage pounding from hidden heavy artillery; though the boats completed their mission, their decks were littered with casualties.

On the afternoon of D-day-minus-2, Blandy's battleships and cruisers resumed their bombardment. Carrier planes were called in to strafe the island, and B-24s from the Marianas flew in to drop fragmentation bombs. But that evening an assessment of the day's damage was discouraging; though some satisfaction was gleaned from the fact that the Japanese had been compelled to reveal some gun positions previously unsuspected by the Americans, very few of the defenders' known installations had been destroyed. A decision was made to spend D-day-minus-1 concentrating U.S. fire on the coastal guns and beach defenses, to clear the way for the Marines to land.

The man designated to command them on Iwo, General Schmidt, was undismayed by the prospect of stiff Japanese resistance. Contemplating the massive assemblage of U.S. might all around him, Schmidt predicted that he would secure the island in 10 days. His estimate was as unrealistic as Tokyo's broadcast claim that five American warships, including a battleship, had been sunk off Iwo and the invasion of the island repelled.

One high-placed Japanese was not taken in by this claim. Foreign Minister Mamoru Shigemitsu knew that the invasion was at hand, and knew what it portended. The Iwo operation, he later wrote, "brought home to the Japanese that the war was at their doorstep."

TARGET FOR THE LIBERATORS

Opening the air war against the strategic island of Iwo Jima, one of a force of 18 B-24s drops bombs on Chichi-jima, a way station for supply ships bound for Iwo.

FRUSTRATING RAIDS ON AN UGLY LITTLE ISLAND

For six months starting in August 1944, a frustrating assignment preoccupied the U.S. Seventh Air Force in the Marianas. With increasing frequency, B-24 crews were called out for bombing raids on Iwo Jima, some 700 miles to the north, or on the nearby islands of Chichi-jima and Haha-jima, which supplied Iwo from Japan. The bombers' ultimate objective was to soften up Iwo for the amphibious invasion planned for February 1945. But on each mission, weary crewmen took off in their Liberators knowing that the odds were against their doing serious damage.

Iwo was, as one pilot said, "the most unpredictable target in the Pacific." Roughly half the time, the ugly eight-square-mile island was covered with heavy clouds, leaving the raiders three sour choices: to bomb blind with radar, to come in under the clouds in the face of fierce Japanese antiaircraft fire, or simply to abort the mission.

When the weather cooperated, the B-24s not only had to face antiaircraft fire but also had to fight off swarms of Japanese fighter planes that rose from Iwo's two airfields. Worst of all, the bomber crews could never be sure that they had done any real harm to Iwo's defense systems, the bulk of which were built underground.

After four discouraging months of strikes, bombing was stepped up a notch. In December and January, the B-24s flew 1,836 sorties; after daylight raids, night missions were dispatched to impede the work of Japanese repair crews. Yet the airfields, even though badly damaged, were not put out of operation for as long as a day. The bombers dropped more than a hundred 55-gallon drums of napalm to burn off the clever camouflage concealing Japanese gun emplacements. But even then follow-up bombers missed many of these installations or failed to penetrate deep enough to knock them out.

As the invasion date approached, the raids were stepped up yet again—with the same results. Ultimately, the B-24s dropped nearly 6,000 tons of high explosives on Iwo. But, according to an intelligence officer, all the bombing only made the Japanese defenders burrow deeper underground.

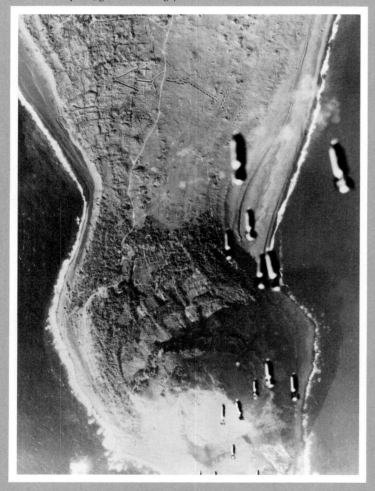

During a November attack on Iwo, bombs from a B-24 plummet toward Mount Suribachi. The bomber crews, who always met furious gunfire from the fortified peak, gave it the angry nickname "Mount Sunovabitchi."

An early intelligence map of Iwo Jima, completed on August 24, 1944, details defenses on the island. To make the map, camera-equipped B-24s took pictures of different sections of the island during the bombing runs of August 17, and a dozen photographs were later pieced together by aerial reconnaissance experts. The superimposed notation "AW" marks the location of automatic weapons; "AA" indicates antiaircraft guns.

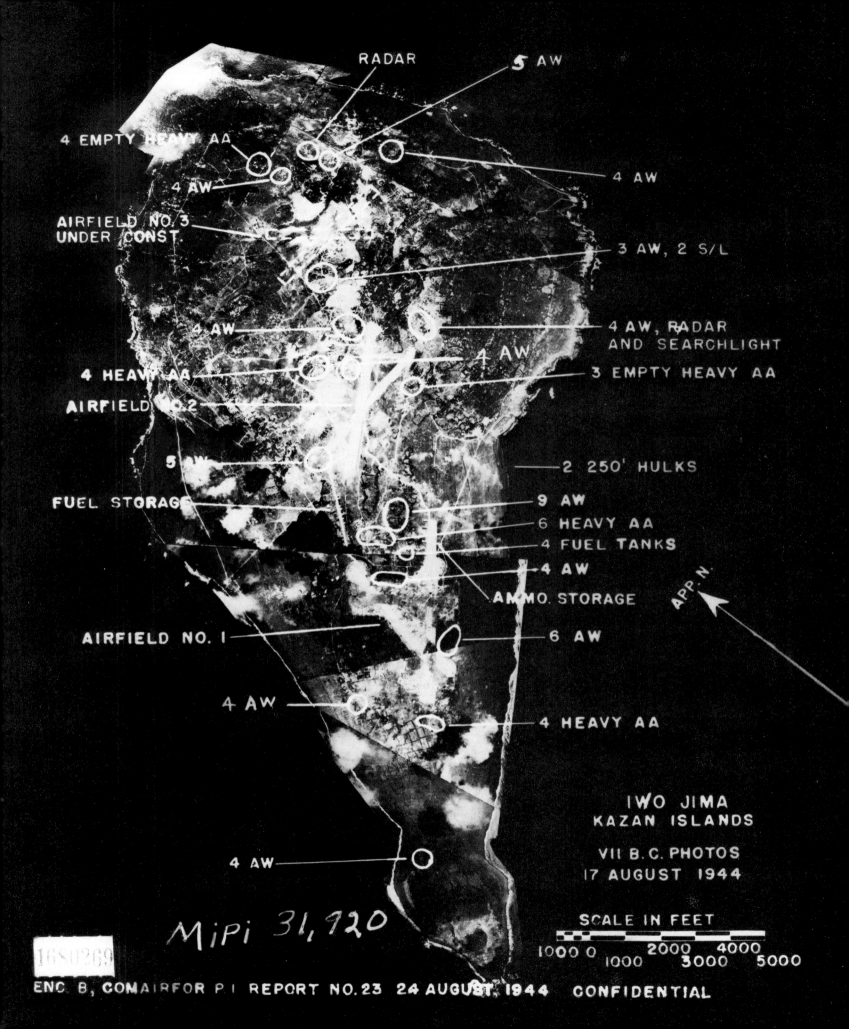

RADAR

5 AW

4 EMPTY HEAVY AA

4 AW

4 AW

AIRFIELD NO. 3
UNDER CONST.

3 AW, 2 S/L

4 AW

4 AW, RADAR
AND SEARCHLIGHT

4 AW

4 HEAVY AA

3 EMPTY HEAVY AA

AIRFIELD NO. 2

5 AW

2 250' HULKS

FUEL STORAGE

9 AW

6 HEAVY AA

4 FUEL TANKS

4 AW

AMMO. STORAGE

APP. N.

AIRFIELD NO. 1

6 AW

4 AW

4 HEAVY AA

IWO JIMA
KAZAN ISLANDS

VII B.C. PHOTOS
17 AUGUST 1944

4 AW

MiPi 31,920

SCALE IN FEET

1000 0   2000   4000
         1000   3000   5000

1680269

ENC. B, COMAIRFOR P.I. REPORT NO. 23 24 AUGUST 1944 CONFIDENTIAL

B-24s crowd a service area on Saipan's uncompleted Isely Field in November 1944. Tents (foreground) housed crewmen before permanent quarters were built.

Getting ready for a night raid on Iwo Jima, ordnance men hoist a 500-pounder into a B-24's bomb bay.

Smoke rises from Japanese planes hit by B-24s on an Iwo airfield. In retaliation, the Japanese from time to time raided the Liberators' bases in the Marianas.

B-24s attempt to strafe a Japanese supply ship hugging the cliffs of Haha-jima. But the Liberators lacked the speed and agility needed to succeed in the task.

Heading home from a raid on Iwo Jima, B-24s pass through a shower of incendiary fragments from two phosphorus bombs dropped by Japanese fighters flying high above. Though this spectacular weapon damaged many planes, it failed to knock down a single Liberator.

2

The private thoughts of a Japanese general
"Every man's position will be his tomb"
Burrowing down into volcanic Iwo
Titanic thunder rolling in from the sea
Nature's own devilish defenses
Monster mortars hurling ash cans of death
"Okay, you bastards. Off this beach."
Rooting the enemy from the heart of Suribachi
A tank named Ateball fights back
Finishing off the Meat Grinder
The B-29 that explained it all
An all-American end gets his revenge
A foredoomed gesture of national honor

Lieut. General Tadamichi Kuribayashi, the garrison commander on Iwo Jima, knew more than most Japanese officers about Americans and their ways. As a captain in the late 1920s, he had taken cavalry training at Fort Bliss in Texas. Later, as military attaché at the Japanese embassy in Canada, he had often revisited the States. These travels had left him with an immense respect for American industry and energy—and with a conviction that he disclosed only to his wife. "The United States is the last country in the world Japan should fight," he wrote her in 1931.

When U.S. Marines went ashore on Saipan in the Marianas in mid-June of 1944, Kuribayashi surmised that it was just a matter of time before he would be doing battle with Americans on Iwo. The island lay only 625 miles north of the Marianas and was a logical prize for the enemy to seek. Small as it was, it had two airfields and a third under construction, from which U.S. planes could conveniently range the western Pacific, hitting Japan and its dwindling outposts at will.

Kuribayashi immediately began preparing for the invasion of his domain. Whatever his admiration for the industrious Americans, he intended to kill as many of them as possible—and by methods as efficient as he could devise.

At the end of June, the general entertained a new staff officer, Major Yoshitaka Horie, at dinner. Horie wielded considerable authority on his own at Chichi-jima, an island 150 miles from Iwo that served as a vital supply funnel. From Chichi, cargoes brought by destroyer and fast transport from Tokyo were transshipped to Iwo in fishing boats and other small craft.

Over dinner the liquor flowed freely, and so did the talk. Kuribayashi asked Horie's opinion of Iwo. Horie had seen enough of it to decide that it was one of nature's lesser triumphs. Though there were some sea birds, it was almost devoid of land birds; he had been unable to spot a single sparrow or swallow on the island. And as a target, Horie had decided, Iwo was as vulnerable as "a pile of eggs."

Ordinarily, the major would have been reluctant to offer his superior officer advice, but in the relaxed atmosphere of the evening he did so, and bluntly. "The best thing to do with Iwo would be to sink it to the bottom of the sea," he said. "It could be done—with enough explosives."

Kuribayashi was none too fond of Iwo himself. It was a

BRUTAL BATTLE FOR IWO JIMA

volcanic ash heap, waterless, barren except for scrub, and it stank of the sulfur deposits that had drawn the Japanese there to begin with. This lone asset, in fact, had given the island the name Iwo Jima—Sulfur Island.

Privately, Kuribayashi may have agreed with Horie that it would be better if Iwo did not exist; in enemy hands it would be a dagger aimed straight at the heart of the homeland. Still, the younger officer's morose dismissal of the island nettled the general. There was a better way to look at it—as a bastion of the Empire, and one that could be made costly in the extreme to its attackers.

"When the enemy comes here we can contain him," Kuribayashi said, "and then our Combined Fleet will come to slap his face."

"There is no longer any Combined Fleet," Horie said. Kuribayashi stared at his guest in astonishment. "You're drunk," he said.

Horie was indeed exaggerating. But his responsibilities involved regular contact with Tokyo, and he was far better informed than Kuribayashi about recent events beyond Iwo. He went on to tell the general about the havoc suffered by Japan's Navy, just a week or so earlier, in a two-day battle off the Marianas in and above the waters of the Philippine Sea. Torpedo hits by U.S. submarines had sunk two Japanese carriers, while U.S. carrier planes had accounted for a third Japanese carrier and damaged four other ships. More than 400 planes, well over half the entire strength of Japan's Naval air arm, had been destroyed.

Horie added other news Kuribayashi had not known, about the ravages inflicted on Japanese shipping by U.S. submarines and the resulting shortages of everything at home—even of food. Kuribayashi was stunned. But he was now more than ever determined to convert Iwo into a rock fortress anchored in the sea. Once the invasion came, Kuribayashi said, "every man will resist until the end, making his position his tomb."

The build-up of Iwo proceeded all through the summer of 1944. The best of Kuribayashi's troops were the 2,700 men of the 145th Infantry Regiment; most of them hailed from the city of Kagoshima on the home island of Kyushu, traditionally a source of superb fighting men. Imperial Headquarters sent in the 109th Army Division, but its largest unit, the 5,000-man 2nd Mixed Brigade, was poorly trained, and many of the officers were overage. A more welcome unit was the 7,600-man 26th Tank Regiment, seasoned in Manchuria. Unfortunately for the Japanese, a ship bearing 28 of the regiment's tanks had been sunk by the U.S. submarine *Cobia*. But Baron Takeichi Nishi, the 26th's commander, was only temporarily discomfited; in time, another 22 tanks arrived. Nishi was a dashing figure, known and admired in the U.S. as Japan's finest horseman; he had won the equestrian gold medal at the 1932 Olympics in Los Angeles, and he still carried a swatch from the mane of his famous jumper, Uranus. Another distinguished officer, Rear Admiral Toshinosuke Ichimaru, a Naval aviator who had been permanently lamed in the peacetime crash of an experimental plane, arrived to take charge of the 7,000 men of Iwo's Naval air and ground forces.

By autumn, Kuribayashi had a total of 21,000 men at his disposal—and a defense plan so radical that it shocked and offended most of his subordinates. He would not fight for Iwo's beaches: From the invasions of Tarawa and Kwajalein, the general knew that pillboxes on a beach stood no chance against the combined weight of an American air, naval and amphibious assault. Nor would he permit suicidal banzai attacks. Instead, his men were to hold out as long as possible; each man was to take 10 American lives for his own.

Kuribayashi's plan called for almost his entire garrison to go underground. The idea was audacious; few places were less suited to subterranean construction than volcanic Iwo. At a depth of about 30 feet, the heat was so intense that it was impossible to work for more than five minutes without returning to the surface for a breather. Nevertheless, a labor force that included hundreds of Korean conscripts was set to digging into the island's rock with every available tool and machine. Engineer specialists in cave fortifications were brought from Japan to lay out the underground works. Cargoes of concrete and reinforcing iron arrived from Major Horie's supply depots on Chichi-jima. A Naval construction battalion came in to cut down quantities of scrub oak to furnish timber supports for the caves. The same fate befell every wooden structure on the island.

Kuribayashi concentrated his warrens inside Mount Suribachi, the 556-foot eminence that commanded the narrow south end of Iwo, and in the tortuous, boulder-strewn ridges and ravines of the north end. Admiral Ichimaru protested these priorities, since they meant that Chidori, the island's largest airfield, from which his fliers would have to operate, was left virtually unprotected. Kuribayashi made a slight concession; the Navy got half of one allotment of concrete, enough to construct 150 pillboxes around Chidori near the beach.

By the start of 1945, Kuribayashi had an intricate underground network of caves, bunkers, command posts and hospitals, connected by 16 miles of tunnels; one tunnel alone was 800 yards long and had 14 entrances. These hidden installations were stocked with food, water and ammunition, provided with electricity and equipped with radio and field telephones for internal communication.

On the surface, the installations terminated in massive concrete blockhouses and pillboxes with earth piled deep around and over them, both for purposes of concealment and as a buffer against bombs and gunfire. In all, Kuribayashi had some 800 gun positions: deeply dug mortar pits with degrees of the compass painted on the walls for guidance in aiming, and blockhouse gun emplacements with firing ports slanted so that they could not be knocked out by direct hits

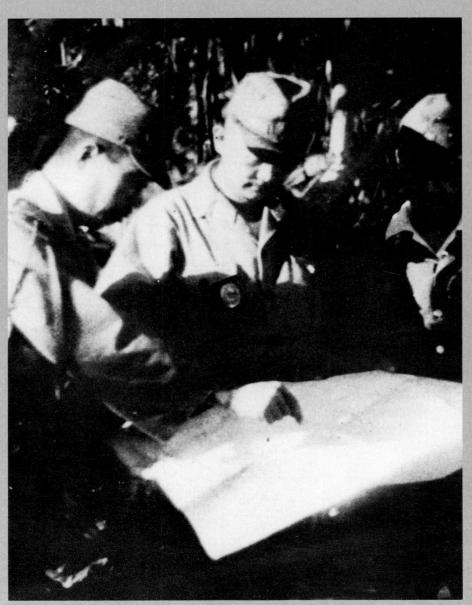

General Kuribayashi (center) scans a plan of underground defenses a-building on Iwo in 1944.

A BEWILDERING MAZE OF UNDERGROUND DEFENSES

The Japanese on Iwo Jima were so thoroughly dug in that little more than the muzzles of their guns showed above the ground; everything else was hidden in a maze of subterranean chambers and connecting tunnels.

Garrison commander Lieut. General Tadamichi Kuribayashi had spent six months supervising the construction of innumerable installations around the island. Mount Suribachi was honeycombed with seven levels of tunnels connecting about 1,000 chambers. The network in the hilly northern quarter of the island had tunnels that branched off to incorporate numerous natural caves. The flat center of the island afforded few natural strong points, and the builders, forced to start from scratch, laid out one section of their underground defenses in a neat grid, as shown in the diagram at right.

In most of the defense systems, multiple entrances allowed the Japanese to mount sudden counterattacks from unlikely quarters. The defenders could outflank advancing Marine units by racing unseen through the tunnels to another entrance in the attackers' rear. In case of naval shelling or aerial bombardment, the defenders could retreat deep into the maze.

Support services for the combat troops were tucked away in well-protected tunnels. Squad rooms and barracks for the enlisted men were sandwiched between storage chambers and kitchens. And for the officers there were comfortable quarters decorated with family photos and portraits of the Emperor.

from the sea. The general himself checked out the positions on his daily rounds of inspection; sometimes, standing at the firing slit of a pillbox, he would raise his swagger stick like a rifle and sight the view.

Iwo's defense build-up went steadily forward in spite of a crescendo of raids by Saipan-based B-24s and, in the late preinvasion stages, by U.S. carrier planes. None of the raids had much effect, except to keep Kuribayashi's men awake.

Kuribayashi himself spent much of his time writing to his family in Tokyo. He did not expect to survive the battle that lay ahead, and his letters were full of husbandly advice and fatherly admonition. He chided his daughter Yoko for her poor grammar and spelling, saying, "In Japan, others will not respect you if you make errors in letters." He fretted over his 20-year-old son Taro's lack of maturity. "Will power is the essence of manhood," he wrote. "You have not yet developed your will, and in your present state you cannot head my household successfully." Kuribayashi's wife, Yoshie, had the benefit of his counsel on what to wear to avoid Tokyo's wintry drafts and how to put the family valuables into safekeeping.

Occasionally, in letters written to his wife, Kuribayashi

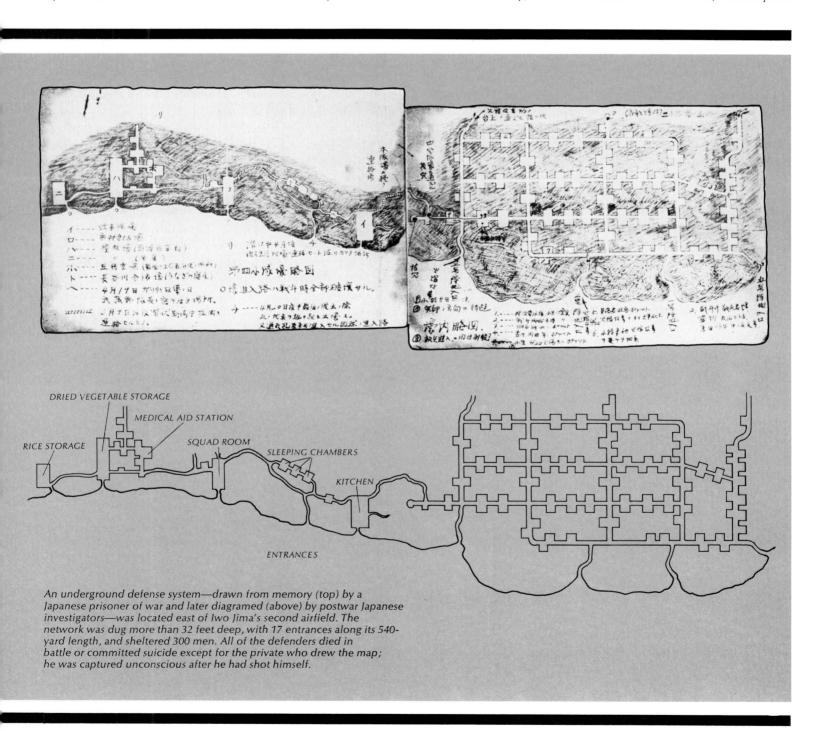

An underground defense system—drawn from memory (top) by a Japanese prisoner of war and later diagramed (above) by postwar Japanese investigators—was located east of Iwo Jima's second airfield. The network was dug more than 32 feet deep, with 17 entrances along its 540-yard length, and sheltered 300 men. All of the defenders died in battle or committed suicide except for the private who drew the map; he was captured unconscious after he had shot himself.

touched on his own situation. "I have lost much weight," he reported. "Somehow I look like Gandhi, the great Indian. The meals consist mostly of dried vegetables, so that I often have a sour feeling in my stomach. We sweat a lot; unfortunately, there is no clear water available here. There are so many flies and mosquitoes that we sometimes cannot open our mouths and eyes."

The general was frank about what he regarded as his certain doom. "It really does not matter much to me where my grave will be," he wrote Yoshie. "If there is really such a thing as soul, then it will stay with you and our children."

February 19, 1945—D-day for Iwo—dawned clear and calm. The hulking gray transports of the invading U.S. armada hove to 10 miles offshore. At 6:40 a.m. the bombardment force, from mighty battlewagons down to small rocket-firing gunboats—"spitkits," the Americans called them—moved in and opened up. All at once, the quiet morning erupted in titanic thunder.

Out at sea, the Marines of the 4th and 5th Divisions began crawling over the rails of the transports and down the high sides, laboriously descending the sagging handholds of the cargo nets into the landing craft below. Now and then, a Marine burdened by a pack that weighed more than 100 pounds lost his footing and fell. The landing craft began to form up in waves. LVTs, the tublike floating tanks known as amtracs, were to go in first; ramp-bowed LCVPs, the so-called Higgins boats, would follow.

Overhead the fire storm of shell and rocket raged on, and Iwo began to disappear from sight under the smoke of the bombardment. Watching from the rail of the transport *Bay-*

field, Robert Sherrod, a correspondent for *Time* and *Life,* reflected that he had never seen a bombardment like it—and he had seen them at Attu, Tarawa and Saipan. "I can't help thinking 'nobody can live through this,' " he jotted in his notebook, "but I know better."

By 7:30 the first waves of LVTs were at the line of departure, two miles off Iwo's southeastern beaches. Just after 8 o'clock the warships stopped shelling to allow 120 low-flying carrier planes to hit the island with napalm, rockets and machine-gun fire. A flight of B-24s from Saipan came across high and unloaded 19 tons of explosives. At 8:25 the naval bombardment force opened up again and in the next 30 minutes hurled 8,000 more shells into the target.

At 8:30 the first wave of 68 LVTs left the line of departure. Soon the churning white wakes of 10 echelons marked the advance toward shore. Many of the men in that disciplined approach to destiny would soon be dead, and nobody knew it better than themselves.

The 5th Division, never before in combat as a unit, although 40 per cent of its Marines were veterans of other Pacific battles, was to land on the beaches designated Red and Green, the left flank of the beachhead, nearest to Mount Suribachi. The task of taking that dormant volcano, now honeycombed with defenses, was assigned to the division's 28th Regiment, at the extreme left. The seasoned 4th Division, making its fourth Pacific assault in 13 months, was to land on beaches Blue and Yellow, on the beachhead's right flank. Nothing ahead looked easy for anybody, but probably the 3rd Battalion, 25th Regiment, 4th Division, confronted the worst task of all—the capture of a heavily fortified hill, surmounting a rock quarry studded with pill-

boxes and blockhouses, on the far right of the beachhead.

Watching from his command ship, Major General Clifton B. Cates, the 4th's commander, remarked: "If I knew the name of the man on the extreme right of the right-hand squad of the right-hand company of 3/25 I'd recommend him for a medal before we go in."

The first LVTs lumbered ashore at 8:59, one minute ahead of schedule. Immediately the drivers found themselves embroiled with Iwo's devilish natural defenses. The beaches were not only steep, rising in a series of terraces each as high as 10 or 15 feet, but they were made of volcanic sand so loose that the tracks of many of the LVTs could not get a grip on it. Instead of being carried inland by amtrac, the leathernecks had to debark at the water's edge, shoulder their heavy packs, and work their way up the terraces on foot, slipping and sliding, sometimes sinking knee-deep. But if the footing was awful, the beaches were at least free of enemy fire. General Howlin' Mad Smith, commander of the Marine expeditionary force, had predicted that "every cook and baker will be on the beach with some kind of weapon." That had been the experience on previous Pacific beachheads, but General Kuribayashi had planned otherwise for Iwo. He intended to let the invaders sweep ashore, then annihilate them with withering fire from both flanks. Three waves, about 1,200 Marines to the wave, were ashore before the defenders began to open up with more than a smattering of small arms and a few vagrant mortars.

The first Marine killed on Iwo may have been a 28th Regiment corporal who reached the crown of the terraces in Suribachi's shadow without attracting fire and set out on

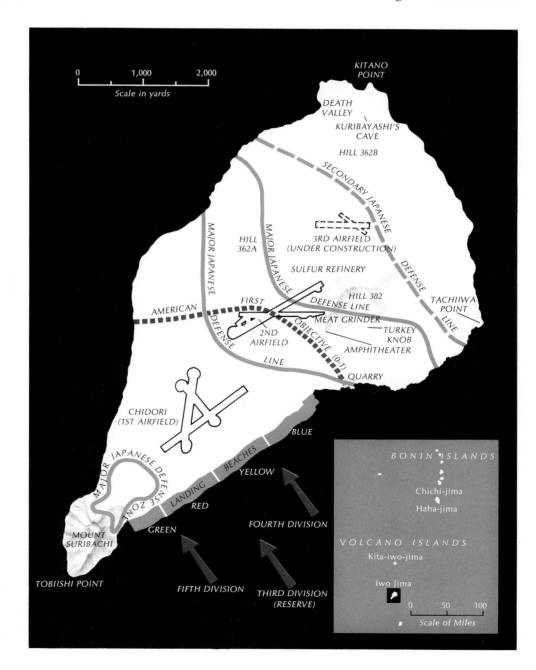

Two black Marines, pinned down by enemy fire, dig into an Iwo beach on D-day, February 19, 1945. Four black Marine companies served with the parties unloading cargo, and they were commended by their white commanding officer, Colonel Leland S. Swindler, for their "marked coolness and courage" under fire.

The U.S. invasion fleet approached Iwo Jima, the largest island in the Volcano chain (inset), from the southeast and landed an initial force of two Marine divisions almost without opposition. But then the Japanese opened a devastating cross fire from Mount Suribachi and well dug-in positions to the north, and turned Iwo Jima into one of the bitterest battlegrounds of the Second World War.

a personal campaign of eliminating pillboxes. After he and a sergeant had tossed grenades into the firing slit of one pillbox, the corporal went inside and emerged with his bayonet bloody. He then raced to another and jumped on top of it. A bullet from a third pillbox killed him in his tracks.

On the far right of the beachhead, near the heavily fortified quarry held by the Japanese, an extraordinary ordeal by gunfire awaited Second Lieutenant Benjamin F. Roselle Jr. of the 4th Division's 25th Regiment. Roselle had charge of a naval gunfire liaison team assigned to pinpoint targets for the ships. The team members were laboring up the terraces beside the quarry, manhandling a load of radio gear through the treacherous sand, when a mortar round came in on them. Roselle's left foot was virtually severed. His men had just applied a tourniquet when another round came in, killing two men and slamming fragments into Roselle's right leg. Roselle and his one remaining man were hugging the ground when a third round came in; it hit Roselle in the right shoulder and blew off his companion's right leg.

Without a word the man crawled away on his elbows, and Roselle was alone with the dead. A fourth mortar round lifted him from the ground, then dropped him. Vaguely he wondered what time it was and lifted his wrist just as fragments from a fifth round sliced away his watch and ripped a red hole through his wrist. Roselle, beyond caring now, was finally found and carried to the beach. He lived.

The invaders soon learned that Kuribayashi's men were equipped with new and monstrous mortars, some as big as 320mm—about three times the size of the largest U.S. mortar. The shells, looking like giant ash cans as they floated through the sky, produced a tremendous explosion on impact, spewing forth larger fragments than did an ordinary shell, and over a much wider radius. Such shells were a principal reason why nearly 8 per cent of the Americans wounded on Iwo were to die of their injuries, against a World War II average of 3 per cent.

The Japanese arsenal had other nasty surprises in store, including rockets weighing hundreds of pounds. One, eight inches in diameter, was fired from a metal trough that could be folded and moved from place to place; a big brother 16 inches in diameter was fired from a wooden chute, like a Fourth of July skyrocket. These weapons were inaccurate—they tended to wobble in flight—and more often than not they overshot their targets and landed in the ocean; the Marines named them "bubbly wubblies" because of the strange whuffling noise they made in flight.

The rapidly intensifying fire from Kuribayashi's positions, plus the difficulties of moving through constantly shifting sand and ash, created a mammoth pileup of men and matériel all along the 3,500 yards of the beachhead. Amid the chaos, a critical task lay with two companies of black Marines, the 8th Ammunition and the 36th Depot. Their responsibilities (later to be shared by two more black companies and a black Army unit, the 476th Amphibious Truck Company) ranged from wrestling landing craft through the surf to unloading, stockpiling and sorting out supplies and equipment—and delivering them to the Marines on the line. Strong backs were essential, but so were courage and coolness in continuing these exertions under fire; though the black Marines were regarded as labor rather than combat troops, the Japanese artillery made no such distinction.

At the far left of the beachhead, the men who were to assault Mount Suribachi were having trouble trying to climb the sands of the intervening terraces. They crowded the shore, uncertain what to do next. A short, stocky Marine officer broke the jam by striding along the waterline and bellowing: "Okay, you bastards, let's get the hell off this beach." He was Lieut. Colonel Chandler W. Johnson of the 2nd Battalion, 28th Marines, and at his imperious shout, the men got to their feet. Johnson's adjutant was carrying the American flag they were expected to plant at Suribachi's summit, and they scrambled onward.

About a thousand yards farther along the beach, the 27th Marines found the going somewhat easier. At that point, the island was only about 1,500 yards wide, and comparatively weakly defended. By late afternoon the 27th had driven all the way across to Iwo's west coast, and had secured a fingernail grip on the southern edge of the largest airfield.

On the right flank of the beachhead, the Marines of the 4th Division were taking a steady artillery pounding from the quarry and the hill behind it. The 4th's travail was witnessed and shared by the Navy's 133rd Construction Battalion—the Seabees. One of them, Machinist's Mate First Class Alphenix J. Benard, had a sickening moment just getting ashore. He was inside the maw of an LSM, mounted

Toiling under enemy fire, Marines pass boxes of ammunition ashore from LSTs and LSMs on D-day at Iwo Jima's Red Beach. This onerous chore fell to the men because trucks bogged down in the soft volcanic sand, and there were not enough tracked vehicles to take up the slack.

on the seat of his bulldozer with its engine already running, as the ship neared the beach. When the ramp went down, Benard saw a number of Marine bodies sloshing in the surf directly ahead of him. There was no other way to put his dozer ashore; he closed his eyes and drove in.

By midmorning 16 Sherman tanks had been brought in to help speed the capture of the quarry. The Marines were of two minds about the tanks. It was great to have them, but not so great to be near them—tanks drew fire. Preceded by an armored bulldozer cutting a road, the 36-ton Shermans waddled up the terraces. On the way, a mine blew a tread off one tank, and three shells hitting in rapid succession completed its ruin. The others kept going, and troops of Captain Masao Hayauchi's 12th Independent Anti-Tank Battalion fought back until their own guns were knocked out by the tanks' 75s. With no other way left to fight, Hayauchi clutched a demolition charge against his chest and threw himself against a Sherman's steel flank, blowing himself up but failing to stop the Sherman.

By 4:30 p.m. the quarry was taken. But taking it had cost Lieut. Colonel Justice M. "Jumpin' Joe" Chambers of the 3rd Battalion, 25th Regiment, all but 150 of some 700 men of his attacking force. The rest were dead, wounded or in battle shock; one company was down from 240 to 18 effectives. And the first objective of D-day—defined on the maps as 0-1, a line reaching from the quarry to Iwo's second airfield to the west coast—was far from realized.

At around 5 p.m. the assault force began to button up. By then, 30,000 Marines were ashore and 566 of them were dead, missing or dying of wounds. Burrowing into Iwo's shifting sands for the night was a struggle. "It's like diggin' a hole in a barrel of wheat," an exasperated private said.

A mass counterattack during the night was expected but it did not materialize. General Kuribayashi was hoarding his men. But his monstrous mortars crumped down on the beachhead, killing Marines in their foxholes. "A nightmare in hell," Sherrod called it.

Kuribayashi himself had a special task to attend to. He put a match to a pile of Japanese currency—in all, 120,000 yen (about $28,000). The money was hardly useful to the Americans on Iwo; still, the general did not want it to fall into their hands. By radio, he informed Tokyo that the bonfire represented a gift to the National Treasury from Iwo's doomed personnel.

At 8:40 a.m. on D-plus-1, the 28th Regiment, 5th Division, turned to the grim work of reducing the Suribachi defenses.

It was to take two more days and part of a third, but there were times when the job seemed unlikely to be done at all.

Just reaching the foot of the mountain was grueling work. The attack got moving with Lieut. Colonel Johnson's 2nd Battalion on the left and Lieut. Colonel Charles E. Shepard's 3rd Battalion on the right. Shepard's men were under simple and explicit orders to "secure this lousy piece of real estate so we can get the hell off it." They had no tanks; eight Shermans were available, but they were out of gas and ammunition. The two battalions did have artillery support—from portable 37mm antitank guns, from 75s mounted on half-tracks and from the guns of a destroyer and a mine-sweeper, one off each coast, operating within 200 yards of the base of the mountain.

But it was still a job for men afoot, for carbine, M-1 and bayonet, Browning automatic rifle, grenade, satchel charge and flamethrower—especially the last two—to flush out the defenders from their concealed positions or incinerate them there. For the most part, Kuribayashi's men were invisible. Even a corpse was a rare find, although Shepard's men found 73 Japanese bodies strewn around some coastal guns, the victims of the U.S. naval bombardment.

The bombardment had knocked out all the big coastal guns at the base of the mountain, but there were still hundreds of concrete pillboxes where the defenders squatted behind machine guns and watched the Marines come on. And inside Suribachi lurked another 1,200 men, free to move through interconnecting tunnels to the best-situated firing points on the surface, ready to pick off the Marines as they drew near.

The best way to attack such positions was from in close. One Marine, lugging a flamethrower or satchel charge and covered by his companions, would crawl up on what he hoped was the blind side of a pillbox. Then, edging toward a firing slit or ventilator, he would shove in the explosive or let loose a roaring tongue of yellow flame. By late afternoon Johnson's men had inched along Iwo's east coast to the foot of the mountain, leaving behind them more than 40 blasted or burned-out positions with the tenants dead inside.

D-plus-2 on Suribachi was a repetition of the day before, except that this time it was preceded by a carrier-plane bombing-and-strafing strike only 100 yards ahead of the Marines. Then the air support was pulled off; the bombs and bullets were coming too close for the Marines' comfort. All day long, LVTs hauled in more flame oil, more satchel charges, more grenades. The Marines devised a new weapon as well. As they climbed the flanks of Suribachi, they could hear Japanese talking deep below. They sent for drums of gasoline, poured it into rock fissures that led downward and set it afire.

From somewhere inside the mountain, Colonel Kanehiko Atsuchi got in touch by radio with Kuribayashi at his headquarters on Iwo's northern plateau. "Enemy's bombardments from air and sea and their assaults with explosives are very fierce," Atsuchi reported. "If we try to stay and defend our present positions it will lead us to self-destruction. We should rather like to go out and choose death by banzai charges." Kuribayashi was still dead set against banzai attacks; his reply was a question: Why was Atsuchi talking of folding after only three days anyhow?

Atsuchi did not have much time to brood over this rebuke. During the day he was hit by a shell fragment. As he lay dying, he ordered some of his men to try to get through the enemy lines and report to Kuribayashi.

On D-plus-3 there was still resistance by the remaining Japanese on Suribachi, but it was growing feebler; occasionally the desperate defenders dislodged a boulder high up on the mountain and sent it crashing down among the Marines. But during the day, in a driving rain that combined with volcanic ash to clog their rifles, Marine patrols got all the way around Suribachi, meeting at Tobiishi Point, Iwo's southern tip. In the afternoon Sergeant Robert L. Whitehead and a four-man patrol crawled well up the north face of Suribachi above a shattered gun position. They saw no Japanese and went back down to report. Whitehead asked whether he should go all the way to the top. But the hour was late and he was told to wait until morning.

That night about half the 300 Japanese still alive inside the mountain crept out and headed north, in accord with their dying colonel's instructions. About 20 of them made it—a tattered band of enlisted men led by a Navy lieutenant. At the headquarters of Captain Samaji Inouye, commander of Iwo's Naval guard force, the lieutenant reported Suribachi's loss. In the Japanese Navy hierarchy on Iwo, Inouye ranked next to Admiral Ichimaru himself, and he was a

F6F Hellcat fighter-bombers, swooping in over Iwo from Fifth Fleet carriers (background), expertly place their bombs on Japanese positions just ahead of the advancing 4th Marine Division. By the battle's end, American bombardiers had pounded the island with more than 1,000 tons of bombs, 12,000 rockets and 400 tanks of napalm.

traditionalist to the core. "You traitor, why did you come here?" he shouted at the lieutenant. "Don't you know what shame is? You are a coward and a deserter. I shall condescend to behead you myself."

The lieutenant knelt and meekly bent his head. Inouye drew his sword and swung it up. It never fell; Inouye's junior officers tore it out of his grip. The captain began to weep, moaning, "Suribachi's fallen, Suribachi's fallen."

At 8 a.m. on D-plus-4, Sergeant Sherman B. Watson and three privates of the 2nd Battalion, 28th Marines, started up Suribachi's north face. They reached the top in 40 minutes without meeting any hostile fire and scanned the volcano's crater. They saw a battery of machine guns and stacked ammunition—but not a living soul. They went sliding and scrambling back down the slope to report. Lieut. Colonel Johnson summoned the executive officer of Company E, Lieutenant Harold G. Schrier, and ordered him to take the crest and secure the crater. "And put this up," Johnson added, handing over the small American flag that he had hoped to raise on Suribachi's summit on D-day.

On the way up, Schrier and the 40 men with him, loaded down with weapons and ammunition, found the going so steep at some points that they had to move on their hands and knees. But they got to the top without enemy interference. Somebody found a 20-foot section of iron pipe lying on the ground, possibly a part of the island's rain-catching system. The flag was lashed to the pole. Half a dozen Marines grabbed it and planted it while Sergeant Louis R. Lowery, a combat photographer for the Marines' magazine, *Leatherneck,* took pictures.

Private First Class James A. Robeson, aged 16, refused to get into the act. He was standing by, hooting at his comrades as "Hollywood Marines," when a Japanese soldier with a rifle sprang from a cave in the crater wall. Robeson fired a long burst from his Browning automatic and the man dropped. Then from the cave came a Japanese officer brandishing a sword and running toward the flag. A rifle volley from the Marines felled him.

General Howlin' Mad Smith was coming ashore with a distinguished civilian from the States—Secretary of the Navy James V. Forrestal. Newly arrived from Washington for a firsthand look at the Navy at work in the Pacific, Forrestal spotted the little banner on the crest and said, "Holland, the raising of that flag on Suribachi means a Marine Corps for the next 500 years."

From the foot of the mountain, Lieut. Colonel Johnson also saw the flag go up. He quickly realized that his battalion's property had turned into a symbol of history. "Some sonofabitch is going to want that flag," he said, "but he's not going to get it. That's our flag." A corporal was sent to scrounge another flag. He got one from a landing craft off the beachhead. It was a proper banner, measuring 56 by 96 inches, almost twice the size of the one already flying.

When half a dozen Marines raised the big flag about two hours later, Joe Rosenthal, an Associated Press photographer, was there—to shoot the most famous photograph of World War II *(pages 72-73).*

On D-plus-4, General Harry Schmidt, V Amphibious Corps commander on Iwo, reiterated his preinvasion prediction that Iwo's subjugation would take a total of 10 days. It would, in fact, be D-plus-25—March 16—before the Marines' grip on the island would be firm enough to call the place secured. With Suribachi taken, about a third of Iwo was in U.S. hands. But the rest of it, to the north, included the island's roughest terrain—a region of rocky outcroppings and fissured hills running down to the sea on both east and west coasts. The natural obstacles alone would have been trying enough, but here also were most of Kuribayashi's man-made defenses—countless caves, tunnels, dug-in tanks, barbed wire, concealed concrete gun and mortar positions, all zeroed in on interlocking fields of fire.

Dominating the north was Hill 382 (the number denoted its height in feet) and its smaller satellite, Turkey Knob, which overlooked a broad natural amphitheater; among other defenses, the amphitheater contained a three-story blockhouse and a number of tanks buried up to their turrets. Both 382 and Turkey Knob were veritable anthills of desperately courageous Japanese. To the Marines, the area was to become known as the Meat Grinder.

On D-plus-6, V Corps headed northward, three divisions abreast. The 4th was on the right, facing the Meat Grinder, and the 5th was on the left; the center was assigned to elements of the 3rd Division, which had been kept in reserve offshore and had started landing on D-plus-3. Following a preparatory barrage by a battleship and two cruisers, a carrier-plane strike and 1,200 rounds of land-based artillery, the 9th Regiment, 3rd Division, moved against the center behind 26 Shermans.

There was no way for the tanks to go except across the exposed airstrip of Iwo's small second airfield. Japanese troops that were dug in on a nearby ridge opened fire, and the three tanks at the point—dubbed "Agony," "Ateball" and "Angel" by their crews—were hit almost at once. Angel and Agony were enveloped in flames. Ateball was stopped in its tracks, but its turret remained operable. Agony's crew squeezed out of the half-open hatch and dived for shell holes on the runway. But one crewman, Corporal William R. Adamson, was unable to follow suit. As he dropped to the ground, a bullet hit him in the leg. While bandaging his wound under cover of the smoke pouring from Agony, he glimpsed the muzzle flash of a Japanese gun. He crawled to a point 30 feet ahead of the disabled Ateball, crouched in the open and waved, pointing out the location of the enemy gun. Ateball's gunner caught his meaning, and its 75 knocked out the gun.

Adamson, still in the open, went on spotting targets; Ateball disposed of four machine-gun nests, a Japanese soldier sneaking up with a demolition charge, and 15 enemy infantrymen creeping amid the rocks of the ridge. Later a special vehicle used as a tank retriever came for Ateball, first straddling Adamson and picking him up through the escape hatch in the bottom of its hull.

The capture of Hill 382, on the right of the second airfield as the attackers moved north, had been assigned to the men of the 4th Division. They were having a bitter time of it, mostly from snipers embedded in the flanks of the hill all the way to the top. When a Marine carrying a bazooka was hit, the man next to him, Private First Class Douglas T. Jacobson, suddenly went berserk. He dropped his rifle, seized the bazooka, raced up to a Japanese 20mm gun emplacement and knocked it out. Still running, he destroyed another pillbox, then a concrete blockhouse. By now he was inside the Japanese lines, surrounded but still firing, somehow protected by a whimsical providence. Before Jacobson cooled off he had killed 75 Japanese. The deed brought him one of the 27 Medals of Honor bestowed for heroism on Iwo.

The next day, still clawing at Hill 382 and Turkey Knob, the men of the 4th Division made a little progress, but they paid dearly for it; nearly four Marines went down for every yard gained. The division's losses for the day were 792 casualties, one of the worst daily totals of the campaign.

While the line companies battled northward, some sort of order was emerging back on the landing beaches. Cranes cleared the wreckage that had jammed up on the shore as a result of storms and high surf on the second and third days of the invasion. At Iwo's biggest airfield, Seabees had cleared an airstrip 1,500 feet long, and artillery-spotting planes were using it. Field hospitals were functioning on the beach, and whole blood was being flown in only 36 hours after it had been drawn from donors in the States. The day

On D-plus-15, a cigar-chomping Lieut. General Holland M. "Howlin' Mad" Smith, leader of the Marine expeditionary force, briefs his top commanders on the drive across northern Iwo Jima that was designed to wind up the campaign. Following Smith's gesture are the V Corps commander, Major General Harry Schmidt (second from left), and the 4th Division commander, Major General Clifton Cates (left), while Cates's second-in-command, Brigadier General Franklin Hart, glances at a battle map.

after the 5th Division hospital took in 375 patients, one of the surgeons, Lieutenant E. Graham Evans, wrote to his wife: "I've seen all the surgery I want for awhile. They come in with wounds that make you sick to look at, and you tell them they must be evacuated and they cry."

The American cemeteries, too, were rapidly filling. All during the day and into the night, litter-bearers brought the bodies and set them down in rows, 50 bodies to a row. Two men went along the rows, taking the print of the right index finger—if it was still there. Others lifted one of the two dog tags from each body that still had them, leaving the second tag for burial. When there were neither hands nor tags nor identification bracelets, the men tried to identify the dead by letters from home, stencils on clothing, scars, tattoos or birthmarks; as a further clue, dental charts were made of the teeth. Sometimes so little remained of a body that the

Graves Registration unit could only make a gesture. They tried to determine from what part of the battlefield the body had come in order, if possible, to learn the dead man's unit; by checking a list of those missing from the unit, they hoped to deduce the corpse's name.

By D-plus-9 the Americans' situation was changing for the better all across the front, but at a pace so agonizingly slow that one day was difficult to tell from the next. At the center—the 3rd Division's sector—the 21st Regiment was moved into the line to replace the 9th and almost instantly encountered Baron Nishi's last eight tanks. Originally, Nishi had expected to use his tanks as a "roving fire brigade," moving from one area of combat to another. But the ruggedness of the terrain had dashed his plan, and he had been compelled either to bury the tanks up to their turrets or to

remove the turrets and emplace them in the ground. Now, however, Nishi knew that the time for static defense was past. His remaining armor was out in the open and shedding shrubbery-and-rock camouflage as it rammed ahead. Three tanks were destroyed by Company I's bazookas and flamethrowers; carrier planes got two more. With only three of his motorized cavalry left, the baron was all but unhorsed.

On the left sector of the front, the 27th Regiment, 5th Division, had the task of capturing a small eminence, Hill 362A (the letter was to distinguish it from two other hills of the same height). The Marines fought all the way up one side of a ridge that guarded the approach to 362A. But when they tried to take the other side, they found themselves up against a wall of small-arms and machine-gun fire; the reverse slopes turned out to be studded with caves and pillboxes. In less than an hour, 94 men were killed trying to cross a space of 100 yards in front of one cave.

The Marines had added reason to remember this cave— an unfamiliar tactic employed by its occupants. A Marine detail posted to keep watch on the entrance suddenly saw a Japanese soldier emerge and sit down on the ground in full view. First Lieutenant John K. McLean, who spoke Japanese, was summoned to talk the man into surrendering. From about 20 yards away, McLean held out the promise of food, water and medical aid—to no avail. The man remained mute. After half an hour, McLean asked angrily: "Naze inochi o suteyō to suru no ka?" ("Why are you throwing your life away?").

Just then, another Marine spotted wires leading from the Japanese soldier back into the cave; he was serving as a sacrificial decoy. Aware of the discovery, the Japanese tried to move, and Marine bullets riddled his body.

On the right of the northern front, the 23rd Regiment, 4th Division, kept chipping away at Hill 382. Trucks carrying multiple launchers that fired 4.5-inch rockets were brought up to supplement the 75s of tanks. The Marines of Company A worked their way around the base of the hill and began fighting up the reverse slope. But the guns at the top held out, and the day ended with the Japanese still in possession.

What was to be the division's final assault on the Meat Grinder began on D-plus-11, March 2. The effort required three days and probably can best be measured by the experience of Company E, 2nd Battalion, 24th Regiment. After a preliminary barrage by corps artillery and rocket trucks, Major Roland E. Carey took E straight against Hill 382. He was on the left; Company F, under Captain Walter J. Ridlon Jr., was on the right. By 9 a.m. one of Carey's platoons, under Second Lieutenant Richard L. Reich, was on the crest, crouched under a wrecked Japanese radar screen. Two of Ridlon's platoons were on a ledge below, stalled under heavy mortar and machine-gun fire. Carey and Ridlon crawled up to Reich's position and conferred; they decided that Carey would send up another platoon and meanwhile dispatch two tanks to the right to try to cut off enfilading Japanese fire. As Carey sped down the hill to issue his orders, he was hit by a machine-gun burst. The firing continued so intensely that his men took an hour to reach him; meanwhile, Captain Fraser P. Donlan, Carey's executive officer, took over Company E.

At 2 p.m. Donlan was hit by a mortar fragment. As First Lieutenant Stanley E. Osborn came up to relieve him, another round burst on top of them, killing Osborn and blowing off Donlan's right leg. Lieutenant Reich was now in command of Company E.

Later that afternoon, First Lieutenant William Crecink came up to the crest to relieve Reich. At nine the next morning, D-plus-12, Crecink was wounded and Reich was back in command—until later in the day when Captain Charles T. Ireland Jr. came up and took over. That day the battalion advanced 350 yards.

Early the next morning, D-plus-13, Ireland was hit in the leg; Lieutenant Reich took command for the third time. But he sent a plaintive message to battalion command: "How about a captain up here?" By now the battalion was so short of officers that Captain Robert M. O'Melia, the regimental band officer, was sent up to take command of Company E. Reich went back to his platoon.

O'Melia stayed in charge for about 24 hours. At 10 a.m., D-plus-14, a mortar shell hit his command post, killing him instantly; he was the sixth commanding officer of the unit to become a casualty. This time Reich did not take charge. Company E no longer existed; its remnants were absorbed into Company F.

But the Meat Grinder was finished. Hill 382 was overrun and Turkey Knob silenced and bypassed. Winning Hill 382

Marine demolition experts take cover as their king-sized charge of TNT seals the entrance to a Japanese cave and sends rubble hurtling hundreds of yards in every direction. Demolition teams paved the way for the Marines' slow advance by blasting or burning their way past as many as three dozen entrances to enemy caves in a single afternoon.

gave the Americans their best observation point of the parts of northern Iwo still to be taken; losing the hill deprived the Japanese of their best view of the enemy's rear areas.

The 5th Division, at the left end of the northern front, was now in possession not only of Hill 362A, but also of the next objective, Hill 362B, seized on D-plus-12 along with an additional 600 yards of enemy territory. The cost was reflected in the experience of Sergeant William G. Harrell of Company A, 1st Battalion, 28th Marines, who had been standing watch the night of D-plus-12 in a foxhole 20 yards above the company command post.

At dawn, after a night of intermittent firing and Japanese star-shell bursts, Harrell was found lying, half alive, at the bottom of the hole. His left hand was off at the wrist, dangling by threads of tendon; his right hand was gone

entirely, and his left thigh was broken. A dozen Japanese bodies lay around the hole, though Harrell was able to account for only five of them. He had killed two of the enemy with a carbine before he was hit by a grenade that shattered his left hand. He had disposed of a third attacker with a .45 pistol held in his right hand. His fourth and fifth victims had crawled into the foxhole with him; one of them had placed a grenade under Harrell's chin and jumped out. With his .45 still in his right hand, Harrell had cut the man down in mid-air, then used the pistol to shove the grenade toward the remaining interloper. The detonation had killed the man—and torn off Harrell's right hand.

The Medal of Honor awarded to Harrell was one of five that were earned in the same day—a measure of the tempo of the fighting and the valor it evoked. The other four

In winning form, Takeichi Nishi takes a jump at the 1932 Olympics in Los Angeles.

THE PLAYBOY OF THE EASTERN WORLD

One of Iwo Jima's Japanese defenders was an officer known to the Western world as a playboy-sportsman. He was Baron Takeichi Nishi, commander of the tank regiment on the island. In happier times, he had kept a string of fast horses and toured Japan in a flashy, gold Packard. On several trips abroad, he was often seen in the company of Hollywood film stars.

The apex of Nishi's career came in the 1932 Olympics. Japan had finished last in the 1928 games, and he vowed to avenge his nation's honor. To increase his odds in the equestrian competition, he paid almost $10,000 for a European jumper named Uranus. Nishi brought home a gold medal in the individual jumping event.

The triumph endeared Nishi to his countrymen—all but his superiors in the cavalry corps. These jealous officers saw to it that he was relegated to inconspicuous jobs, such as the procurement of horses. When he was ordered to Iwo Jima in July 1944, Nishi welcomed the assignment, foreseeing a fight worthy of his warrior lineage. As he left for Iwo, he told his son, "Your father will not die meaninglessly."

The baron fell in battle—but not before he and his tank crews had held off a division of Marines for six days in a rocky ravine. Nishi was found dead with a pistol in one hand. In his other was the whip he had used in his Olympic victory.

awards, three posthumous, went to two of Harrell's fellow Marines and to two Navy medical corpsmen.

D-plus-13, a Sunday, witnessed an equally memorable event. The radioman on a ship of the covering U.S. fleet heard an unexpected call on the air-sea rescue frequency.

"Hello Gatepost, this is Nine Baker Able. We are running low on gasoline. Can you give us a bearing on Iwo?"

"Hello Nine Baker Able, this is Gatepost," the radio operator answered. "Who are you?"

"We are a monster, short on fuel. Give us instructions, please."

The "monster"—slang for a B-29 bomber—was in trouble out there somewhere, and it was trying for Iwo. After a quick check of the air-sea code index to verify the plane's identification number, the radio operator ordered, "Look for Kita Iwo, 30 miles north of Iwo Jima."

"We see it, we see it," the B-29 replied.

"Roger. Course 167 for 28 miles. Do you prefer to ditch or try to land on the strip?"

"We prefer to land."

The pilot, First Lieutenant Raymond F. Malo, may have had some second thoughts about that preference when he brought his plane, *Dinah Might,* past Suribachi for his first look at ragged, dusty Chidori; nothing at the airfield in any way resembled the 8,500 feet of smooth blacktop back on his base at Guam. After two passes over the field, Malo decided it was this or nothing. He came in skirting the west flank of Suribachi and set the plane down. *Dinah Might* rolled 3,000 feet before stopping; less than 500 feet of runway remained. When Malo turned the big plane, the Japanese were reaching for it with mortars and artillery.

The bomber had been burning so much gasoline that it could never have made it back to Guam; the problem turned out to be a faulty fuel valve. It was quickly repaired; 30 minutes later, the B-29 was airborne again and slowly climbing out of Japanese flak.

If anything was needed to tell the Marines why they were dying on this unholy island, the successful landing of *Dinah Might* furnished the demonstration.

By that Sunday, the Americans' death toll since the landing stood at more than 3,000. The body count of dead Japanese came to 12,864, and probably several thousand more had been cremated in caves or sealed up in tunnels. Kuribayashi had only about 3,500 effectives left. But they were not quitting. Some were moving in and out of Marine lines with impunity. Japanese bodies were found dressed in Marine garb and in possession of Marine weapons. A Japanese diary picked up on the field bore a notation: "I tasted Roosevelt's rations for the first time and they were very good."

The fighting went on with undiminished ferocity. On the morning of D-plus-17, Company E, 2nd Battalion, 27th Marines, 5th Division, was driving for Iwo's north coast, its objective somewhat east of Kitano Point, the island's northernmost tip. Only about 300 yards separated the men from the coast, but every crag and crevice along the way concealed enemy troops bent on blocking the U.S. advance. Company E stalled in its tracks.

But the leader of one rifle platoon, First Lieutenant Jack Lummus, sprinted ahead. Lummus knew how to gain yardage; he had once been an all-American end at Baylor University in Texas. When the concussion of a Japanese grenade knocked him down, he got up and kept going. He had rushed and destroyed an enemy gun emplacement when another grenade knocked him down, tearing a hole in one shoulder. Again he got up, rushed a second enemy position and killed all the occupants. He was still running, shouting at his men to follow, when one of his feet came down on the detonator of a land mine. Lummus vanished in a cloud of dust and flying rock. When the cloud cleared, he seemed to be standing in a hole. The mine had blown off both his legs, but he was holding himself erect on the stumps, still shouting the men on.

In the 5th Division's hospital that afternoon, Lummus raised himself on one elbow and told Dr. E. Graham Evans, "Doc, it looks like the New York Giants have lost a damn good end." By nightfall he was dead.

By then Lummus' men were on the last ridge of Iwo's northeast coast, looking down on the sea after a wild and furious rush through the Japanese trying to bar their way. As the official Marine account later put it, "Love and compassion for their leader, mixed with anger and frustration, had supplied the spark." The result, the account noted, was "the American equivalent of the traditional banzai charge."

About two miles farther down the coast, near Tachiiwa Point, a true banzai charge was in the making—under the direction of Captain Inouye, the Japanese Naval land force commander who had wept over the fall of Mount Suribachi. Inouye and about 1,000 of his men were encircled by two Marine regiments, the 4th Division's 23rd and 24th, and the pocket was growing steadily smaller.

Inouye, a champion swordsman and member of a samurai family—Japan's hereditary warrior caste—had no intention of dying in a trap. He decided to break out and, despite General Kuribayashi's ban on wasteful attacks, to launch a banzai charge against the American lines. March 8, D-plus-17 for the Marines, was Inouye's chosen date, for a particular reason. Ever since his country's attack on Pearl Harbor—which, by Japan time, had taken place on the eighth day of December of 1941—the eighth day of every month had held a special significance for the Japanese. Inouye intended to turn his banzai attack into an appropriate tribute to the occasion. He planned to go all the way through the Marine lines to the south of Iwo, and once more raise the Japanese flag on Suribachi.

An hour or so before midnight, Inouye and his men set out for an area held by the 2nd Battalion, 23rd Marines. Some of the Japanese had rifles, grenades or demolition charges strapped on their chests; others carried only sharpened bamboo stakes. They crept silently to within 10 yards of the battalion's command post, then charged, screaming. The sky came alight with flares and star shells. The attackers were raked by mortars, machine guns, rifle fire and grenades; one Marine company alone used up 20 cases of grenades. Captain Inouye was last seen by his orderly brandishing his sword and shouting *"Tsukkome!"* ("Charge!"). Some of his men penetrated the American lines, and close fighting continued through the night. In the morning, the Marines counted 784 Japanese bodies. The American losses were 90 killed and 257 wounded.

Lieutenant Satoru Omagari, once commander of a rocket battery, had taken part in the banzai charge. Greatly to his shame, he had survived it and retreated back to his cave. He now resolved to make amends. He fitted himself out as a human bomb, with a box of dynamite strapped to his shoulders, and sallied forth to ambush a tank.

In a gully that seemed a likely route for Sherman tanks, he found five dead Japanese. He smeared himself with the blood and entrails of his compatriots and lay down among them, feigning death, to wait for the noise of approaching tank treads. The sun blazed down, the gigantic bluebottle flies swarmed, and the smell of the five corpses nauseated him. But not a tank appeared all day. When Omagari could no longer stand the decay about him, he crept back to his cave and tried to clean up. The stench would not come off.

Omagari was still determined. The following day he went out and once more lay down among his dead comrades. He began thinking over his life, following himself in memory back to childhood, Naval training, his embrace of the feudal code of Bushido, which valued honor more than life itself. Was this the way it was to end—to become a putrid mess like the corpses around him for the glory of the Emperor? No American tanks came, and after a while Omagari stood up among the dead. He removed the dynamite from his back and retreated to his cave.

Heretical thoughts continued to plague Omagari, but he kept on the move as the Americans mopped up one place after another. He was to hold out for several months—and then to become one of the 1,083 Japanese on Iwo who surrendered to the enemy.

On D-plus-18 the attackers of Iwo suddenly glimpsed the battle's end. That day, a 28-man patrol under Lieutenant Paul M. Connally of Company A, 1st Battalion, 21st Marines, 3rd Division, finally reached the sea on the island's north coast. The patrol climbed to the top of a bluff above the water and looked down past the wreckage of pillboxes long since destroyed by U.S. naval gunfire. The men went down to the beach; some peeled off their combat boots and waded in the surf to coddle their aching feet. A canteen was filled with sea water for proof of the company's breakthrough to the coast and was sent back to the division's commander, Major General Graves B. Erskine, with the label, "For inspection, not consumption." Company A was not the same outfit that had come ashore 18 days before; of the original 200-plus Marines, only three remained.

General Kuribayashi's last substantial stand was made on Iwo's roughest terrain—a deep, winding gorge, some 700 yards long and from 200 to 500 yards wide, extending from southwest of Kitano Point, the island's northern tip, down the west coast. The Marines, their depleted rifle companies now padded with artillerymen and rear-echelon troops, called the gorge Death Valley.

In such a place, mortars were of little help and tanks could barely move. To rout the Japanese from their positions, explosives were lowered over cliffs by rope, rockets brought up on bulldozers were hurled at hillsides, and grenades were dropped from low-flying spotter planes. Finally, Death Valley was burned out, cave by cave and pillbox by pillbox; some 10,000 gallons of flamethrower oil were used up every day of the operation.

On D-plus-22 a patrol from the 26th Marines almost got Kuribayashi himself. Some time earlier he had moved his headquarters to a cave not far from Kitano Point. Candles provided the only light. Kuribayashi's orderly heard the enemy patrol and saw a Marine silhouetted against the cave entrance. He blew out the candles and threw a blanket over the general. Kuribayashi murmured his thanks and walked deeper into the cave. Several Marines, one of them carrying a flamethrower, stepped through the entrance, came in a little way, then stopped, turned and walked out. The orderly took a deep breath.

On D-plus-23, March 14, General Schmidt, feeling that for practical purposes the battle was won, held a ceremony a few hundred yards north of Suribachi. The U.S. flag was run up the halyards on an 80-foot pole planted atop a ruined Japanese bunker, and a colonel read a proclamation from Admiral Nimitz saying: "United States forces under my command have occupied this and other of the Volcano Islands. All powers of government of the Japanese Empire in these islands so occupied are hereby suspended."

In his cave that day, Kuribayashi listened to one of a series of special radio programs from Tokyo designed to express his countrymen's support for his efforts. A choir sang "The Song of Iwo Defense," composed by men under his command before the American landing. Prayers for victory were voiced by boys and girls from Kuribayashi's birthplace in the prefecture of Nagano.

That night he sent a message by courier to Colonel Masuo Ikeda at his post south of Kitano Point. The general asked how much remained of the 145th Infantry, once his best regiment. Back came the courier with Ikeda's report: Only six men remained. Again Kuribayashi dispatched the messenger, this time with an order to Ikeda to burn the regimental flag. "Do not let it fall into the hands of the enemy," Kuribayashi warned.

On March 17, at Guam, Admiral Nimitz issued a statement. As of that day, American casualties on Iwo were 4,189 killed in action and 19,938 wounded—the highest casualty rate of any engagement in 168 years of Marine Corps history. "On Iwo island," Nimitz said, "uncommon valor was a common virtue." (The toll of Iwo was not quite finished. Many of the wounded died; the ultimate count was to total 6,821 killed in action, missing, or dead of wounds, and 19,217 wounded.)

That same day General Erskine of the 3rd Division dispatched two Japanese prisoners to Kuribayashi's headquarters; they carried a letter from Erskine noting that Kuribayashi's situation was now hopeless and suggesting that he could surrender with honor. No reply came.

Kuribayashi's compatriots believed that he lived to take part, on March 26, in a final gesture of national honor—a foredoomed attack in which 262 Japanese and 53 Americans were killed. Reportedly the general was badly wounded and later committed suicide. His soldiers, it was said, buried him deep. The body was never found by the Marines.

Despite the final, futile attack by Kuribayashi and his men, the battle for Iwo had really ended the day before—March 25, D-plus-34—with the elimination of the last Japanese stronghold in Iwo's northwest corner. That day a ragged pickup band of 5th Division Marines, put together from the remains of the 26th, 27th and 28th Regiments, closed out a pocket of 50 square yards in Death Valley. In the group were a few men from the 3rd Platoon, Company B, 1st Battalion, 28th Marines, including Private First Class G. C. Burk Jr., who for eight days had led the platoon while it had no officers. Burk had shrapnel in his belly and he could not stand erect. But he would not quit. He was one of a tiny elite. He had gone all the way through on Iwo from D-day to the end.

TO THE TOP OF SURIBACHI

Approaching Iwo Jima, the first waves of landing craft churn shoreward. Those at upper left carry Marines assigned to storm defenses on nearby Mount Suribachi.

A DECEPTIVE START TO A FURIOUS FIGHT

"We were still some distance from the island when Mount Suribachi, craggy and forbidding, began to loom up on our left-front," wrote Marine Corporal Richard Wheeler, describing his landing on Iwo Jima. "We would beach on the landing zone's extreme left flank, only a few hundred yards from the volcano's base. I hunched lower as it occurred to me that high positioned snipers might already have us in their sights."

Wheeler's outfit, the 28th Regiment of the 5th Division, was about to assault Suribachi, a knobby 556-foot peak dominating Iwo's southwestern tip. The mission was vital. The extinct volcano was a formidable fortress, studded with defense installations, and its guns could raise havoc among units coming ashore. It was also a superb observation post, from which the Japanese could monitor American movements on two thirds of Iwo. For these reasons, the Marine command wanted to take Suribachi swiftly.

When Wheeler's landing craft ran aground, the chances for a quick conquest looked good. During heavy bombardment by U.S. naval guns and carrier-based aircraft, the Japanese artillerymen on Suribachi were relatively quiet, and only light fire came from defenders manning a thick belt of machine-gun nests and mortar pits that girdled the volcano. There were no enemy troops in sight, and Wheeler's buddy, Private First Class Louie Adrian, asked in surprise, "Where's the reception committee?"

But there would be no banzai charges in the fight for Suribachi—and no easy victory, either. The Japanese, hidden in their underground defenses, were playing a waiting game, and when the U.S. warships shifted their bombardment out of fear of hitting Marines, the enemy guns opened a furious fire. "Artillery and mortar shells were whoomping along the beach," Wheeler said, "and small-arms fire was weaving an invisible criss-cross pattern just above it."

Wheeler's unit began taking casualties as the Marines tried to advance. For the next four days, as one of them said, "there probably wasn't a man among us who didn't wish to God he was moving in the opposite direction."

Marines display enemy flags captured early in the fight. The flags, bearing well-wishes, were considered good-luck charms by the Japanese soldiers.

An LCVP carries Marines of the 5th Division on their 30-minute journey from the larger LSTs offshore to a landing beach in the shadow of Mount Suribachi.

While U.S. naval shelling raises clouds of smoke and dust on Suribachi, Marine riflemen of the 28th Regiment struggle to advance up a steep terrace of soft volcanic sand on the beach. One of the regiment's battalions attacked across the narrow neck of the island, while the other two deployed for their fight against enemy positions defending the volcano.

Casualties of the D-day fighting, a stranded Marine howitzer and burning amphibious tractors lie abandoned on a shell-pocked rise leading toward the volcano.

Surrounded by ammunition cases and spent cartridges, a Marine machine-gun crew keeps up steady fire at a Japanese installation near the foot of the mountain.

Returning enemy fire, Marines manning a 37mm gun pour shells at Japanese artillery emplaced in caves dotting the northern slope of Mount Suribachi.

BLASTING OPEN A CONCRETE RING

On D-plus-1, the 28th Regiment struck at Suribachi's main line of defense, a ring of concrete pillboxes and fortified caves around the volcano's base. The Marines attacked with tanks and artillery, and were given awesome covering fire. Air strikes roared in with bombs and napalm. Gunboats fired rockets from barely 200 yards offshore, and destroyers, cruisers and battleships lobbed shells that dropped a mere 100 yards in front of the Americans.

But in the end the Marine infantry had to dig out the Japanese. Using flamethrowers and demolition charges to reduce the fortifications, the Marines slowly advanced, surrounding the mountain. The regiment paid a high price for each yard gained, suffering most of its losses in this grueling struggle. By nightfall on D-plus-3, more than 800 Marines in all had been killed.

A Marine calls to a Japanese soldier lying half-buried in the volcanic ash with a cloth covering his face and a hand grenade lying inches from his right hand.

A LUCKY ENCOUNTER IN A SHELL CRATER

During the fighting on D-plus-3, a handful of Marines made a fortunate discovery. Accompanied by photographer Louis R. Lowery, who was covering the invasion for *Leatherneck* magazine, they dived for cover in a shell hole and found a wounded Japanese there. This was a rare chance to interrogate a Japanese; most either fought to the death or committed suicide.

One Marine hurried off to get an interpreter. The wounded soldier turned out to be an embittered local conscript; he willingly told the Marines about his former comrades' defenses on Mount Suribachi.

Armed with this information, a 40-man Marine patrol started climbing the mountain the next morning. Lowery went along to photograph the action, but there was surprisingly little for him to record—until they got to the top.

The wounded soldier, his grenade knocked away with a stick, is given a smoke by the interpreter.

The Marines, fearing that the captive may be booby-trapped, cautiously pull him out with a rope.

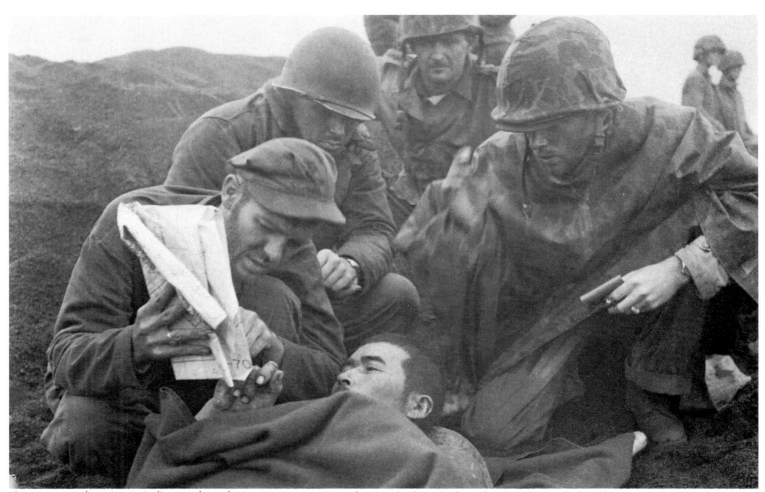

Shown a map, the prisoner indicates where the Japanese are positioned on Suribachi and where the mountain paths have been mined and booby-trapped.

Watching out for enemy action on Suribachi, a Marine sniper hugs a steep slope above the beach.

Skirting a mined pathway up the slope, Marines climb past the body of a dead Japanese soldier.

Marines use flamethrowers to wipe out enemy soldiers in a cave. The Japanese caught in such attacks, said one who survived, were like "chickens being fried."

Snapping in the breeze, the Stars and Stripes in Louis Lowery's photograph flies over Suribachi even as skirmishing goes on. One Marine, his face taut with strain,

A Marine takes down the small U.S. flag, while in the background others raise the large flag.

A TALE
OF TWO FLAGS

At the top of Mount Suribachi, the patrol fanned out and charged over the rim into the crater. They were greeted with rifle fire from Japanese soldiers in caves on the inside slopes. During a brisk little skirmish, a few Marines found an iron water pipe and raised their flag on it *(left)*.

A Japanese grenade came flying at photographer Lou Lowery as he snapped the action. He hit the ground—and slid 50 feet down the crater. The patrol soon silenced the Japanese, sealing the caves with demolition charges. A few hours later, four more Marines reached the summit carrying a larger flag to replace the small one flying on the pipe staff. The switching of the flags was captured *(above)* by Marine photographer Bob Campbell. But neither Campbell nor Lowery shot the flag-raising picture *(overleaf)* that became the most famous photograph of the War.

stands with his rifle at the ready while a second heads into the crater to answer fire from enemy caves.

Six men—five Marines and a Navy medical corpsman—hoist the second American flag on Mount Suribachi about 30 feet from the spot where the first one had flown. So dramatic was this photo by Associated Press cameraman Joe Rosenthal, who had just climbed up from the beach, that there were rumors it was posed. In fact it was absolutely unrehearsed.

3

The best way to comprehend the power of the U.S. Pacific Fleet was to see it at rest. At sea and at work, the ships were scattered, often only smudges on the horizon. But in their anchorage at the Ulithi atoll in the western Caroline Islands, they were massed—row upon row of carriers, battleships and their smaller sisters, variously dressed in geometrical camouflage or dull gray, looming as solid as so many First National Banks. Even in the quiet waters of Ulithi's lagoon, they exuded an air of cold menace.

Ulithi itself was to play a vital role in the outcome of the Pacific war. Ironically, it had come into American hands without a fight; the Japanese, who had used it as a seaplane base, had found it of dubious value and had abandoned it. To the new occupants, taking over in September of 1944, Ulithi's potential was clear. The atoll lay 900 miles southwest of Iwo Jima and 1,200 miles southeast of Okinawa—a handy springboard for both invasions and, indeed, for the Pacific Fleet's forays closer to Japan. Ulithi's huge lagoon, 112 square miles of deep water, could accommodate nearly 1,000 ships at a time; between engagements with the foe, the fleet's fighting ships could return there for replenishment and minor repairs.

American ingenuity and organizing skill had turned the expanses of Ulithi's lagoon into an enormous supply warehouse. Instead of building storage facilities on the islets surrounding the lagoon, the Navy brought in a number of concrete barges, collectively known as the "crockery fleet." Freighters arriving with supplies from the States deposited the goods in the barges, which were moored in the harbor. To service newly arrived fighting ships, the barges merely weighed anchor and chugged to their berths, transferring aboard everything from ammunition to flour. Added to the barges were six types of specialized repair ships; one type did nothing but fix damaged radio and radar equipment.

Commodore Worrall R. Carter's Service Squadron 10 was the unit charged with managing the warehouse operation. Another unit, Service Squadron 6, under Rear Admiral Donald B. Beary, resupplied the fleet once it departed to seek out the enemy; Servron 6 included oilers, cargo carriers, ammunition ships, refrigerator ships, salvage ships, tugs and even a hospital ship.

Beary's seagoing general store routinely performed prodigies. In just one two-and-a-half-day period of replenish-

BOLD FORAYS BY THE FLEET

ment, Servron 6 supplied the fleet's fighting ships with 379,157 barrels of fuel oil, 555,000 gallons of aviation gas, 2,000 barrels of diesel oil, 6,369 tons of ammunition, 99 replacement airplanes, more than 1,000 replacement personnel, transferred by boatswain's chair, enough fresh food, including meat, butter, eggs, apples and oranges, to feed a fair-sized city for a month, and an item even more prized by men who had been at sea for weeks—5,822 bags of mail.

Sometime near the end of 1944, the top command of the U.S. Navy arrived at the conclusion that from then on, the Pacific Ocean would be *mare nostrum*—a sea ruled by American ships as totally as the galleys of ancient Rome had ruled the Mediterranean. The unique logistical support enjoyed by the Pacific Fleet was making it more and more independent of the land; its task forces would soon be able to stay at sea without touching base for as long as two months. And supposedly, they would be encountering less and less enemy opposition; Admiral Halsey himself had pronounced Japan's Navy "beaten, routed and broken" as a result of the Battle for Leyte Gulf at the time of the Philippines invasion in October.

The new confidence in the fleet's potency was not altogether justified. Though the fleet was, indeed, increasingly the master of its domain, it was by no means impervious to harm. When assault landings were under way, as at Iwo Jima and later at Okinawa, the fleet was forced to function as a bodyguard, limited to a confined area while it provided protection for the men on the beaches. In such exposed circumstances it was highly vulnerable.

The admirals much preferred the fleet's other role—as a massive, mobile strategic weapon, roving freely and hammering at enemy strongholds around a 3,700-mile arc of ocean. But even in this capacity, the mighty armada was not immune. Though it was no longer seriously threatened by the Imperial Navy's surface ships, it was still subject to savage aerial attack.

The fleet also faced the recurrent possibility of another sort of deadly confrontation—with an enemy of far more awesome power than any that men could muster. This force was the raging, whirling windstorm known in that part of the world as the typhoon. Like the hurricanes of the Atlantic and Caribbean, typhoons could ravage land as well as sea.

But such storms packed a particularly vicious punch in their sweep across vast, unobstructed stretches of water—as Admiral Halsey and the men under his command learned to their grief in mid-December of 1944.

A small portent of the disaster that befell Halsey and his men appeared on the morning of December 17. The fleet was then about 500 miles east of the Philippines. It had just completed a three-day strike in support of General MacArthur's impending invasion of the island of Luzon, and it was trying to refuel for another three-day strike. The area in which the ships lay was known to be along a track that typhoons traveled, but it had been selected anyhow, as the nearest location to Luzon that was beyond the range of Japanese fighter planes. The destroyers were taking on fuel from the heavy ships—which were then to refill their bunkers from the fleet oilers—when a cross-swell and high winds parted some of the fueling hoses. At 1:10 p.m. Halsey ordered fueling suspended and began feeling around for a course to evade a "tropical disturbance" reported 500 miles to eastward.

When his staff meteorologist estimated that the disturbance was moving north-northwest, but that it would veer northeast after colliding with a cold front, the admiral decided to send the fleet northwest to a new rendezvous with the oilers. An hour later a corrected forecast indicated that the storm was 300 miles nearer than previously thought, and likely to hit the new rendezvous area. Halsey then decided to send his ships southwest.

All through the night they ran southwestward, and at 7 a.m. on December 18, they began another attempt to refuel. But mounting seas and winds clocked at 43 knots doomed the effort, and Halsey radioed MacArthur that the fleet would be unable to launch the second strike at Luzon. At 8:30 a.m. it was learned that the storm, instead of curving northeast, had continued in a westerly direction; its center was reported only 150 miles away and rushing toward Halsey's ships. At about 10 a.m. the plunging barometer and the counterclockwise movement of the wind certified the storm as a typhoon.

By noon the wind was gusting up to 110 knots, the barometer had gone off the low end of the scale, and the seas—barely visible amid the wind-whipped spray—had grown to monstrous proportions. Even the heaviest ships had trouble keeping a course. Halsey, aboard the 57,000-ton (full-load) battleship *New Jersey,* was to recall that the typhoon tossed her about "as if she were a canoe."

Anything smaller was being hurt even more. The escort carrier *Altamaha* recorded rolls of 31 degrees on her inclinometer; 43 airplanes, in addition to assorted jeeps and tractors, were so heavily damaged that they later had to be shoved overboard as junk. The light carrier *Monterey,* unable to maneuver, wallowed helplessly. Scout planes blew off the catapults of the battleship *Wisconsin* and the cruiser *Boston.* On the decks of the light carrier *Cowpens* and the escort carrier *Cape Esperance,* airplanes broke loose and, thrashing from port to starboard like battering rams, broke electrical connections and touched off fires. The light carrier *Independence* reported three men overboard and beyond any hope of rescue.

But it was among the destroyers that the storm turned mass murderer. Loaded topside with the extra weight of antiaircraft guns, radar and gunfire-direction gear, destroyers rolled abominably even in moderate seas. Some of them, unable to refuel, had nearly empty oil bunkers and were, therefore, even more top-heavy than usual. Against the force of the raging typhoon, they were just about defenseless. A number of the destroyers lay on their sides, their stacks almost horizontal, while sea water rushed into the ventilators, shorting electrical circuits, knocking out steering gear, lights and communications and flooding the engine and boiler rooms.

Finally three of the ships went under. The human toll was devastating: 244 men lost of the 250 on the *Monaghan,* 305 of the more than 325 on the *Spence,* 200 of the more than 250 on the *Hull.* At dusk, when the seas had abated somewhat, Halsey began a search for survivors that was to last for three days. Some were found on life rafts, holding rifles to ward off sharks. Others, incredibly enough, were found swimming—and able to summon help with the whistle the Navy had forehandedly ordered attached to all life jackets.

A number of the survivors told their stories to a court of inquiry convened at Ulithi. Lieut. Commander James A. Marks recounted the ordeal of the destroyer *Hull,* which was the first command of his career. "I tried every possible combination of rudder and engines with little avail. . . . The

ship was being blown bodily before the wind and sea, yawing between headings of 100 and 080. . . . The force laid the ship steadily over on her starboard side and held her down in the water until the seas came flowing into the pilothouse itself. . . . I remained on the port wing until the water flooded up to me and I stepped off into the water as the ship rolled over on her way down."

Joseph McCrane, Water Tender Second Class, senior of the *Monaghan's* six survivors, had struggled amid a welter of crashing gear and loose oil drums to open valves that would permit flooding the destroyer's empty tanks with sea water to give her some stability. He then joined about 40 other men topside in the after deckhouse. The ship was rolling heavily to starboard and the lights went out.

"At that point we were all just plain scared," McCrane remembered. "One of the fellows was praying aloud. Every

The typhoon that battered the U.S. Third Fleet in December 1944 appears on a radar screen aboard the carrier Wasp. This photograph, the first to capture a typhoon on radar, shows the eye of the storm, a small dark circle of calm six miles across, and surrounding it a light area of thick clouds and torrential rains swirling counterclockwise at nearly 150 miles an hour.

time the ship would take about a 70 degree roll to starboard he would cry out, 'Please bring her back, dear Lord. Don't let us down now! Bring it back, O God, bring it back.' Soon a few other guys would join in. Then when we came back, we'd chant, 'Thanks, dear Lord!'

"We must have taken seven or eight rolls to starboard before she went over on her side. . . . A gunner's mate by the name of Joe Guio, with absolutely no thought of his own safety, was standing outside of the hatch pulling everyone out. . . . Some of the men who had been knocked into the sea or who had jumped . . . were being pounded into a pulp against the side of the ship. Finally a wave came along and knocked me off. . . . It seemed like I was out there for an eternity before I heard Joe Guio yell that there was a raft right in back of me."

At length Guio joined the men on the raft. He was naked,

cold and in pain from a gash that had torn off part of one foot. That night McCrane held him in his arms to keep him warm. Guio thanked him and went to sleep. "About half an hour later I had a funny feeling come over me," McCrane told the court, "and I tried to wake him up only to find he was dead."

Nearly 800 men in all lost their lives during the fleet's encounter with the typhoon. In addition to the three destroyers sunk, 21 ships were damaged, nine of them so badly that they were put out of action. And aboard the light carriers and escort carriers, some 150 planes were ripped from their steel-cable lashings and wrecked.

The court at Ulithi pinned the responsibility for the damage and losses on Halsey. It also noted, however, that any mistakes in handling the fleet were "errors in judgment committed under the stress of war operations and stem-

The light carrier Langley rolls wildly as she battles 70-foot waves during the terrible typhoon of December 1944. Despite the battering, the Langley lost not a single plane to the storm. Several sister carriers were less fortunate: On the Monterey, 34 planes went overboard or were damaged, while the Cowpens and the San Jacinto lost eight planes each.

ming from a commendable desire to meet military require-ments." Halsey himself thought the cause of the disaster was incompetent weather forecasting.

By early January 1945, Halsey was once again his old confident self. Since the previous October, he had been champing to go big-game hunting in the South China Sea. This 2,000-mile-long stretch of water—bounded on the south by the Dutch East Indies and the Malay Peninsula, on the west by the Indochina and China coasts, on the north by Formosa and on the east by the Philippines—had been off limits to American surface ships for more than three years. Though U.S. submarines had done much mischief to enemy shipping in the South China Sea, the Japanese were still using it as their highway for moving essential oil, rubber and tin from Southeast Asia to the home islands.

Halsey's aim was to polish off what remained of the Japanese Navy. His thirst for action was newly whetted by a report that two Japanese hybrid battleship-carriers, the *Ise* and the *Hyuga*, had been spotted at Camranh Bay on the southeastern Indochina coast. He promptly sought and got approval from his boss, Admiral Nimitz, to go after the prey; such a mission would also serve the immediate purpose of safeguarding the U.S. supply lines for the impending landings at Lingayen Gulf, on the west coast of the main Philippine island of Luzon.

A move into the South China Sea required considerable temerity, since the U.S. task force, once there, would be surrounded by Japanese airfields at every point of the compass. On the night of January 9, an armada of 13 fast carriers, six battleships, 13 cruisers and 48 destroyers slipped, apparently undetected, through the narrow waters between Luzon and Formosa. A group of oilers, guarded only by destroyers and escort carriers, followed.

On the 12th, the U.S. carrier planes, sent aloft with Halsey's blessing—GIVE THEM HELL. YOU KNOW HOW TO DO IT—struck Camranh Bay. To the admiral's intense annoyance, the two Japanese battlewagons were gone; they had retired to Singapore after U.S. submarines had torpedoed and sunk their tankers. Still, Halsey's fliers had a profitable day. They sank 13 cargo ships, 10 tankers and 11 small warships—a total loss of 126,000 tons and, as it turned out, Japan's second worst shipping disaster of the War. (A U.S.

raid early in 1944 on Truk, Japan's island stronghold in the western Pacific, had accounted for 37 ships and a total loss of 191,000 tons.)

Two other victims of the U.S. attack on Camranh Bay were the Japanese light cruiser *Kashii* and the French cruiser *Lamotte-Picquet*, which the Japanese had disarmed. For good measure, the American pilots shot up airfields, fuel dumps and other installations around Saigon and along 300 miles of the Indochina coast.

For the next eight days, alternately refueling and striking, the task force ranged up and down the sea. The carrier planes hit Saigon again, destroying 50 Mitsubishi "Betty" bombers on the ground, turned north to strike Formosa, then hit Japanese shipping and airfields in the Chinese ports of Canton, Amoy and Swatow, the island of Hainan and the former British crown colony of Hong Kong. At Hong Kong the Japanese put up formidable resistance; there was intense antiaircraft fire and a swarm of planes rose to meet the attackers. The Americans lost 61 planes, the Japanese 47

In the chart-filled flag plot of the carrier Bunker Hill, Vice Admiral Marc A. "Pete" Mitscher (right) and his chief of staff, Commodore Arleigh A. Burke, review plans for an air strike to be mounted on the following day by their Task Force 58. Mitscher's calm, courageous leadership won him the affection of officers and men alike. "He never lost his temper and never raised his voice," said his old friend Admiral William F. "Bull" Halsey. However, Halsey added, Mitscher was "high-strung to tension hardly endurable," and he "kept it bottled up inside."

—one of the rare aerial encounters in which U.S. losses were more than the enemy's. This blow to American pride was somewhat mitigated when clandestine broadcasts from Indochina revealed that five of the downed carrier fliers had fallen into friendly hands and had been spirited to safety in China's interior.

Tokyo broadcasters made much of the Hong Kong episode, claiming that the U.S. task force was now bottled up in the South China Sea. Japan's celebrated English-speaking propagandist, Tokyo Rose, issued this taunt: "We don't know how you got in, but how the hell are you going to get out?" On January 20 Halsey gave his answer: he took his fleet back into the Pacific through the same gate that he had used to enter the South China Sea. On the following day, as the fleet was running eastward past Formosa, the carrier planes launched a farewell strike. They hit Formosa's harbors and airfields and a number of neighboring smaller islands, destroying more than 100 Japanese planes on the ground and sinking 10 ships.

Then, abruptly, Halsey's luck turned sour. In 11 days in the South China Sea, no Japanese aircraft had come within 20 miles of his ships, thanks to the vigilance of his combat air patrol (CAP)—the Hellcats and Corsairs that served as an aerial shield over the fleet. Now, however, enemy planes from Formosa found the maneuvering fleet and moved in. Four managed to penetrate the CAP shield. One hit the light carrier Langley with a small bomb, killing three men and ripping a hole in the flight deck. The other three planes were Kamikazes—flown by suicide pilots. One Kamikaze dived into the destroyer Maddox, hitting amidships and killing seven of her crew.

The carrier Ticonderoga had the worst of it. A Kamikaze bearing a 550-pound bomb knifed through the flight deck and exploded between the gallery and hangar decks. The last Kamikaze hit the carrier's superstructure. The two Japanese pilots targeted on the Ticonderoga exacted a high price for their lives, killing 143 men, wounding 200—among them Captain Dixie Kiefer—knocking out all radio and radar, setting off raging fires on the hangar deck and leaving the flight deck temporarily inoperable.

With the crippled carrier under special escort, Halsey went off on yet another mission—a combined bombing strike against the Ryukyu island chain and photographic reconnaissance of its largest island, Okinawa. Finally, on January 22, the admiral set course for the Ulithi atoll. His men badly needed rest and he, personally, had an important date to keep. On January 26 Halsey turned over his command to Admiral Spruance and prepared to leave for a rest in Hawaii before reporting to Washington for temporary duty.

Halsey had held the command since taking over from Spruance in August of 1944; in four more months Spruance would turn it back to Halsey again. The ritual, unique to the Pacific Fleet among all the world's navies, not only afforded the departing commander a respite from battle but also provided the fleet with a fresh new "backfield," as one Navy football fan put it. Some of the officers who witnessed the ceremony at Ulithi welcomed the shift from the visceral Halsey to the cerebral Spruance. With Halsey, one of them said, "you never knew what you were going to do in the next five minutes or how you were going to do it." Spruance, he noted, was more orderly; the printed instructions issued to the officers were kept up to date, and "you did things in accordance with them."

In the change-over, the fleet itself underwent a numerical transformation. When Halsey was in command, it was called the Third Fleet, and the fast-carrier groups, generally under Vice Admiral John S. McCain, were designated Task Force 38. Under Spruance, the fleet became the Fifth Fleet and the carriers became Task Force 58, under Vice Admiral Marc A. "Pete" Mitscher. An incidental effect of this numbers game was to confuse the Japanese; some of them were convinced that they were alternately confronting two fleets.

As Halsey was about to depart on leave—and "moping around," he later confessed—he received a farewell message from General MacArthur. The gesture was not surprising—Halsey came closer than most Annapolis men to being considered an acceptable warrior by the general —but the message was a mite baffling. It read: YOUR DEPARTURE FROM THIS THEATER LEAVES A GAP THAT CAN BE FOULED ONLY BY YOUR RETURN. Halsey chose to believe that the dispatch had been garbled in transmission and that the general had meant to say "filled."

On the 10th of February the newly renumbered Task Force 58, under Admiral Mitscher, sortied from Ulithi for a series of air strikes against Tokyo and its environs—the first aerial attack on the Japanese capital since Lieut. Colonel Jimmy Doolittle's raid in April of 1942, and the first ever to be attempted by carrier planes. The mission, which was aimed at airfields and aircraft plants in and around Tokyo, was important both tactically and strategically. The assault on Iwo Jima was only nine days away; the danger that Japanese planes might disrupt the landings had to be minimized. At the same time, the enemy's air arm might be dealt a permanently crippling blow.

The stately parade of ships leaving Ulithi's lagoon included 16 carriers; two of them—the *Bennington* and the *Randolph*—were brand-new. Mitscher had a few aces up his sleeve as well. Because of the Kamikaze menace, his air groups had been rearranged to allow for a heavy preponderance of fighters over bombers and torpedo planes. To make up a deficit of carrier-trained Navy fighter pilots, Marines flying Corsairs had joined the fleet.

Moreover—since nobody could with any confidence predict what to expect on this first run up to the enemy's coast—Task Force 58 had been supplied with extra eyes and ears. Submarines scouted ahead to look for and dispose of Japanese picket boats that might warn of the fleet's approach. B-29s and Navy Liberators from the Marianas prowled the skies near the coast, and a screen of five destroyers took the van 35 miles ahead of the main fleet. These cautionary measures yielded only small game: one snooping Betty bomber and a picket boat whose sinking produced a single wet, cold and terrified prisoner.

The U.S. fliers had expected to launch their strike from a distance of 100 or more miles off the main home island of Honshu. But by the time the first fighter pilots manned their planes and began taking off before 7 a.m. on February 16, Mitscher had brought them within 60 miles of Honshu's shoreline—only 120 miles from Tokyo. The weather was discouraging, with a solid overcast at 4,000 feet, scattered clouds at 1,000, and squalls of snow and rain.

The pilots were braced for a furious counterattack; they were, after all, challenging the spirit of *Bushido* on its own home grounds. Over the Chiba Peninsula east of Tokyo the overcast broke, and the first strike of 40 fighters ran into about 100 enemy fighters; in the ensuing melee, the U.S. group claimed 40 Japanese planes shot down to two of its own. Elsewhere, the opposition proved scattered and rarely

very aggressive, though there were exceptions. Preparing for a strafing run on an airfield bordering Tokyo Bay, Lieutenant Donald G. Kent watched his flight leader, Commander Philip H. Torrey Jr., engage in a head-on duel with a new Tojo fighter. The Hellcat and the Tojo swept toward each other, closing at perhaps 700 miles an hour, both planes with their guns flaming. The charge ended when the Japanese plane went down trailing smoke. Kent thought Torrey had won until he saw the Hellcat suddenly begin to climb, then dive, then go out of control and spin downward. Evidently, the Tojo pilot had managed to kill Torrey before his own fatal plunge.

Throughout the day and into dusk, when night fighters from the veteran carriers *Enterprise* and *Saratoga* went to work, the U.S. pilots strafed, bombed and rocketed airfields in the Kanto Plain around Tokyo, and got in an apparently effective strike at the Nakajima airframe assembly plant 40 miles from the city.

On the morning of the 17th, low black clouds scudded over the sea, and Mitscher's ships were sporadically lashed by rain and sleet. Nevertheless, strikes by more than 200 aircraft, half of them bombers, were launched against the Tachikawa and Musashi aircraft-engine plants near Tokyo. Somewhat more aggressive than the day before, Japanese fighters picked at the fringes of the attackers from the coast to the target and out again. Then, shortly after 11 a.m., the weather socked down so tight on both sea and targets that Mitscher recalled all aircraft and headed south.

Adding up their score, the American pilots claimed a total of 341 enemy planes destroyed in the air and another 190 on the ground—probably exaggerated in both categories—three aircraft plants damaged and numerous airfield installations knocked out. Further damage was done in the harbors; many small craft were strafed and rocketed, and one ship of more than 10,000 tons, the cargo vessel *Yamashio Maru*, was sunk in Yokohama harbor.

For their part, the Americans had lost 60 planes in combat and 28 in operational mishaps. One survivor by a narrow margin was Ensign Louis A. Menard Jr., the pilot of a Hellcat that was hit by a 40mm burst at 6,000 feet over Tokyo Bay. The Hellcat began to spin, but Menard managed to pull out at 2,000 feet; he found that his right aileron had been smashed but that he could manage the plane so long as he kept the speed below 185 miles per hour.

Menard headed out to sea and went looking for help in the murk, knowing that his plane's delicate condition would not permit landing on a carrier and jeopardizing the other planes on the deck. He found the destroyer *Taussig,* but as he prepared to bail out his troubles multiplied. When he tried to roll open the Hellcat's canopy, it stuck on a jagged edge of metal that had been torn by enemy flak. The pins that secured the canopy proved to be rusty, and Menard had difficulty budging them with his cold, stiffened fingers. When the canopy finally did break loose, it pulled a safety cable across his chest and pinned him in the cockpit. At last

he hacked through the wire with a jackknife, went out over the trailing edge of the wing and pulled his rip cord.

When he hit the water, his parachute failed to deflate, and he could not cut it loose because his knife was back in the cockpit, nor could he inflate his life jacket. Then the wind gusted, and the chute, as Menard later recalled, "started to drag me along the water. The waves were pretty big. I would blow through one, then skip along in the trough and then be dragged through another wave. I tried to breathe while I was in the valley and hold my breath while going through the waves. . . . Then things got dimmer and dimmer and finally I blacked out."

In an extraordinary feat of seamanship, the *Taussig's* skip-

Hangars and workshops at the Omura Aircraft Factory on Kyushu belch black smoke during a bombing raid staged by carrier-based planes of U.S. Task Force 58 on March 18, 1945. The attack, coming two weeks before the invasion of Okinawa, was part of a bombing campaign intended to cut Japan's production of airplanes to be used as Kamikazes.

per, Commander Josephus A. Robbins, stopped his ship dead in the water with its stern just downwind of Menard's skittering parachute. The chute billowed up against the fantail, and sailors heaved the unconscious flier aboard. More than an hour's labor by pharmacist's mates revived him. Two days later, Menard was aboard his own ship, the carrier Randolph, ready though not anxious to fight again.

From the Honshu coast, Task Force 58 sped south to provide close-in support for the Iwo landing and to fend off any enemy aircraft intent on hobbling the operation. While some of TF 58's pilots bombed, rocketed and strafed Japanese installations ashore in a coordinated effort with the Marines fighting to root out the enemy cave by cave, other carrier pilots struck at the neighboring islands of Haha-jima and Chichi-jima; both had small airfields from which harassing attacks could be launched.

Meanwhile, the combat air patrol shielded the transports and other ships of the U.S. amphibious force so effectively that they enjoyed total immunity from danger overhead. But three carriers—the preferred target of the Japanese planes—were less lucky. On February 21, the third day of the Iwo Jima invasion, a Kamikaze torpedo bomber hit the escort carrier Lunga Point; though the plane exploded before contact and ended by plunging into the sea, it started a fire as it skidded across the carrier's flight deck. Lunga Point's crew doused the fire, and she was able to keep going. In the next 10 minutes, two more Kamikazes dived into the escort carrier Bismarck Sea, touching off a series of explosions that engulfed her in flames. Three hours later, abandoned by her crew, she sank.

The big old carrier Saratoga—Sara to her many admirers—had been detached from Mitscher's task force to furnish a nightly combat air patrol over the invasion armada. Just before 5 p.m., 35 miles off Iwo, six Japanese planes came through a lowering cloud cover at 3,500 feet and dived in on the carrier. Two, aflame from her antiaircraft fire, hit the water, then skipped and plunged against the ship's side at the waterline. Their bombs penetrated the hull and exploded inside. Almost simultaneously a third plane dropped a bomb that detonated on an anchor windlass, wrecking the forward section of the flight deck. A fourth plane went into the water, but the fifth crashed into the ship

and blew up on the port catapult. The sixth, already in flames, crashed into an aircraft crane on the starboard side and flopped over into the sea. The Saratoga was severely hurt topside, but her engineering plant was whole and by 6:46 the fires were under control.

Just at that juncture, parachute flares lighted up the scene and five more Kamikazes dropped through the clouds. Four were shot down, but the fifth dropped a bomb that blew a 25-foot hole in the flight deck while the plane struck and bounced overboard. By now Sara had been hit in seven places and had lost 123 men killed and 192 wounded. The planes she had sent aloft for night patrol had been compelled to land on other carriers. But by a little after 8 p.m.

Crippled by two Japanese bombs, the carrier Franklin erupts in a chain of fiery explosions, forcing the assisting cruiser Santa Fe to pull away temporarily for her own safety. Sailors on the Santa Fe had slung their fire hoses between the ships for use by crewmen on the listing carrier. The fires were finally put out, and the Franklin remained afloat, although more heavily damaged than any other ship of the War that did not sink.

she was able to take them back aboard and was on the way, under her own power, to a three-month repair job on the U.S. West Coast.

On the reasonable assumption that at least some of the attacking planes had come all the way from Japan, Mitscher was eager for another go at the enemy's homeland. On February 23, his task force left Iwo, bound for the waters off Nampo Shoto, the archipelago directly south of the home island of Honshu. A repeat strike at the Tokyo area was planned for February 25, and a first strike at aircraft plants in the heavily industrial Nagoya area for the next day.

Then the weather took a hand. It turned foul not only over the projected targets but in the vicinity of TF 58.

Visibility was poor and the carrier pilots took off from pitching decks. The Nagoya strike had to be canceled; the Tokyo strike was a disappointment. In the late winter that had settled on Japan, snow covered the targeted airfields; in any case, they were virtually empty of planes. The Japanese had begun taking special measures to conceal their remaining aircraft from aerial hunters, hiding them under haystacks, trees or camouflage netting along country roads up to five miles from their runways.

In mid-March, after a period of rest and replenishment at Ulithi, Task Force 58 returned to Japanese waters, this time on a mission of utmost urgency. The U.S. assault on Okina-

wa was set for April 1, and both the seas and skies around it had to be swept clear for the invading force. Mitscher's top-priority targets now were some 45 airfields on the home island of Kyushu, within fighter range of Okinawa, and the enemy's big naval bases at Kobe and Kure on the home island of Honshu. Mitscher had reason to be confident. Task Force 58 was at peak strength: 16 fast carriers in four task groups, eight new battleships, two new cruisers with guns nearly as large as those on the battleships, 14 lesser cruisers and attendant destroyers.

The strike took place over two days. It began at 5:45 a.m. on March 18, with fighter sweeps launched about 100 miles east of Kyushu's southern tip. The pilots hit all 45 of the targeted airfields and claimed 387 Japanese aircraft destroyed, mostly on the ground. That night the task force steamed northeastward, and next day it hit Kobe and Kure. The day's score added up to 17 Japanese warships damaged, including the great battleship Yamato and four carriers.

The initial Japanese response to the strike was largely ineffective. On the first morning, shortly after the early sweeps were launched, a Japanese plane slid through the combat air patrol and dropped a bomb on the Enterprise's flight deck. The weapon was a dud. It failed to detonate, bounced as high as the bridge, fell and rolled off the stern. Nobody was hurt. A Betty swept down on the Intrepid, but smashed into the sea after running into a curtain of anti-aircraft fire. Parts of the plane ricocheted against the hull and killed two men. In the afternoon three Japanese planes dived on the Yorktown; two missed, but a bomb from the third struck the signal bridge, skidded down the ship's side and exploded, tearing holes in the hull and killing five men. All three carriers continued flight operations.

But the Japanese were not yet done. Soon after sunrise the next morning, an enemy aircraft suddenly appeared over the Wasp and scored a direct hit with a bomb. The carrier's flight deck was partially clear; two thirds of her planes had already gone off on strikes. The Japanese bomb did not explode until it had sheared all the way through to the third deck, where cooks and mess attendants were preparing to serve breakfast; they were the first victims among a toll of 101 dead and 269 wounded. The fires touched off by the explosion—and stoked by leaking aviation gas—spread to five decks. But thanks to improved damage-control methods aboard the newer U.S. carriers, the fire was contained within 15 minutes. Within the hour, the Wasp was able to begin receiving her returning planes. She was to remain in operation for several days before heading back to base for repairs.

The ordeal of the carrier Franklin was by far the worst. A few minutes after seven that morning, she was launching her second strike for Kure. Most of the planes were still on the flight deck, armed, gassed and manned. A third strike was being readied on the hangar deck below, also armed and gassed. Out of nowhere, seen by nobody and showing on no radar screen, a Japanese plane came over the bow and dropped two 550-pound bombs. The first went through the flight deck near the forward elevator and exploded on the hangar deck; the second struck the flight deck and went off among a number of aircraft warming up to launch.

Both bombs set off huge fires, fed by high-octane gasoline and, as the heat swiftly built up, by bombs bursting in their racks. Then a dozen "Tiny Tim" rockets, each packing more than 1,200 pounds of explosives and slung under the wings of fighter-bombers, began to go off. "Some screamed by to starboard, some to port and some straight up the flight deck," the Franklin's executive officer said later. "The weird aspect of this weapon whooshing by so close is one of the most awful spectacles a human has ever been privileged to see." The ship's vitals were torn by a series of explosions so powerful they could be heard aboard the carrier Bunker Hill beyond the horizon. Hundreds of men were killed at once, some when they were flung against steel bulkheads. The impact of the explosions threw hundreds more into the sea.

The Roman Catholic chaplain aboard the Franklin, Father Joseph Timothy O'Callahan, crouched beneath a table in the wardroom, where seconds earlier he had been breakfasting on French toast. Shielding his head against bits of glass that showered down from broken light fixtures, he listened to the death-dealing explosions all around him and began to utter the words of general absolution from sins. Then he made his way up ladders to his cabin two decks above. From his safe he took out the vial containing the holy oils for the dying, put on his steel helmet with the white cross on it, and "went in search of my proper work."

He found the forward flight deck littered with the bodies

of the dead, dying and burned. One of the *Franklin's* surgeons, Lieut. Commander Samuel R. Sherman, was tending to the men who were still alive, helped by pharmacist's mates. Father O'Callahan joined them "to administer spiritual treatment," as he said. After a while, with all the patients attended to, he and the surgeon took a moment to rest, and exchanged experiences. It turned out that Sherman had been briefly knocked unconscious by one of the explosions; Father O'Callahan had suffered a gash in his leg from a flying hunk of steel, and Sherman now patched the wound. "Amidst the fire and explosion in this moment of respite," Father O'Callahan was later to recall, "the Jewish doctor and the Catholic chaplain said a prayer together."

Rear Admiral Ralph E. Davison, commander of one group of Task Force 58, was aboard the *Franklin*. He ordered a destroyer alongside to transfer his flag to another ship. As he left, he advised Captain Leslie E. Gehres, the *Franklin's* skipper, to get ready to abandon. Gehres demurred and a few minutes later got off a message to Admiral Mitscher, aboard his flagship *Bunker Hill*. The message was a terse one that was in time to become a Navy classic: "This is the commanding officer of *Franklin*. You save us from the Japs and we'll save this ship." Mitscher, watching the black clouds of smoke boiling above the horizon, said to his chief of staff, "You tell him we'll save him."

At about 9:30 a.m. the wounded ship began to get outside help. The cruiser *Santa Fe* veered in and came alongside, holding there with her engines, taking the heat of the *Franklin's* fires and the risks of her exploding ammunition. The cruiser put her hoses across to help the carrier's struggling fire fighters. She also began receiving the wounded, some by breeches buoy, others carried out on the carrier's horizontal antenna masts and lowered to the cruiser's deck. In half an hour, the *Santa Fe* had taken in 832 men.

One got there almost entirely by accident. Storekeeper Second Class Edward D. Mesial had been trapped below in one of the *Franklin's* burning compartments. Somehow, gasping for breath, he found his way through a hatch and onto the catwalk alongside the flight deck. "I heard people yelling for me to crawl over the side and onto a cruiser that was picking up wounded men," Mesial recalled. "I tried, and my legs wouldn't move any more. So I just lay there on the catwalk, hoping and praying that my strength would

return. Then the ship listed heavily to starboard—and I tumbled off, right onto the deck of *Santa Fe*."

At 10 a.m. the build-up of heat drove the remaining crew out of the engine areas, and the *Franklin* was dead in the water. But by noon the fires were nearly under control and the list was stabilized at 13 degrees. Captain Gehres' prayerful boast had been realized.

In early afternoon, the cruiser *Pittsburgh* slid in close and passed a towline, which was secured to the *Franklin's* bow. By degrees the cruiser worked its 36,000-ton burden around to a southerly course and eventually built up to six knots—a job made doubly difficult because the *Franklin's* rudder was jammed hard left and she wanted to yaw. But men were at work down in the tormented carrier's bowels. They managed to free the rudder and get the boilers lit again. By 11 a.m. on March 20, they had two shafts turning well enough to give the carrier seven knots under her own power. At noon the tow was cast off and, guarded by her sisters, the *Franklin* was on her way to Ulithi and, eventually, to the Brooklyn Navy Yard.

She had lost 724 killed; about 1,700 men had been evacuated or rescued from the water. Some solicitous skippers thought the *Franklin* might need additional manpower—since there were only about 700 of her original complement still aboard—and that perhaps she could use provisions as well. An offer was made but Gehres replied, "We have plenty of men and food. All we want is to get the hell out of here." A little later, as the speed built up, he reported: "Down by the tail but reins up!"

The airplane that had touched off the fearful carnage on the *Franklin* was not a Kamikaze. It was a conventional bomber and surely the most successful of its breed, even though it was shot down. But as the crippled *Franklin* made her slow way home, other ships of the Pacific Fleet were about to confront the full fury of the Kamikazes.

The fleet was now shifting into its other function as static bodyguard for the work ashore on Okinawa. This was expected to be a stint of no more than a few days. But, as it turned out, the difficulties of the Okinawa operation compelled the fast-carrier groups to be confined to the narrow seas around the island for more than two months—while the Kamikazes, knowing exactly where to find them, came at them in waves.

PLAYGROUND IN THE PACIFIC

Lounging in the shade of coconut palms, officers of the U.S. Pacific Fleet enjoy the tunes of a Navy band on the beach at Mogmog Island, the fleet's rest center.

A GOB'S PARADISE ON MOGMOG

The U.S. Navy got an unexpected bonus when, in September 1944, it took over the Ulithi atoll in the western Caroline Islands as a convenient forward base for operations against Japan. Mogmog, one of many islands inside the huge coral reef, was a splendid place for sea-weary sailors to stretch their legs while their ships were being resupplied in the harbor. So the Navy brass persuaded the local chieftain, King Ueg, to move Mogmog's 300 residents to another island. Then a small staff built a chapel, a movie theater and refreshment stands, transforming Mogmog into a recreation center for the men.

During the eight or 10 days that a ship spent in the harbor, each crewman was allowed one or two days ashore on Mogmog. As many as 15,000 eager sailors a day swarmed onto the small (about 60 acres) island at 1 p.m. and stayed until 6 p.m., when everyone was required to return to his ship. So many men were milling about on the island that, according to a Navy report, "Mogmog resembled a sandwich discarded near an ant heap."

The sailors' favorite activities on the island were the four B's—bathing, baseball, boxing and above all beer drinking. The beer was free but strictly limited, at least for enlisted men. Each sailor was given ration coupons that entitled him to exactly two cans of beer. Of course it was no great trick to stretch the limit, and every day a fair number of gobs managed to get thoroughly drunk on the brew. Thirsty sailors would buy their shipmates' beer coupons for large sums of otherwise useless cash. And some men were willing to pay an even higher price for a couple of extra cans, swapping their first leave in San Francisco.

After a sojourn on Mogmog, the men came away with mixed feelings about the place. A destroyer captain snorted that "it's just a couple of logs and beer cans," and Navy wags cracked that it had "no wine atoll, no women atoll, no nothing atoll." But most of the sailors agreed with the officer who described the island—pompously but not inaccurately—as "a welcome oasis of relaxation in the long drive to crush the Japanese Empire."

A visitor on Mogmog studies a map of the island, which shows the areas that were reserved for officers, enlisted men and a battalion of Seabees.

In the busy harbor at Ulithi, small boats ferrying sailors to and from Mogmog weave their way in and out among destroyers, supply boats and repair ships.

Two sailors manning a refreshment stand wait to hand out free beer and soft drinks to enlisted men.

Lolling gobs guzzle beer—no less a treat for the fact that it was often as warm as the tropical weather.

Sun-baked sailors take a dip in Mogmog's crystal-clear waters. Canny swimmers wore sneakers to protect themselves from the sharp coral of offshore reefs.

Inside the junior officers' club, Navy pilots relax and chat over beer. No matter where their conversation started, they invariably ended up comparing notes on aerial tactics.

RANK AND PRIVILEGE ON A PRIMITIVE ISLAND

Rank had its privileges even on Mogmog: A choice area known as Officers' Country was off limits to enlisted men. Here commissioned officers lounged about in their thatch-roofed clubs, purchased as much beer as they pleased and—between 3 p.m. and 6 p.m.—sipped Scotch or bourbon at 20 cents a shot.

The officers, too, were neatly segregated by rank. There was a separate club for junior officers and another for lieutenant commanders, commanders and captains, while the admirals took their ease in King Ueg's former palace, a hut that actually boasted tables and chairs. But there was one conspicuous exception to this rigid caste system: off-duty Navy nurses were permitted to circulate freely among the officers' clubs and converse with anyone from admiral to ensign.

A volunteer band of black sailors performs outside a clubhouse in Officers' Country. Blacks throughout the Navy were relegated to the positions of ship's steward and cook.

Navy nurses, the only women allowed on Mogmog, prepare to return to their hospital ships. As officers, nurses were expected to avoid social encounters with enlisted men.

Boisterous sailors crowd a boat ferrying them back to the carrier Intrepid following an afternoon on Mogmog. At island-closing, the thousands of gobs jamming

the island's single jetty were so rambunctious that sailors were often bumped overboard and had to be fished out of the water soaking wet and fighting mad.

4

On the morning of March 29, 1945—three days before the American assault on Okinawa—a number of U.S. landing craft appeared off the island's southwestern beaches about 500 yards from shore. Under a covering bombardment by the guns of the Pacific Fleet, they discharged an odd sort of cargo into the water: 1,000 swimmers in trunks, rubber flippers and face masks, their bodies camouflaged with silver paint. The gear each of them carried looked innocuous enough: a reel of fishing line knotted at 25-yard intervals, a length of sounding line and a lead weight, a stylus for making notes and, as a writing surface, a sheet of plexiglass wrapped around the left forearm.

The crews aboard the landing craft, watching the swimmers head toward the enemy shore, could understand why they were fondly known as "half fish and half nuts." These superbly conditioned men were all volunteers—members of the Navy's Underwater Demolition Teams and participants in some of the riskiest ventures of the War. UDTs had helped scout the way for the invasions of Sicily, Normandy, Kwajalein, Saipan and, most recently, Iwo Jima. Their mission at Okinawa posed its own complexities.

Okinawa was one of the largest Pacific islands thus far targeted for capture by the Americans. But it had one topographical feature more often associated with atolls—a fringing coral reef. Nourished by the warm waters of the Japan Current, the reef had grown into a tortuous trap for the unwary. To cross it safely, assault-craft crews had to know its extent and the depth of the water above it; without such information, a boat could be hung up or smashed to bits. Americans had learned this the hard way as far back as their first amphibious operation in the central Pacific, the invasion of the Tarawa atoll in November of 1943.

After that, UDT techniques had been refined to a science. Each swimmer off Okinawa began by securing one end of the fishing line to the reef's outer edge. Moving shoreward, he gradually unwound the reel, pausing every 25 yards—at each knot in the line—to take a sounding with his lead; at depths of a fathom or less, he could use his own body as a gauge. Each measurement was noted by stylus on the plexiglass sheet, along with the location of safe channels and of protruding coral knobs and other obstacles.

All the while, the UDTs faced the unnerving possibility of being cut down either by stray shells from their own bom-

ASSAULT ON OKINAWA

barding ships or by gunfire from the Japanese on the island. But that morning they were in luck; the shelling was on target and the attention of the Japanese was further diverted by a carrier-plane strike. About an hour after the swimmers had begun their labors, they were hauled back aboard the landing craft, no worse the wear except for a few coral scrapes and leg cramps.

The plexiglass data went into the speedy revision of charts of the projected Okinawa beachhead; the UDTs themselves were closely questioned as to what they had seen. As it happened, one of their answers compelled a repeat performance the following day. The swimmers confirmed that though they had encountered no mines—that problem had been previously disposed of by U.S. minesweepers—they had found another menace to the assault craft: hundreds upon hundreds of wooden stakes, four to eight feet high and laced with barbed wire, planted everywhere in the reef.

When the teams reappeared off the beaches the next morning, they had small explosive charges in tow and an incredibly exacting task ahead. For three hours, much of the time underwater, they moved from stake to stake—about 2,900 in all—attaching the charges and interconnecting the detonators. They then set off the fuses and raced seaward. In one shattering chain explosion, the path the U.S. attackers would have to take to shore was effectively cleared.

Some 15 miles west of Okinawa, another operation designed to ease the difficulties of the impending invasion met with equal success. At dawn on March 26, five battalion landing teams of the U.S. 77th Infantry Division went ashore on five rocky islands of a small group known as Kerama-retto. For the next three days, the landing teams swept through the group until by the 29th all eight islets that make up the Keramas were declared secured.

The Japanese had not foreseen an attack on the Keramas and had not bothered to build up the defenses there; in fact, more than half of the 2,300 troops previously on the islands had recently been shifted to Okinawa. But to the Americans, the Keramas were well worth taking. They sheltered an excellent roadstead, about eight miles long and four miles wide, whose waters could hold about 50 large ships; moreover, both ends of the anchorage could be closed off with antisubmarine nets. Instead of refueling and

replenishing near Okinawa, thus inviting enemy surface and air attacks, ships of the invasion armada would be able to use the haven of the Keramas for these services.

The islands yielded an unexpected bonus as well. Unknown to the Americans, the Japanese had intended the Keramas as an operating base for *renraku tei*—explosives-laden suicide boats that would hurl themselves against U.S. ships off Okinawa. The boats, made of plywood, were about 18 feet long and five feet wide; powered by an 85-horsepower engine, they could attain a speed of 20 knots. Each of the boats was equipped with two 264-pound depth charges. According to captured Japanese instructions, the boats were to travel in threes, run alongside an enemy ship—preferably a transport "loaded with essential supplies and material and personnel"—then trip the depth charges, causing them to roll from their rack and over the stern. The pilots had five seconds in which to make their getaway before the charges exploded. No one expected them to survive the blast.

Mopping up in the Keramas, troops of the 77th Division came upon more than 350 of the suicide boats, which had been camouflaged and hidden in caves and coves. The Americans splintered them.

The 77th followed its seizure of the Keramas with the take-over of Keise Shima, a smaller group of islands only six miles off Okinawa's southwestern coast. On the morning of March 31, just 24 hours before the assault on Okinawa, a battalion of the 77th landed on Keise's four sandy islets. Opposition was minimal; again the Japanese had misjudged the worth of the prize. On Keise Shima, the Americans were able to emplace 155mm artillery that could reach all the way to the area around Naha, Okinawa's largest town, and provide massive fire support as the U.S. invaders advanced.

The eve of the invasion found its planners satisfied. The preliminaries had gone as hoped. Okinawa had been deprived of the use of two of its satellite island groups. Its perilous fringing reef had been given a thorough going-over. And the island itself had been subjected to six days of ferocious pounding by the Pacific Fleet—twice the duration of the softening-up process at Iwo Jima.

The Americans were under no delusion that the landing, or its aftermath, would go anywhere near as smoothly as the preliminaries. Okinawa was 60 times the size of Iwo and, according to the latest U.S. intelligence estimate, harbored about 75,000 troops. The defenders were certain to put up at least as fierce a fight as at Iwo. The Japanese were well aware that Okinawa was logically the last stop on the road to Japan, only 300 nautical miles away; and, unlike tiny Iwo, it could accommodate a major U.S. staging base for a direct assault on the homeland.

Expecting the stiffest sort of resistance, the Americans were instead about to be enveloped in euphoria. By the end of the first day's action, 60,000 men would be safely ashore on Okinawa, at a cost of no more than 28 lives.

That day, April 1, happened to be Easter. For the military record, it was designated as L-day, for Landing-day. The choice of the new designation had been made to avoid confusion during the hectic period when the Iwo and Okinawa campaigns were being simultaneously mounted; the right to the customary term, D-day, had been assigned to Iwo's planners. The matter meant little to the fighting men who landed on Okinawa on April 1. Later, the cynics among them would remember the date as April Fool's Day.

But at the time, the landings seemed miraculously free of hitches. Four divisions moved in abreast, their assault craft churning up a froth of white wakes eight miles wide. On the left were two Marine divisions, the 6th and the 1st, of Major General Roy S. Geiger's III Amphibious Corps. On the right were two Army divisions, the 7th and the 96th Infantry, of Lieut. General John R. Hodge's XXIV Corps. Their destination was a long, straight stretch of sandy beach fronting on a village named Hagushi, on Okinawa's lower western coast. The Hagushi area had been wisely chosen. Behind it the land sloped gently upward, offering easy passage from the beachhead to two top-priority objectives, the Yontan and Kadena airfields, each lying only about a mile inland.

The veteran newspaper columnist Ernie Pyle, who went in with the Marines, marveled at the peaceful scene around him. "Never before had I seen an invasion beach like Okinawa," he reported. "There wasn't a dead or wounded man in our whole sector of it. Medical corpsmen were sitting among their sacks of bandages and plasma and stretchers, with nothing to do. There wasn't a single burning vehicle, nor a single boat lying wrecked on the reef or shoreline. The carnage that is almost inevitable on an invasion was wonderfully and beautifully not there."

Troop-carrying amtracs begin the 4,000-yard run to Okinawa's Hagushi beaches at 8:10 a.m. on April 1, 1945. Behind them the battleship Tennessee adds one more salvo to the heaviest preinvasion bombardment of the Pacific war.

In the invasion of Okinawa, the main assault force of four divisions went ashore on the west coast (straight arrow) while one division made a feint (curved arrow) at the south coast. Of the four outfits that landed at once, the 1st and 6th Marine Divisions were assigned to move north and east, leaving the 7th and 96th Infantry Divisions to attack the principal Japanese line of defense in the south.

To the poetic eye of Marine First Lieutenant David Tucker Brown Jr., the landing was "more like a pastoral than a battle." Inland from the beach, he wrote to his family back in Virginia, "were furrowed fields or patches of ripe white winter barley, and tiny bright field flowers were scattered over the light earth. We were all incredulous, as if we had stepped into a fairy tale."

By 10:30 a.m., two hours after the first Americans had come ashore, patrols from the 7th Infantry Division had reached and moved beyond the Kadena airfield; an hour later the Yontan airfield was firmly in the hands of 6th Division Marines. So tranquil was the scene at Yontan that in the afternoon a Japanese Zero dipped through the clouds and landed. The pilot was out of the plane and walking toward the hangars before he noticed anything unusual about the soldiers lounging there. When he did, he drew a pistol—an error that cost him his life.

By nightfall on L-day, the U.S. beachhead was 5,000 yards deep and 15,000 yards wide, and so many Okinawa civilians had flocked to the American lines that a camp was set up to receive them. By nightfall on L-plus-1, units of the 1st Marine Division were almost across the Ishikawa isthmus,

the narrow neck of land between the southern third of Okinawa and the rest of the island. On L-plus-2 the Americans completed their sweep across the isthmus and on L-plus-3 secured a broad stretch of the east coast, cutting off the defenders in the north from those in the south.

In just four days, the assault on Okinawa had achieved what its planners had figured would take three weeks. Lieut. General Simon Bolivar Buckner Jr., who as head of the newly created Tenth Army was in charge of the U.S. land operation on Okinawa, was still aboard the command ship *Eldorado*. At his direction, the battle plan was amended to lift the limitations on day-to-day objectives. The III Amphibious Corps, with the 6th Marine Division in the vanguard and the 1st Marine Division covering the rear, was to move immediately against the upper two thirds of the island. The XXIV Army Corps, with the 7th and 96th Infantry Divisions side by side, was to move southward for the assault on Okinawa's lower third.

Thus far, the Japanese had given little sign of their presence. Here and there, the Americans had run into scattered sniping and occasional rounds of enemy artillery; few of the fire

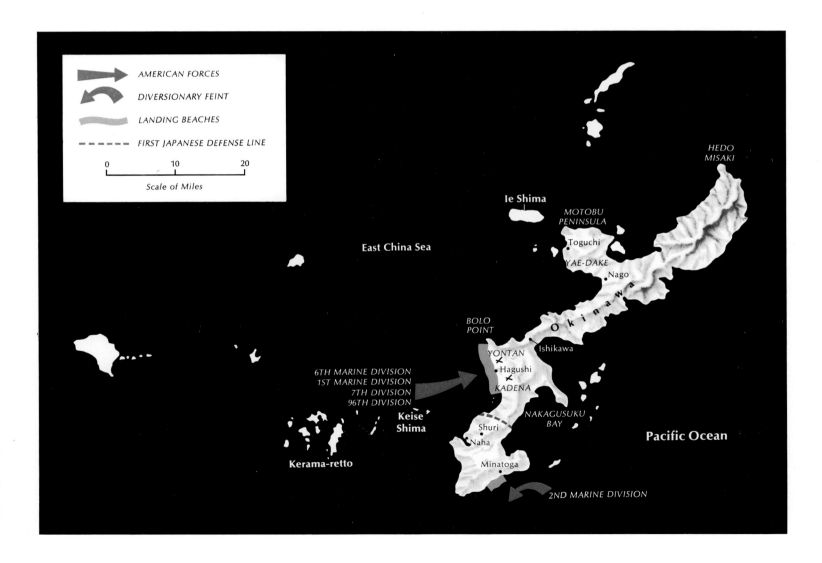

AMERICAN FORCES

DIVERSIONARY FEINT

LANDING BEACHES

FIRST JAPANESE DEFENSE LINE

0   10   20

Scale of Miles

HEDO MISAKI

Ie Shima

MOTOBU PENINSULA

East China Sea

Toguchi

YAE-DAKE

Nago

BOLO POINT

Okinawa

Ishikawa

YONTAN

Hagushi

KADENA

NAKAGUSUKU BAY

6TH MARINE DIVISION
1ST MARINE DIVISION
7TH DIVISION
96TH DIVISION

Keise Shima

Shuri

Naha

Pacific Ocean

Kerama-retto

Minatoga

2ND MARINE DIVISION

fights had lasted for more than minutes. Otherwise, the U.S. advance had been virtually unhindered. Lieut. General Mitsuru Ushijima, the Japanese commander on Okinawa, had planned it that way.

Like his counterpart on Iwo, Ushijima assumed from the start that he would be fighting a lost cause. But he proposed to exact as high a toll as possible from the enemy, both in manpower and in time; the longer he could hold out on Okinawa, the longer he could stave off an assault on the homeland. His superiors in Tokyo had encouraged him in this resolve, promising to launch a succession of suicide attacks on the U.S. invasion armada and its supply ships.

Ushijima was superbly equipped to wage a war of attrition. He had more weaponry than had been available for the defense of any Pacific island previously targeted by the Americans; a large part of this arsenal had been intended for the Philippines but had been retained on Okinawa because of transshipment problems. Ushijima also had a much larger defense force than U.S. intelligence had estimated—substantially more than 100,000 troops.

The principal elements of Ushijima's Thirty-second Army were the veteran 62nd Infantry Division out of China, the 24th Infantry Division from Manchuria and the 44th Independent Mixed Brigade from the home island of Kyushu—all told, about 34,000 frontline foot soldiers. Another 10,000 foot soldiers had been put together from Japanese Navy personnel based on Okinawa and the nearby islands. All together, with service and construction outfits, the general had 80,000 men at his disposal. The infantry was supported by the normal divisional field guns and mortars; in addition Ushijima had a tank regiment, three artillery regiments—two of 150mm howitzers and one a mixture of 75mm and 120mm guns—and a regiment of the giant 320mm mortars that had wreaked havoc among the Americans on Iwo.

A part of Ushijima's defense force was Okinawan. The Boeitai, a home guard organized in mid-1944, had recently been absorbed into the Thirty-second Army. Its 20,000 members were dubious combat material but dependable workers, relieving Ushijima's regulars of such sweaty tasks as excavating the countless dugouts that now dotted Okinawa's hills; women members handled various rear-echelon chores and served as nurses.

Rounding out the Okinawan contingent were about 1,700 high-school boys, some as young as 14; many had received their induction notices along with their diplomas at the Shuri Middle School's graduation ceremonies only the night before the invasion. These striplings were organized in so-called Tekketsu ("Blood and Iron for the Emperor" duty units) and were mostly assigned to the Thirty-second Army's communications system. At Ushijima's order they were also being schooled in guerrilla tactics—training that the general felt would be increasingly useful as the tide of battle inexorably ran against him.

But the first few days of the invasion had given Ushijima reason to hope that he could make the fight a long and brutal one for the enemy. None of the American moves thus far had altered his basic defense plan—or ruffled his characteristic calm. From the ramparts of Shuri Castle, the 15th Century fort that had once housed Okinawa's feudal kings, he had watched impassively as the Americans swarmed ashore. Their sheer numbers were enough to confirm his belief that any attempt to deny them the beachhead would have entailed a needless expenditure of his men.

Ushijima proposed instead to let the Americans come on until they ran up against his first major defense line. The Americans were far from certain where that would be. U.S. aerial reconnaissance had revealed a sharp difference of terrain between the north and the south of the island. Much of the lower third of Okinawa was gently rolling country, a patchwork of fields and villages. The upper two thirds was mostly mountainous, a jumble of pine-forested peaks and thicketed ravines from which defending troops would presumably be harder to dislodge. But what the Americans did not know was that Ushijima had, in effect, written off northern Okinawa, leaving fewer than 2,000 men to fight essentially delaying actions. A stronger defense of so large a region and its intricately curving coastlines would have required too great a dispersal of his forces.

Ushijima chose to make his main stand in the south, in a rugged area below the Ishikawa isthmus. Before the Americans moving down from the landing beaches could reach the gentler terrain at the island's southern end, they would have to break through a formidable natural barrier—a succession of jagged ridges, some rising to 300 feet, stretching

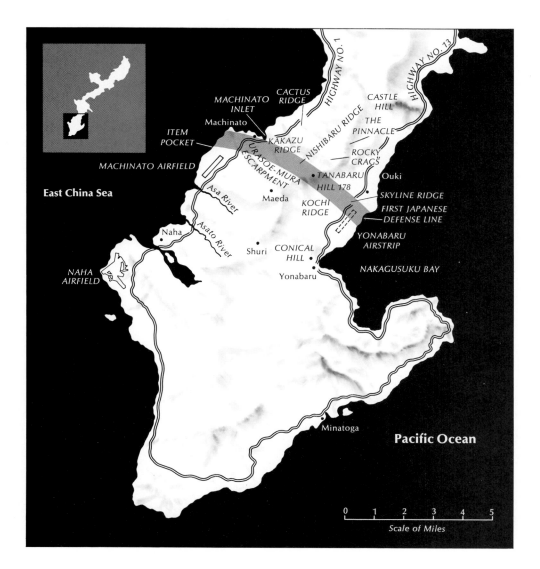

Rumbling inland from their landing craft, U.S. tanks roam at will across the farmers' fields behind the invasion beaches. Japanese opposition to the Okinawa landing was so slight that a correspondent who came ashore with the Marine vanguard wrote, "It was almost as though we were the original explorers."

Okinawa's defenders concentrated their forces in the southern third of the island, taking advantage of a series of natural barriers formed by ridges and cliffs that ran roughly east-west from coast to coast. The first line of defense, extending from Kakazu Ridge on the west to Skyline Ridge on the east, fell only after three weeks of bloody fighting.

clear across the island. Ushijima's plan called for defending this escarpment ridge by ridge, chewing up the Americans piecemeal as they tried to advance.

To complete his resistance in depth, Ushijima positioned a number of outposts in the area forward of the wall and several roughly concentric rings of defenses behind it, with Shuri Castle, his own headquarters, as anchor. Caves, both man-made and naturally formed out of the local limestone, provided ample room for additional gun emplacements. An ancient Okinawan funerary custom also served Ushijima's purposes. Families preserved the bones of their dead above-ground, inside masonry burial vaults. These tombs, studding the hillsides by the thousands, were ready-made rifle and mortar pits and machine-gun nests.

Belowground, Ushijima's labor units had dug hundreds of chambers, some large enough to shelter an entire company, and hundreds of connecting tunnels, including some that went all the way through the ridges from front to back. The complexity of this subterranean network was to win wide-spread American respect; at one point, when a U.S. tank fired six phosphorus smoke shells into one entrance of a single tunnel, the tank crew counted smoke spurting from more than 30 other entrances.

It was on April 5—L-plus-4—that the American troops moving southward on Okinawa began to realize that the real resistance had just begun. One chronicler of the cam-paign tersely summed up the new situation: "The honey-moon was over."

At first the three miles that separated the Americans from General Ushijima's defensive wall of cliffs and ridges did not look especially difficult. Parts of this terrain were fairly flat, with patches of cultivated farmland and open rice paddies. The hills that rose here and there were, with few exceptions, little more than knobs.

Ushijima himself did not expect to hold this outpost area for long—just long enough to give the Americans a blood-ing. For the first time since the invasion, they were to encounter defenses that had been presited for maximum effect and troops who were under no restraints. "Do your utmost," the soldiers had been told. "The victory of the century lies in this battle."

At the age of 57, Ushijima was a veteran tactician who

had held infantry commands in China during the late 1930s and in Burma in 1942, during Japan's conquest of Southeast Asia. On Okinawa he had arranged his defenses in masterly fashion. Minefields and tank traps guarded the approaches to the hills. At the foot of the slopes were trenches occupied by riflemen with grenades, light machine guns and knee mortars. Behind them, crews manned heavy machine-gun nests. Mortars were emplaced atop the hills and on the reverse slopes, and artillery observers were strategically spotted to call in the bigger guns along the main defense line to the south.

The defenders' primary strategy was to isolate the oncoming U.S. infantrymen from their protecting tanks. The armor would first be halted by artillery fire from the hills, then attacked close up by Japanese tank-destroyer teams hurling satchel charges and flaming bundles of rags. The tank crews would be shot and bayoneted as they popped out of their hatches to flee. U.S. infantrymen trying a frontal assault on a hill would then quickly find themselves pinned down without adequate cover or would be engaged in hand-to-hand combat with Japanese springing from caves, crevices and spider holes—dugouts with tightly fitting lids.

The Americans soon discovered the effectiveness of the Japanese tactics. The 7th Infantry Division, assigned to seize the eastern half of the outpost area, took seven days to cover the 6,000 yards from its jump-off point to its objective: the village of Ouki near the eastern end of Ushijima's main line. On the way, the men of the 7th had secured the eminences they would long remember as Castle Hill, The Pinnacle, Red Hill, Tomb Hill and Triangulation Hill. But, as Ushijima had intended, they had paid for their gains yard by yard—with more than 1,120 casualties.

The 96th Infantry Division, charged with taking the western half of the outpost area, had equally rough going. Seizing one hill alone—Cactus Ridge—took three days of furious frontal and flanking attacks. But the capture of that hill was vital: it lay only 1,200 yards north of the 96th's objective—the western end of Ushijima's first line, a rocky hogback named Kakazu Ridge.

To Colonel Edwin T. May, commander of the division's 383rd Regiment, the opportunity to be the first to crack a key sector of Ushijima's first line was irresistible. From where he stood on Cactus, Kakazu did not look particularly forbidding. At 280 feet, it was not as high or as precipitous as other parts of Ushijima's defense barrier, and some of its inclines were gentle enough to have been used by Okinawans as sites for their family tombs. The ridge was, in fact, two hills, connected by a saddle. Together, Kakazu and its western extension—soon dubbed Kakazu West—formed a ridge that ran for 1,000 yards.

One substantial hazard the Americans would have to deal with was a deep gorge directly in front of the ridge on the north side—the side from which the attack would have to come. The gorge, its depth partially concealed by trees and brush, was a natural tank trap. May decided that his infantrymen would have to go it alone, without any help from the Shermans. Moreover, he decided to dispense with any artillery preparation, the better to surprise the foe.

Before dawn on April 9, May threw four rifle companies against the ridge. Companies A and C of the 1st Battalion were to take Kakazu's crest; Companies L and I of the 3rd Battalion were to take the crest of Kakazu West. The assault was launched without incident, and by dawn Companies A and C were on Kakazu's crest, a fairly level strip of land about 25 yards wide, and Company L was partway up Kakazu West. The ascent had gone undetected except by a few sleepy Japanese pickets, swiftly bayoneted into silence. But at daylight a Japanese soldier in a pillbox near the top of Kakazu spotted the Americans there. All at once, the thunderous roar of a mortar and artillery barrage erupted along the entire ridge, followed by Japanese charging through their own fire—a demonstration of reckless courage they were to repeat again and again.

At 7:45 a.m. Captain Jack A. Royster, in charge of Company A, radioed his battalion commander that unless reinforced, his men faced a choice of withdrawing or being wiped out. Reinforcements were sent, but were pinned down by Japanese fire. Colonel May, reluctant to yield the high ground his troops had reached, and convinced that they would lose as many men in withdrawing as in staying put, ordered them to "hold the ridge at all costs."

But it was impossible. Soon after Royster called for help, he was hit in the face by mortar fragments and almost blinded. First Lieutenant Dave Belman, commanding Company C nearby, had also been wounded. In desperation,

Japan's two top officers on Okinawa were a seemingly mismatched pair. Lieut. General Mitsuru Ushijima (top), the Army commander, was a humane, fatherly man who deplored shows of anger, which he considered a base emotion. Ushijima's chief of staff, Lieut. General Isamu Cho (bottom), was a quick-tempered zealot who was not above slapping junior officers in rage. Yet the two combined effectively, with Cho's explosive energy and clever mind complementing Ushijima's mature judgment.

Royster called in smoke from a chemical-mortar battalion to cover a retreat by the two battered companies. A capricious wind kept blowing the smoke back toward the American lines until shortly before 10 a.m., when the withdrawal could at last begin.

In that agonizingly protracted maneuver, a 23-year-old Chicagoan, Private First Class Edward J. Moskala, of Company C, was to earn—posthumously—the regiment's first Medal of Honor. Atop the ridge, Moskala had singlehandedly silenced two Japanese machine-gun nests after a 40-yard run in full view of the enemy. Now, serving as rear guard with a handful of his buddies while the others crept down the slopes, Moskala knocked off at least 25 Japanese soldiers. Twice he returned to the crest to retrieve the last of the wounded. On the second trip he was fatally hit.

On Kakazu West, Company L—commanded by First Lieutenant Willard F. "Hoss" Mitchell, an affable and heavy-set Louisianian whose rallying cry was: "Here comes the Hoss and God's on the Hoss's side"—was undergoing its own frightful ordeal. When the Japanese barrage began at daybreak the men were still on the way up. They managed to make it to the top but they immediately found themselves locked in a furious fight with the Japanese on a nearby knoll, the troops of Colonel Munetatsu Hara's 13th Independent Infantry Battalion.

Company L was outnumbered and outgunned. The Japanese had rifles, grenades, 22-pound satchel charges, light and heavy machine guns, small-bore knee mortars and the new supersized 320mm variety. Six of Mitchell's men were able to put one of these giant weapons out of action after they spotted it being rolled out of a cave on a 40-foot-long track. Knowing that one shell from the monster could blow them off the hill, they raced through a curtain of enemy fire to the mouth of the cave and satchel-charged the crew of four beside the weapon.

All morning and well into the afternoon, Company L dueled the Japanese from the skimpy cover of a small draw near the crest. Mitchell's men beat back four separate attacks on their positions. But at 4 p.m. Mitchell radioed that his situation was critical. Of the 89 men he had led to the crest, 15 were dead and all but three of the survivors were wounded. About the only ammunition left was what could be removed from the dead and injured. Under smoke and artillery cover, Company L withdrew from Kakazu West.

The day had cost the 383rd Regiment 326 casualties—23 killed, 47 missing and 256 wounded. The Japanese, too, had suffered. Colonel Hara's records later revealed that on the following day he could muster only about half of his original 1,200 men.

The 381st Regiment joined the 383rd in the assault on April 10. Together they threw four battalions—twice the number originally deployed—against the ridge after it had

been subjected to heavy air strikes from the carriers off-shore, a bombardment by the battleship *New York* and a rolling barrage by eight field-artillery battalions. In reviewing the previous day's debacle, the American commanders had concluded that overwhelming firepower was the only solution. They now discovered that it was inadequate. Eventually the carrier planes left and the shelling ceased, so that the U.S. infantrymen could launch their assault. Then, from the reverse slopes where the Japanese were entrenched, mortar shells poured down on the attackers at the rate of more than one per second.

All that day and the day following the Americans futilely hurled themselves at the ridge. Ammunition, food, water and medical supplies began to run low.

Occasionally, an inventive American soldier scored a momentary triumph. Sergeant Beauford T. Anderson of the 381st Regiment emerged from a cave in which his mortar squad was huddled to try to deal, singly, with some approaching enemy troops. He had only his carbine and a few grenades; in desperation, he picked up a Japanese mortar dud, threw it and heard it explode. That gave Anderson an idea. He ran back into the cave, tore his own mortar shells out of their casings, pulled the safety pins, activated the shells by banging them against the cave wall, then hurled them. He repeated the process 15 times; the next morning he found 25 dead Japanese in a gully in front of the cave.

Anderson's feat won him a Medal of Honor, but ingenuity alone could not wrest Kakazu from the Japanese. On April 13 it was still firmly in their hands. The 96th Division was stalled at the western end of Ushijima's first main defense line and the 7th Division was stalled at the eastern end. In the nine days since the two divisions had moved south, they had inflicted at least 5,000 casualties on the foe but had incurred more than 2,500 of their own. Clearly, the Americans needed to reassess their situation.

The only good news coming in to General Buckner's headquarters offshore was from the northern part of the island. And there, where U.S. planners had anticipated fierce resistance, a decisive victory was in the making. Moving north by way of the roads that edged the east and west coasts, the leathernecks of the 6th Marine Division had set so fast a pace that their supporting artillery battalions were hard put to keep up. Japanese soldiers were seldom seen except in stray bands encountered by patrols probing the trails that led inland. Furthermore, as a result of General Ushijima's decision to let most of the north fall to the Americans by default, enemy defenses along the coastal roads were uncharacteristically careless. Mines were easily spotted because they had not been planted deep enough. Abatis—roadblocks formed by felled trees—lacked the usual booby-trap attachments. Bridges had been only partially blown.

A DUK-W pulls up at a horseshoe-shaped Okinawan tomb, converted into a bivouac by Marines preparing to move north in search of the enemy. Such tombs, roomy enough to shelter 10 men, also served as ready-made pillboxes for the Japanese defenders.

Topping a hill on the Ishikawa isthmus, a Marine reconnaissance team (center) spies another patrol marching unchallenged into a thatch-roofed village below. These Marines, some of whom were veterans of jungle battlefields on Guadalcanal and Cape Gloucester, were pleasantly surprised by Okinawa's open fields of ripe wheat, sugar cane and sweet potatoes.

By April 13—eight days and 40 miles from the division's jump-off point on the Ishikawa isthmus—advance Marine elements were at Hedo Misaki, the northernmost tip of Okinawa. On the west coast, Marine contingents controlled the port of Nago and a number of smaller towns with usable harbors; the Marines' supplies could now be brought in directly by sea instead of by the arduous overland route. Most important, the leathernecks had sealed off the landward side of the Motobu peninsula, the one area of northern Okinawa where the enemy had chosen to make a stand.

Except for its coastal perimeters, the peninsula was almost all wilderness—a 10-mile-long, eight-mile-wide tangle of densely wooded hills cut by deep ravines. Photographing it from the air had proved largely fruitless; scanning the recon pictures, the Americans could find few distinguishing features that might serve them as landmarks. Such roads as there were lay concealed from the sky beneath the forest growth, and only one watercourse was clearly visible.

The sole inhabitants of the wild interior were mountain farmers and a small Japanese garrison commanded by a Colonel Udo. The Udo Force, as it came to be known, was made up for the most part of elements of the 44th Independent Mixed Brigade—infantry, machine-gun units, and light and medium artillery.

In preparing to defend the only sizable bastion in northern Okinawa, Udo had the advantage of months of studying the terrain. Since much of it was impassable to vehicles of any sort, he had ordered horses brought in for transport, setting up corrals and paddocks fully equipped with veterinary supplies. Since the heavy forest provided excellent concealment against air strikes, Udo had converted his antiaircraft guns to ground use. The colonel's shrewdest move was his choice of a defensive position. In the southwest quadrant of the peninsula rose its tallest peak, Yae-dake, 1,200 feet high. A twisted complex of ridges and ravines, wooded on the lower slopes and with scraggly trees and

In an occupied village on Okinawa's Motobu peninsula, Marines attend a memorial service for their Commander in Chief, President Franklin D. Roosevelt, who died on April 12, 1945—12 days after their landing. On first hearing of his death, many men at the front thought the news was a Japanese propaganda trick. The propaganda came later (bottom), in the form of crudely mimeographed leaflets.

American Officers and Men

We must express our deep regret over the death of President Roosevelt. The "American Tragedy" is now raised here at Okinawa with his death. You must have seen 70% of your CV's and 73% of your B's sink or be damaged causing 150,000 casualties. Not only the late President but anyone else would die in the excess of worry to hear such an annihilative damage. The dreadful loss that led your late leader to death will make you orphans on this island. The Japanese special attack corps will sink your vessels to the last destroyer. You will witness it realized in the near future.

grassy patches at the top, Yae-dake was surrounded by ridges nearly as daunting. Udo set up his command post in a ravine on Yae-dake; he had full radio and telephone communications with his units, as well as the customary cave network inside the mountain and adjoining ridges. By early April he had every conceivable approach to his position mined and was waiting for the Americans to find him.

For several days the 6th Marine Division tried to pinpoint Udo's position. They knew they were getting closer from the increasingly fierce fire they ran into as they probed ever deeper into the interior of the Motobu peninsula. But capturing a Japanese soldier who might reveal his commander's secret was a vain hope. The troops who manned the approaches to Yae-dake vanished into the underbrush as soon as they had finished firing; on reaching the scene, the Marines would find neither guns nor live or dead Japanese—nothing except bloodstains on the ground. "It was like fighting a phantom enemy," one officer recalled.

But on the night of April 12, units of the 29th Marine Regiment made a lucky find. Near Toguchi, a town on the peninsula's west coast, they came upon some friendly Okinawans, several of whom had once lived in Hawaii and spoke English. These civilians reported that the Udo Force was concentrated on the ridges south of the Manna River. The information confirmed a conclusion already tentatively reached by Marine intelligence officers. The Manna River—the sole watercourse that had shown up clearly in aerial photographs—ran east-west across the peninsula at about midpoint. And the fire from the high ground south of the river had given Marine combat patrols most of their trouble.

The 6th Division now had a specific, if hugely complicated, assignment: to wrest control from the Japanese over an area whose steep and broken terrain precluded the use of tanks and whose dominating peak, Yae-dake, commanded every approach route.

The assault on Udo's stronghold began on the morning of April 14, with the 4th Marine Regiment moving in from the west and the 29th from the east. The plan was more than usually hazardous; though Yae-dake loomed between the two regimental positions, they were, in effect, facing each other, with the consequent risk of overlapping fire. The utmost coordination of artillery was required and, fortunately for the Americans, the gunners of the supporting artillery battalions were at their precise best. Supporting their efforts, in turn, were the rockets and bombs of U.S. carrier planes and the main and secondary batteries of the battleship *Colorado,* stationed off the Motobu peninsula.

By nightfall the 4th had taken one ridge in its sector, and the 29th had advanced 800 yards up another. But in the process, the Marines had learned yet another costly lesson about the enemy's aptitude for ambush. The Japanese, well concealed and holding their fire, would let an entire U.S. platoon pass along a trail, then open up on the troops that followed, with devastating results. Officers, the higher their rank the better, were a favored target. Major Bernard W. Green, commanding the 4th Regiment's 1st Battalion, was standing with his operations and intelligence officers on either side of him when he was cut down by Japanese bullets; his subordinates were untouched. As one account of the day put it, Marine officers were suddenly made aware "that it was dangerous to show a map, wave a directing arm, or even to carry a pistol instead of a carbine."

On April 15, the vise around Yae-dake began to tighten. The 29th Regiment moved from east to southeast and gained the high ground to the rear of the peak. On the west, the 4th found the going a lot tougher than on the day before. The Marines were no longer dealing with small hit-and-run groups of Japanese who faded into the forest, but with defenders in caves and pillboxes, dug in on the heights and loosing torrents of fire on the leathernecks as they climbed. The Marines' losses were heavy—one company alone lost 65 of its men and three commanders—but that night they held a key hill just southwest of Yae-dake. The mountain was now surrounded on three sides.

At a little past noon the next day, Companies A and C of the 1st Battalion, 4th Marines, were on Yae-dake itself, working their way up its rocky slopes toward the summit. Company A got to the top first but the troops were thrown back under a hail of grenades and small-arm and knee-mortar fire. The Marines called in a powerful artillery barrage from a nearby ridge. Then Company A and Company C charged the ridge together. This time they were able to dig in on the crest. But their situation was critical: the two companies had lost 50 of their 400 men and were almost out of ammunition. Unless they were resupplied, they would

A COSTLY SIDESHOW ON IE SHIMA

In mid-April 1945, landing teams from the 77th Division were sent to invade Ie Shima, a small island three miles from Okinawa. Their objective was to capture Ie Shima's air base, which boasted three runways long enough to accommodate heavy bombers.

But what was envisaged as a brief sideshow developed into a six-day nightmare as one battalion after another was bludgeoned by Japanese troops. The struggle went on round the clock, with the GIs inching forward by day and fighting to repel suicide raiders at night. When the infantrymen secured their final objective, the summit of Mount Iegusugu, on April 21, they had lost 1,155 men killed, wounded and missing out of 6,100 engaged.

One casualty was Ernie Pyle, the Pulitzer Prize winner whose compassionate columns on ordinary GIs had endeared him to fighting men as well as to the folks back home. On April 18, Pyle fell with a sniper's bullet in his head. GIs emplaced a marker that read: "On this spot the 77th Infantry Division lost a buddy, Ernie Pyle."

Before going to Ie Shima, Ernie Pyle scans an Okinawa invasion site.

Mount Iegusugu, which was honeycombed with enemy defenses, rises 587 feet above Ie Shima, an otherwise table-flat island near Okinawa.

be helpless against the inevitable Japanese counterattack.

Watching from below, other Marines reacted instinctively. One officer was later to recall: "That 1,200-foot hill looked like Pike's Peak to the tired, sweaty men who started packing up ammunition and water on their backs. Practically everyone in the 1st Battalion headquarters company grabbed as much ammunition as he could carry. A man would walk by carrying a five-gallon water can on his shoulder and the battalion commander would throw a couple of bandoleers of ammunition over the other. Stretchers also had to be carried up, and all hands coming down the hill were employed as stretcher bearers."

The men at the crest were resupplied in time to beat back a banzai attack that evening by 75 savagely charging Japanese. With the aid of Marine artillery from the nearby ridges, the attackers were virtually annihilated.

The summit was secure; the rest of Yae-dake was cleaned out in two more days. In the course of the mop-up, the Marines came upon Colonel Udo's command post, with its elaborate radio and telephone equipment. Udo was gone. He had left for parts unknown on the 15th—the night before the assault—to pursue his war against the Americans in guerrilla style. The Americans never found him.

General Buckner had shifted his headquarters from the *Eldorado* to shore on April 14. He was impatient for the campaign to be wrapped up; only then would the assault on Japan itself be feasible. Buckner was looking forward to the thrust against the enemy's homeland with a certain zest; his favorite toast, over a bourbon and water, was: "May you walk in the ashes of Tokyo."

Once on Okinawa, the general let it be known—in the drillmaster's voice never mistaken by any GI who heard it —that he wanted Ushijima's first defense line across the southern part of the island taken without further delay. For more than a week, since the 7th and 96th Infantry Divisions had been stalled at the eastern and western ends of the line, the XXIV Corps had been feverishly preparing for a renewed attack all along the front. It was launched on April 19.

A third division, the 27th Infantry, had been brought out of reserve to fight alongside the 7th and the 96th. Formerly a National Guard unit from the state of New York, the 27th had most recently seen action on Saipan. Its assignment on Okinawa was the western third of the Japanese defense line, including Kakazu Ridge, where the 96th had been bloodied. The 96th was shifted to the center of the front, and the 7th was assigned the eastern third.

By way of overture, the attack of April 19 was preceded by the most massive and concentrated artillery pounding of the Pacific war. A total of 27 artillery battalions, 18 Army and nine Marine, took part, raking the front from east to west with 324 pieces of artillery—from 105mm to 8-inch howitzers—and firing a total of 19,000 shells into the Japanese lines and rear areas. When the morning mists cleared, a bombardment by six battleships, six cruisers and six destroyers thundered in, and 650 Navy and Marine planes struck at the Japanese positions with bombs, rockets, napalm and machine-gun fire. Shuri Castle, where General Ushijima had his headquarters, was hit by 1,000-pound bombs. But the general's command post, excavated out of the rock 100 feet below the surface, was undamaged.

After 40 minutes, the U.S. ground forces moved out. At first they were unopposed. Then, as the Japanese emerged from cover to man more and more of their positions, the assault gradually slowed.

By evening, it was painfully clear to the Americans that the day's attack had failed. Not one of the three divisions had been able to achieve a breakthrough on its sector of the front. The knife-edged crest of Skyline Ridge, the eastern anchor of the Japanese line, was reached by units of the 7th Division after flame-throwing tanks had seared and sealed the defenders' positions on the forward slope. But the Americans' hold on the crest was brief and bloody; Japanese swarming from the reverse slope drove them off with heavy casualties. The 7th's other objective of the day, a key point to the west known as Hill 178, could not be reached at all. The attackers were pinned down in an intervening zone called Rocky Crags (*pages 114-125*), under murderously precise fire from preregistered Japanese weapons.

The weary 96th Division was ordered to capture no fewer than four objectives: the Tanabaru escarpment and two ridges, Tombstone and Nishibaru—all on the first defense line—and beyond them, the towering eminence that was the chief bulwark of Ushijima's second defense line to the south, the Urasoe-Mura escarpment. The 96th's luckless lot that day was reflected in an incident involving the 382nd

Regiment. As its tanks moved toward Tombstone Ridge, a Japanese soldier jumped out of a small roadside cave and hurled a satchel charge at the lead tank. The explosive slued the Sherman around and toppled it over on its side, blocking the road to the rest of the tanks in the column. By day's end, units of the 96th had only a tenuous hold on just one of the division's objectives, Tombstone.

For the 27th Division, April 19—its first day of battle on Okinawa—began auspiciously. During the previous night its engineers, working in total darkness and silence to avoid enemy detection, had thrown two Bailey bridges and a footbridge across the 380-foot expanse of Machinato Inlet, one of the division's jump-off points on the west coast. By dawn, two battalions of the 106th Regiment had moved south on the coastal road and scaled the far-western end of the Urasoe-Mura escarpment; a third battalion reached it after daylight.

The maneuver had involved an end run around the ill-famed Kakazu Ridge—which also figured in the division's plans for the day. Units of the 105th Regiment were not only to assault the ridge frontally but also to accomplish what the 96th Division had been unable to do earlier in April: to move down the reverse slope to the village of Kakazu. Meanwhile, the battalion's tanks were to punch around the east end of the ridge, meet the men coming down the reverse slope and move on with them to Urasoe-Mura, 500 yards to the south.

But the plan fell apart almost immediately. The frontal assault on Kakazu Ridge was halted in its tracks by withering fire from the heights. The tanks made it around to the village of Kakazu only to run into awesome Japanese fire. Of the 30 tanks that set out on the mission, 22 were destroyed—victims of mines, antitank guns, artillery and mortar fire. The loss was the greatest incurred by U.S. armor for any one day on Okinawa.

On April 23 General Buckner held a somewhat strained conference with his superior, Admiral Nimitz. The Commander in Chief, Pacific Ocean Areas, had flown in from Guam the night before, landing at the Yontan airfield—one of the two captured on L-day and since greatly improved. Now, after a tour by jeep of the American-held parts of Okinawa, the admiral wanted to discuss ways of speeding up the U.S. operation so that the fleet could end its unexpectedly protracted and perilous stint as static guard offshore. In an uncharacteristically sharp tone, Nimitz told Buckner that unless he got his ground operation moving within five days, "we'll get someone here to move it."

Nimitz' visiting party included Lieut. General Alexander A. Vandegrift, architect of the successful campaign on Guadalcanal in 1942 and now Marine Corps commandant. Vandegrift suggested that an amphibious landing to the rear of the Japanese lines in southern Okinawa would hasten the day of U.S. victory; moreover, he had the men available to do the job—the 2nd Marine Division. The division had played a brief role in the original Okinawa landing. It had feinted an invasion of the southeastern beaches near Minatoga, across the island from the real beachhead near Hagushi, sending four waves of landing craft almost to shore before heading them back to sea. Then the division had been returned to reserve on Saipan. Vandegrift estimated that it could be under way for Okinawa in six hours.

Buckner opposed a new landing. He had already rejected a similar plan put forth by Major General Andrew D. Bruce, commander of the Army's 77th Division. Bruce's outfit had just taken the little island of Ie Shima just off the Motobu peninsula in northern Okinawa and could be freed for a new amphibious operation. Relying on findings by his own staff, Buckner had concluded that the cliff-rimmed beaches along Okinawa's southern and southeastern coasts would expose the landing force to strong enemy counterattack, thus posing the threat of "another Anzio, but worse." At this reference to the Italian beachhead where Allied troops had almost met with disaster in early 1944, the conferees remained silent.

Then Buckner raised a more immediate point: The proposed new Okinawa operation would complicate his supply problems. The general made it plain that his solution to stepping up the pace of the campaign was to throw more manpower into the frontal assault on the Japanese defenses. At bottom, Buckner was asserting that tactics on Okinawa was the business of the Army, and that the Navy should not interfere. For his part, Admiral Nimitz was willing to concede the general's point—but only if Buckner produced quick results.

As it happened, a tactical decision by the Japanese on the

In a hazardous advance on May 4, GIs use a cargo net to scale a cliff along the Urasoe-Mura escarpment, a jagged limestone ridge that blocked the final approaches to the Japanese stronghold at Shuri. Through two weeks of savage fighting, grenades and explosives had to be hoisted, case by case, to the rugged plateau atop cliffs 30 to 70 feet high.

night of the conference soon gave Buckner reason to hope that a U.S. breakthrough might be near. In the few days since their failed attack of April 19, American troops had gained a growing hold on Skyline Ridge, Nishibaru Ridge and the Tanabaru escarpment, and the Japanese had concluded that their first line of defense was no longer tenable. Hours after Nimitz and his party had left the island, an intensive barrage by Japanese artillery hit the American positions, with at least 1,000 rounds pouring in on each frontline regiment. The barrage, combined with a heavy fog that shrouded the area, provided the cover for a Japanese withdrawal south to the Urasoe-Mura escarpment and beyond. The first line of defense, including the once bitterly contested Kakazu Ridge, was now there for the taking.

In the last week of April, the XXIV Corps set to work grinding down the complex of fortifications the Japanese had installed in the area between the abandoned line of defense and Urasoe-Mura. On the east the 7th Division tackled the task of capturing two strategically important eminences called Kochi Ridge and Conical Hill. On the west the 27th doggedly mopped up a jumble of little gullies and crags that the GIs called Item Pocket, where the Japanese were so thoroughly dug in that they even had a narrow-gauge railway running through their tunnels on which they carried ammunition to the firing points. In the center, the 96th moved against the Maeda escarpment, the eastern end of Urasoe-Mura.

To reach the crest, the men of the 307th Infantry Regiment had to deal with the forbidding north face of the ridge, a sheer cliff. Finding it too steep to climb, the first troops went up on 50-foot scaling ladders, then hauled up cargo nets borrowed from the Navy and draped them down the cliff face for the following troops to use. On the crest, the men ran into the now-familiar Japanese tactic of attack-

ing from the reverse slope, firing mortars and machine guns, and hurling satchel charges and grenades.

With the troops was a medical-aid man, Private First Class Desmond T. Doss, a Seventh-Day Adventist and conscientious objector—and future Medal of Honor winner. Because of his beliefs, Doss refused even to touch a gun—but he took the wounded men into his heart. On Okinawa he was engaged in standard medic duty; whenever a man fell, Doss would crawl to him, dress his wounds as carefully as possible under the circumstances, then let him down to safety in a rope litter.

At midnight a furious Japanese charge drove the Americans off the crest and down the nets and ladders. In the darkness some missed their handholds and fell to the base of the wall. The next morning the uninjured went up again, held through the night, and on the next day made their presence stick. With Private Doss still tending the wounded, a bucket brigade of GIs clung like spiders to the cargo nets and passed up grenades for the men at the crest to drop on the Japanese on the back slope. The Japanese answered not only with grenades but also with knee-mortar fire. The exchange was so brutal that some GIs fell back to the north rim of the crest in tears. Five minutes later, a platoon leader reported, "those men would be back there tossing grenades as fast as they could pull the pins." Gradually the Japanese fire subsided. A day later the 307th was all over the back slope, systematically blasting and burning out the caves.

At the end of April, General Buckner took steps to put fresh muscle into the force confronting the Japanese bastions. The 1st and 6th Marine Divisions were brought down from northern Okinawa; the 1st was to relieve the 27th Division on the west, and the 6th was later to take over the seaward flank of the same sector. The 77th Division, moving out of Ie Shima, was to relieve the battered 96th. Then, after 10 days of rest in the rear, a revitalized 96th would replace the 7th Division in the east sector of the front; until then the 7th was to stay put.

Buckner was none too early with these moves. His rein-forcements were still moving in when something new occurred in the Americans' struggle to take Okinawa—an all-out Japanese counteroffensive.

On the night of May 2, a stormy dispute took place in General Ushijima's headquarters beneath Shuri Castle. The occasion was a Thirty-second Army staff conference, well lubricated with sake, and the protagonists in the clash were two very different personalities. Colonel Hiromichi Yahara, the senior staff officer in charge of planning, was a cool and thoughtful soldier who made his decisions only after careful deliberation. He was 42, fifteen years younger than Ushijima, and he was unimpressed by traditional military precepts; banzai attacks, for example, struck him as sheer wasteful stupidity. Ushijima's chief of staff, Lieut. General Isamu Cho, 51, however, was an extremist by inclination who had mellowed little since his hotheaded youth. He had been a conspirator in the infamous Cherry Society plot to establish a military dictatorship in Japan in 1931, and he had been the one who issued the kill-all-prisoners order that had preceded the rape of Nanking in 1937.

General Cho, his every instinct in rebellion against the static defense plan, demanded that a massive effort be made to smash the Americans back at least two miles. Yahara was dead set against the proposal, insisting that "the army must continue its current operations, calmly recognizing its final destiny—for annihilation is inevitable no matter what is done." But Yahara stood alone. Every other staff officer sided with Cho—and so, in the end, did Ushijima. The general order he issued to his troops called on them to "display a combined strength," and declared: "Each soldier will kill at least one American devil."

The counteroffensive was set for May 4, with the 24th Infantry Division designated to make the attack. Small infiltration units were to move out in advance to create confusion in the American lines. Two engineer regiments were to make amphibious landings behind the American positions on both coasts. Ushijima's heaviest artillery was to be pulled out of its caves and revetments and moved to more open positions farther south to permit wider arcs of fire.

The movement of the big guns first puzzled, then confused Buckner's observers. They believed that Ushijima was retreating. But they were forced to reconsider this notion around 10 p.m. on May 3, when the enemy artillery opened up and dropped 900 rounds on forward elements of the 77th Division in the central sector of the American lines. Thereafter, shelling continued sporadically until 4:30 a.m. on May 4, when Ushijima's armory turned loose one of the heaviest barrages fired by Japanese artillery in the Pacific war. Some 5,000 shells came in on the 7th Division, another 4,000 on the 77th. But the Americans were dug in "deep and dry," as they put it, and casualties were light.

Around midnight on May 3, the two Japanese engineer regiments took to the water. On the east coast several hundred engineers sortied in landing craft and Okinawan barges, intending to come ashore behind the Americans at Skyline Ridge. U.S. Navy vessels on patrol in Nakagusuku Bay picked them up almost at once and began systematically blowing their frail craft out of the water. Some of the Japanese made it to shore alive, but by then reconnaissance troops of the 7th Division were alert and slaughtered them on the beach. Dawn revealed what remained of the attack: bodies floating in the water, ripped and bloody clothing strewn on the beach.

On the west coast, several hundred more Japanese engineers made a navigational error and instead of landing behind the Americans came ashore square up against elements of the 1st Marine Division. They were destroyed on the reef, their banzai yells serving as an aiming aid to Marine gunners.

The Japanese attack by land was set for 5 a.m. on May 4. The key to the success of the entire operation was a breakthrough several hundred yards east of the Urasoe-Mura escarpment. It turned into a debacle.

Two assault battalions of the 24th Division failed to reach their jump-off point in time. At daybreak the troops were caught milling in the open and were mowed down by U.S. artillery and mortars. Troops sent against the 77th Division, in the center, were also late in getting into position. Their attack never developed any real momentum. The only sharp fire fight was a two-hour engagement in a sector held by the 306th Infantry Regiment. But the Americans went into a perimeter defense and beat back the Japanese with fearful casualties. Only two Japanese tanks got anywhere near the action. Both were knocked out by Private First Class James E. Poore, who, despite a shoulder wound from a shell fragment, got the pair with a bazooka.

Neither Cho nor Ushijima was as yet willing to admit that the gamble had failed. Shortly after dark on May 4, two Japanese battalions attempted to take the Tanaburu escarpment behind the American lines. One was battled to a standstill by the 7th Division's 306th Regiment; the Japanese lost 248 men before retreating. The second, commanded by Captain Koichi Ito, penetrated the American lines and surrounded a 7th Division supply dump at the Tanaburu escarpment. But there, at daylight, Ito and his 600 men were trapped by the Americans. Ito dug in on the crest, and 7th Division troops pressed in so closely on all sides that the attacking Americans could hear the hand-cranked generator of Ito's radio when he called headquarters. Finally, under cover of darkness that night, Ito and about 230 of his men— all that survived the day's fighting—retreated along the same road they had used to get to Tanaburu.

By the afternoon of May 5 the outcome of Cho's offensive was unmistakably clear to Ushijima. At 6 p.m. he called it off—what was left of it—and ordered all units to resume their preoffensive positions. Shocked by this decision, several junior staff officers, still full of fire, drew their swords and crowded around Cho, demanding an explanation. Sadly Cho apologized and turned away.

Ushijima, too, had an apology to make. He called Yahara to his quarters and, with tears in his eyes, promised that henceforth he would be guided by the colonel's advice. But Ushijima still proposed to make the Americans pay a fearsome price for Okinawa.

SLUGFEST ON A RUGGED RIDGE

Attacking up a steep ridge a mile inland from Okinawa's southeast coast, two GIs cling to a narrow ledge as an enemy mortar shell explodes dangerously close by.

THE SAME OLD STORY AT ROCKY CRAGS

On April 19, 1945, the first day of a major American offensive in southern Okinawa, a battalion of the U.S. 7th Infantry Division ran into unexpected resistance at the eastern end of the enemy defense line. It was the beginning of a four-day battle that in many ways typified the fighting all over the island: The Japanese were deeply dug in, and the question was whether American superiority in firepower and manpower could root them out.

The enemy position was a long ridge capped by what the GIs called Rocky Crags: two high coral knobs laced with tunnels and crammed with mortars and machine guns. The whole front had been shelled for two days before the offensive began, and the GIs advanced on Rocky Crags behind a heavy barrage. Yet they were stopped cold by intense enemy fire before they reached the slope leading up to the Crags.

"This don't look good," a platoon leader told *Life* photographer W. Eugene Smith, who shared the GIs' peril to take the close-up pictures shown on these pages. "Everybody's pinned down—we just lost a squad with a direct hit." Casualties piled up, and when Smith started for the rear to send out some film, a soldier said, "Tell them we're getting hell kicked out of us."

An attack the next day got nowhere, so the division commander, Major General Archibald V. Arnold, committed fresh troops. And into the fight came a deadly new weapon—flame-throwing tanks. The flamethrowers scorched the slope, roasting the Japanese crouched in trenches and shallow caves. But when the GIs attacked up the slope, they were driven back by more deeply dug-in defenders on top.

General Arnold had still more firepower brought up. A 155mm howitzer systematically pounded Rocky Crags at point-blank range, blasting off great chunks of coral. Then in a following charge, the troops came so close to the Crags they could hear rifle bolts clicking inside the tunnel entrances. But they too were driven back.

Finally, on April 23, disbelieving GIs walked virtually unopposed up the slope where 243 of their buddies had fallen dead or wounded. The Japanese had pulled out during the night—to fight again on the next line.

GIs seek shelter in a ditch near Rocky Crags on the first day of the battle, which Smith called "one of the toughest the veteran 7th had ever run into."

In preparation for an infantry assault, artillery fire rocks the ridge line on the 7th Division's front, obscuring the Japanese positions with smoke and dust.

Attempting to slip past Rocky Crags toward the east, riflemen (left) and a machine gunner (above) of the 7th Division scramble for cover as enemy fire from the two high fortresses begins to rake the area. Unable to outflank the position, the Americans joined the grueling frontal battle to eliminate the Crags.

A Japanese soldier, burned to death by a flame-throwing tank, lies on the slope with his clothes still smoldering. The Japanese on the slope stood no chance of surviving the flames in their trenches and machine-gun pits.

A flame-throwing tank scorches the face of a Rocky Crags fortress while a second tank moves up to fire. The flamethrowers, installed in place of the standard 75mm guns, could shoot a stream of burning liquid 125 yards. But the streams of fire had little effect on many of the defenders tenaciously dug in deep inside the coral stronghold on top of the ridge.

Deployed as skirmishers, infantrymen scramble up the scarred ridge, still smoking after 35 minutes of fire from the flame-throwing tanks. As two platoons of

GIs neared the top of Rocky Crags, Japanese soldiers hidden in caves hurled grenades and satchel charges in their faces, knocking them back yet again.

123

At the foot of Rocky Crags, a GI wounded in the head and foot is tended by a medic while awaiting evacuation. "Although he was in great pain, they did not give him morphine because of the head wound," Smith wrote. "He lay there with his hands clenching and unclenching. Finally he brought his hands together in the position of prayer." A head wound just as agonizing almost killed Smith himself while he was covering the 7th Division in a battle four weeks later.

THE HOMELESS ISLANDERS

A frightened Okinawan, his head swathed in a towel to protect him from the heat, is flushed out of his underground hiding place by cautious U.S. Marines

"OVERWHELMED WITH HIDEOUS FATIGUE"

"Wandering and lodging here and there in the mountain caves and riversides, crying and weeping, they are near death, overwhelmed with hideous fatigue." Thus wrote a Japanese doctor on Okinawa of the several hundred thousand homeless civilians on the island, and he might have added that many of the displaced Okinawans were sick, injured or starving when the Americans came upon them. Another 50,000 to 100,000 died, many of them killed in the cross fire or buried alive when their cave shelters were sealed shut by shellbursts.

At first, the Okinawans feared the invaders. Influenced by Japanese propaganda, they believed that American soldiers were "barbarians" and "devils" who would rape the women, commit wholesale slaughter and grind up their remains for dog food. In panic, some men slew their daughters and even their whole families to spare them the expected horrors. The Americans had to use cajolery and guile—with hasty reference to their Japanese phrase books—to lure the Okinawans out of their hide-outs. One of the more successful coaxers was a private of the 7th Infantry Division who talked out 500 refugees in the first days of the fighting.

As they were collected, the civilians were taken to processing stations, where they were screened by counterintelligence agents. For security reasons, able-bodied Okinawan men were quickly separated from their families and sent to special detention centers. But the Americans' fears, like those of the civilians, were for the most part unfounded; the Okinawans had long been treated as inferiors by the Japanese and consequently showed little loyalty toward their former rulers.

From the processing centers, the great masses of civilians were parceled out among a dozen refugee camps established around the island by the U.S. Military Government. There the Okinawans jammed into surviving villages or built makeshift shelters in which as many as 30 people shared a single room. There they received food, medical treatment and clothing to replace their rags. And there they waited, bereaved and bewildered, for an end to the fighting.

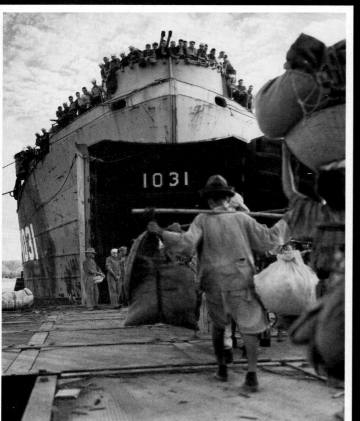

Carrying their meager belongings, civilians trudge into the cargo deck of an LST scheduled to take them up the Okinawan coast to a refugee camp.

Shepherded to safety by an American soldier, a group of civilians stops to rest for a moment while two gaunt, elderly women try to catch their breath

Crouching on a ledge, two civilians mourn a
dead relative lying on a stretcher. "Utter
horror," recalled an Okinawan schoolteacher.
"The dead everywhere . . . everywhere."

In a gesture of friendship, a Marine shares his
rations with a frail old woman. Each American
division brought along special supplies of
fish and rice to distribute among the civilians.

Organizing a group of uprooted Okinawans
an American officer explains through an
interpreter that they will be treated fairly and
given food and shelter. The officer, a trained
administrator of the U.S. Military Government
had been assigned to the invasion staff

Truckloads of homeless civilians are brought to
a U.S. Army reception center at Taira in
northern Okinawa. There they were registered,
examined, then absorbed into camp life.

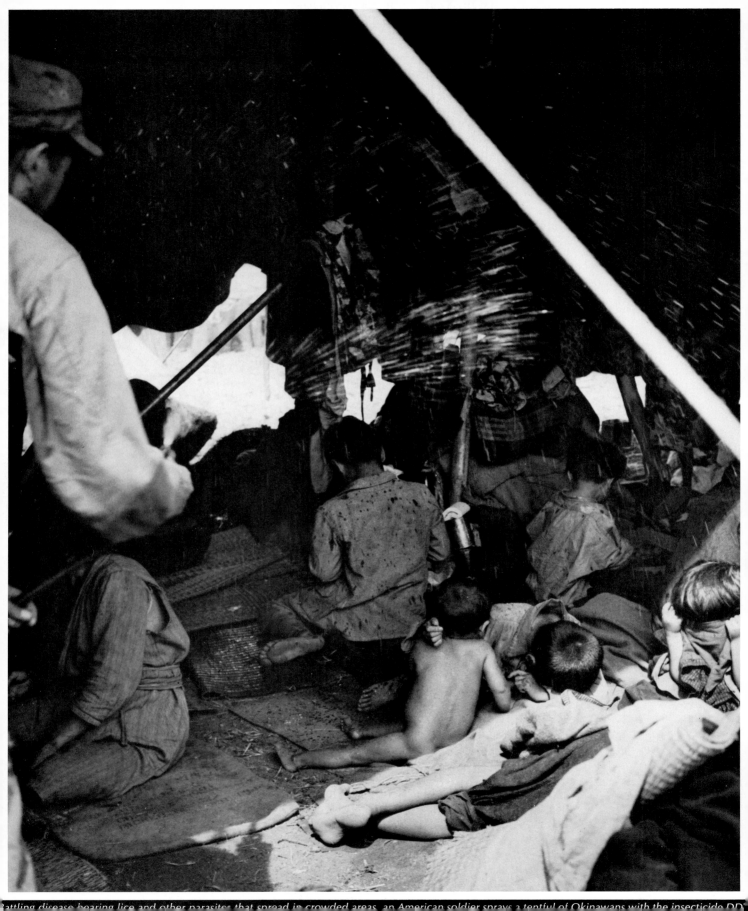

Battling disease-bearing lice and other parasites that spread in crowded areas, an American soldier sprays a tentful of Okinawans with the insecticide DDT.

An aged patient with a tattooed hand is treated for a shrapnel wound by an officer of the U.S. Navy Medical Corps at Nago in northern Okinawa.

Stoic in spite of her multiple wounds, a woman sits motionless while U.S. soldiers and an Okinawan aide bandage her arm at the camp in Shimobaru.

Two Army doctors gingerly move a child wounded in the buttock. The latter Marines bore the brunt of much of the toughest fighting in

Soldiers organize civilians in a village that survived on the island of Iheya off Okinawa's northwest coast. The area became a U.S. Military Government camp.

Setting up housekeeping in a camp, civilian fill the area with ramshackle lean-tos and tent of branches, cloth and hand-woven matting

WORKING IN THE CAMPS, WAITING FOR WAR'S END

Until the Okinawans could safely resume their normal lives, they made the best o their stay in the overcrowded American camps. The big camp at Shimabuku in the center of the island was soon inundated with 14,000 homeless civilians. By earl July of 1945, the Americans were caring for more than 260,000 people.

To help Okinawans regain their self sufficiency, camp commanders appointed village headmen—called "honchos" by the Americans—to communicate orders, help with maintaining the camp and lead work details. The honcho's main job was to get farming started again. Par of the cropland on Okinawa had been churned up and shell-pocked in the fighting, but in undamaged areas the head men led work parties to the fields to harvest staples: sweet potatoes and rice

Every able-bodied civilian kept busy Some men worked for the U.S. Army—a about 23 cents a day—digging ditches and helping in hospitals. Women tended the young and infirm, and milled grain and wove mats. "Our main concern," re called one Okinawan who directed the valuable service of evaporating sea wate for salt, "was to keep alive."

Receiving their daily allotment of food, hungry civilians in the camp at Toya crowd around with pouches and baskets as a headman doles out rice from a sack provided by the American Military Government.

Tending to chores at the Shimobaru camp, a woman breaks the hard shell of rice by pounding it with a wooden mallet in a hollowed log, while other women separate the grain from the hull in a "whirlmill."

houldering their pickaxes and shovels, and carrying baskets, cheerful civilians set out for the nearby fields to harvest sweet potatoes and other root crop.

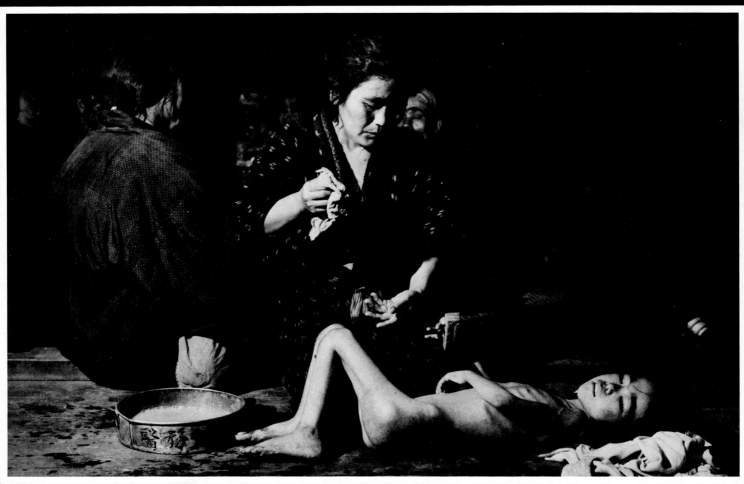

mother at the Sobe camp hospital tends ba bathes her child, who is suffering from malnutrition after weeks of deprivation in the mountains of Okinawa

*Patiently awaiting a share of the food that
they themselves raised, refugees in a camp
surround a mound of sweet potatoes,
soon to be distributed by the headmen. These
men were interned until the end of the War,*

5

As the Japanese strategists in Tokyo had foreseen, General Ushijima's tactics of delay ensnared the American invaders in a prolonged and costly battle of attrition on Okinawa. As they also had anticipated, Ushijima's shrewd ploy pinned down the prodigious invasion armada, forcing it to act as bodyguard and lifeline for the soldiers fighting on land. Thus restricted, unable to disperse or to operate freely, the naval forces were highly vulnerable to aerial attack—exactly as Tokyo had planned. For the Japanese high command intended not only to defend Okinawa but to destroy great numbers of Allied warships and supply vessels that would be essential to an invasion of the home islands.

The Japanese strategists had begun planning their massive counterattack against the U.S. fleet as early as January, when it seemed likely that Okinawa was to be the next American target. Imperial General Headquarters faced huge obstacles and a nearly insuperable fuel and weapons shortage. The majority of Japan's aircraft carriers, battleships and cruisers had either been sunk or severely damaged, victims of a long series of devastating encounters with the U.S. Navy.

With a conventional naval attack out of the question, the Japanese were compelled to pin their hopes on air strikes by land-based planes. Even that approach would not be easy. Airfields on Kyushu, the southernmost of the home islands, and on Formosa were well within range of Okinawa. But aircraft production, reduced by heavy U.S. bombing raids, lagged far behind the enormous loss rate, and experienced pilots were even harder to come by than airplanes in spite of a vigorous training program.

So Japan tapped its one plentiful resource: thousands of young volunteers, ill-trained but devoted to the *Bushido* code and ready to lay down their lives for the Emperor and the homeland. The planners began molding a massive corps of Kamikaze pilots, to be flung, in wave after wave, at the American fleet off Okinawa.

The decision to expend the finest of Japan's young manhood in what amounted to a giant suicide pact was a desperate measure, but it seemed to be justified by recent experience. Conventional bombing of the U.S. fleet had failed, primarily because such attacks required large numbers of seasoned pilots. The Kamikaze, introduced as a weapon in the battle for the Philippines in late 1944, had been more successful: Almost any pilot who was willing to

ORDEAL BY KAMIKAZE

die could manage to aim his airplane at an enemy warship.

The Japanese plan for the great Kamikaze offensive was named *Ten Go* (Heavenly Operation). It would consist of a series of mass-formation attacks, called *kikusui* (floating chrysanthemums); the name was meant to reflect the spiritual purity of the Kamikaze. On paper, the plan was to be executed by 4,500 Navy and Army aircraft. In addition, a small number of piloted buzz bombs would be used. These rocket-propelled cylinders, known as *ohkas* (cherry blossoms), lacked the fuel capacity needed for sustained flight; they would be carried to the attack zone strapped to the bellies of old Japanese bombers, which would launch them when in range of the targets.

Vice Admiral Matome Ugaki, whose Fifth Air Fleet would execute *Ten Go,* realized that the up-to-date aircraft at his disposal would soon be exhausted, and he put out an urgent call for any plane that could fly with a bomb slung beneath its fuselage. In the two months preceding the American landing on Okinawa, hundreds of such planes from all over Japan were assembled at airfields on the home islands of Kyushu, Shikoku and Honshu: obsolete fighters, twin-engined bombers, reconnaissance planes, seaplanes, even wood-and-canvas training biplanes. The collection process continued all through *Ten Go.*

Admiral Ugaki anticipated an ultimate battle when the homeland was invaded, and he had no intention of sacrificing his meager force of experienced pilots at Okinawa. So he assigned his trained fliers and best planes to escort duty. Like Judas goats, the expert pilots would guide groups of Kamikazes to their targets, defending them along the way from enemy fighter planes. Then the veterans would return to base for another suicide contingent.

The Kamikaze pilots were given only rudimentary flight training. Even so, the training took time, and that slowed down Ugaki's Kamikaze build-up. The admiral was also haunted by mechanical breakdowns of his obsolete planes and by a critical shortage of aviation gasoline, which limited practice flights. All this, plus the U.S. bombing raids, prevented Ugaki from launching his first wave of Kamikazes on April 1, when the Americans landed on Okinawa.

April 6 was finally set for the first *kikusui.* Besides hitting Task Force 58, the Kamikazes would attack Vice-Admiral Sir Bernard Rawlings' British fleet, designated Task Force 57, which was operating in the Sakishima-gunto, a group of islands between Formosa and Okinawa. Fighter-bombers from the four British carriers of Task Force 57 had been assigned to neutralize the Sakishima airfields, preventing their use as way-stops for Japanese planes en route to Okinawa as Kamikaze reinforcements.

Meanwhile, Japan's top admirals were considering a naval sacrifice as part of *Ten Go.* A controversial plan was afoot to offer up the remnants of the Second Fleet—the enormous battleship *Yamato,* the light cruiser *Yahagi* and eight destroyers—to lure the carriers of Task Force 58 away from Okinawan waters, so that Ugaki's planes would have a better chance of getting through to the ships around the island. If any of the warships happened to survive their encounter with the American carrier planes, they would sail on to Okinawa, beach themselves and serve as stationary gun platforms, blasting any U.S. ships that challenged them. And when the ammunition for the warships' guns was expended, the sailors would fling themselves at the American soldiers and die fighting as skirmishers.

The sticking point of the plan was the idea of sending the *Yamato* to her death. The great vessel, crewed by some 3,300 men, was the biggest and most powerful battleship in the world *(pages 154-163).* Yet the *Yamato* had not distinguished herself in combat. Although she had been present at the key sea battles from Midway on, the *Yamato* had seldom fired her huge guns at enemy ships. At the disastrous Battle for Leyte Gulf in October 1944, she had spent most of her time in vain pursuit of an American carrier force and had then broken off from the fray. Her failure to close with the U.S. ships had drawn stinging criticism from some factions of the Japanese government. The *Yamato* was being spoken of, one admiral admitted ruefully, as "a floating hotel for idle, inept admirals."

Such barbs wounded the pride of Admiral Soemu Toyoda, Commander in Chief of the Combined Fleet, and pushed him and his staff toward a decision: It was better to sacrifice the *Yamato* in a bold assault than to see her flee ignominiously from port to port to escape Allied bombs. And so, despite vehement protests by many subordinates, Toyoda gave the fatal order to Vice Admiral Seiichi Ito, Second Fleet Commander, on April 5, in a message that began:

"The fate of our Empire truly rests upon this one action."

The *Yamato* and her little fleet made preparations for their final voyage in the harbor of Tokuyama, in Japan's Inland Sea, against a backdrop of terraced hills alight with blossoming cherry trees. All that day, the *Yamato* took aboard 1,170 shells for her main battery and the precious 2,500 tons of fuel that the ship would need for the one-way trip to Okinawa. Much sake was consumed that night in a mood that Ensign Mitsuru Yoshida described as "solemn gaiety." Captain Tameichi Hara, skipper of the cruiser *Yahagi*, drank to excess with Rear Admiral Keizo Komura, commander of the destroyer squadron. Their revelry ended in a crying jag, with Hara clinging to a stanchion and yelling "Banzai!" Enlisted men were issued as a farewell gift packets of *onshi no tabako*, cigarettes of the imperial brand.

On the next day, April 6, the ships steamed out of Tokuyama Bay, threaded their way through Bungo Strait, the narrow neck separating Honshu and Kyushu, and turned southward toward Okinawa.

Simultaneously with the *Yamato's* departure, Admiral Ugaki unleashed Kikusui No. 1, the first of the massive aerial suicide attacks. On April 6 and 7, from fields on Formosa and Kyushu, some 700 Navy and Army planes—355 of them Kamikazes—took off and set their course for Okinawa. Each of the suicide pilots had been fully indoctrinated in the priority of targets; they were to make a supreme effort to crash-dive into the big Allied aircraft carriers, the enemy's most potent weapons. But the first potential victims that these *kikusui* airmen saw were dangerously exposed American destroyers, and many of the pilots were simply too excited to look further.

The perilous deployment of the destroyers was a calculated risk taken by the commander of the invasion fleet, Admiral Turner. He had stationed the destroyers at 16 radar picket stations spaced in an irregular circle around the island, along flyways likely to be taken by incoming attackers. Each picket ship carried a team of radar experts who maintained a constant watch for enemy planes—"bogeys" in airman's lingo. When bogeys were sighted, the destroyers would warn the fleet around Okinawa. But the picket ships, some stationed as far out as 75 miles, lacked the antiaircraft firepower to fight off swarms of Kamikazes. Moreover, their

steel plate was so thin that in two wars they were inelegantly known as "tin cans."

On the afternoon of April 6, the destroyer *Bush* was guarding picket station No. 1, with the *Colhoun* to starboard at station No. 2 and the *Cassin Young* next, at No. 3. The three destroyers were spread out at intervals on a 60-mile arc northeast of Bolo Point on Okinawa. Theirs was the hottest sector in the picket screen, just under the flyway from Kyushu to Okinawa. Around 3 p.m., their radar picked up more than 40 bogeys coming down from the north, stacked at altitudes from 500 to 20,000 feet.

One group orbited the *Bush*, with the planes peeling off one by one to make runs on the ship. The destroyer's gunners shot down two and drove off two more. Shortly after 3 o'clock a Kamikaze was spotted coming in low. The skipper, Commander R. E. Westholm, gave the order to open fire. The plane kept coming, jinking erratically just above the sea. It was repeatedly hit, but it held together long enough to crash into the *Bush* right between the stacks. The plane's single bomb exploded in the forward engine room, wiping out the watch there and killing most of the men in the firerooms. The *Bush* began to flood and quickly took on a 10-degree list. The fires set by the blast were soon smothered by damage-control parties. But the destroyer was dead in the water.

By 3:30 Commander G. R. Wilson on the *Colhoun* had heard the *Bush's* distress call and was racing to her assistance at 35 knots. By 4:35, when the *Colhoun* drew up alongside the *Bush*, a dozen "Zekes" and "Val" dive bombers were orbiting the position just out of range. A Zeke dived at the *Colhoun* but missed and crashed into the watery gap between the two destroyers. The *Bush* was still firing her 40mm and 20mm guns, but her 5-inch main battery was jammed. The *Colhoun* shot a wing off a Zeke at 4,000 yards and brought down another with a 5-inch shell square on the nose. But the next Kamikaze, already aflame, hit the main deck forward, killing the crews of two 40mm guns. Its bomb pierced the deck and exploded in the after fireroom, killing everybody and rupturing the main steam line in the forward engine room. An engineer, running for cover, paused just long enough to adjust cross-connection valves to divert steam to the after engine room. Thanks to the switchover, the *Colhoun* was still able to make 15 knots.

A sequence of photographs taken off Okinawa on June 10, 1945, shows the destroyer William D. Porter going down after a Kamikaze exploded nearby, crushing the ship's hull below the waterline. Another ship (top left) comes alongside to pick up the Porter's crew, and the men escape (top right) over the destroyer's forward quarter. With the last crewman safe, the Porter rolls over on her side (bottom left), then flips her bow into the air (bottom right) and slips into the depths of the Pacific.

But not for long. Three more planes dived down on the ships at 5:17. The *Colhoun* shot one down less than 200 yards away. The second missed, and as it zoomed up, it was destroyed by fire from the *Bush* and a gunboat. But the third rammed into the *Colhoun's* forward fireroom, wrecking both boilers. Its bomb exploded, blowing a four-by-20-foot hole below the waterline and breaking the ship's keel. Now the *Colhoun,* too, was dead in the water.

Yet her crew would not quit. By 5:25 they had the fires smothered with foam and were jettisoning torpedoes and depth charges to relieve the topside weight. Gunners still manned the main battery, but with the power out they had to point and train the guns manually—a task so arduous that the men needed relief in two-minute relays.

The battered tin cans now had to endure another swarm of Kamikazes. Four came in, three on the *Colhoun's* bow and one on the quarter. Three were hit; one of them plummeted into the sea 150 yards away. But the other two, though they were blazing wrecks, kept on coming. A Val clipped its wing tip on the after stack, spun and crashed on

a gun mount. Its gas tank burst into flame, and its bomb fell overboard and exploded alongside the hull, blasting a hole three feet square below the waterline. By a lucky fluke, the waterspout from the bomb fell back on deck and put out the gasoline fires.

The third plane missed the *Colhoun*. But instantly the pilot changed course and crashed into the *Bush* between her stacks. The force of this impact nearly sliced the *Bush* in two; only the keel held bow and stern together.

The fourth Kamikaze pilot, flying a Zeke, perished in a flashy maneuver. After missing the *Bush* by five feet on his first pass, he pulled up in a classic wing over. Then he dived vertically and plowed into the ship's wardroom, where the wounded had been taken. The flaming crash killed them all.

At 6 p.m., the *Colhoun* took yet another hit, its fourth. A flaming Kamikaze hooked a wing on the pilothouse and crushed itself against the port side. By now, the *Colhoun* and the *Bush,* which had taken three Kamikazes aboard, had both suffered too much damage to be saved.

The sea had been running heavy all day, and at 6:30 a big

THE PLANE CALLED "WHISTLING DEATH"

The most versatile plane in the skies over Okinawa was a gull-winged beauty that combined the speed and agility of a fighter with the ruggedness and payload of an attack bomber. Its U.S. designation was the F4U Corsair. To the Japanese, who feared the shriek of its wing-mounted air intakes, it was known as "Whistling Death."

Flat out, the Corsair could fly at 417 miles per hour, 66 mph faster than the swiftest Zeke, and its six .50-caliber machine guns could saw an enemy plane in half in seconds. The Corsair could carry either two 1,000-pound bombs or eight rockets. And it could deliver this deadly payload in 85-degree dives or scorching on-the-deck runs.

The Corsair first appeared in 1943 as a bomber escort in the Solomons; later it was based on carriers, where its speed and superior rate of climb (3,000 feet a minute) were vital in intercepting Kamikazes. On Okinawa, the plane performed with such deadly brilliance in all its roles that pilots called it the "Bent-Wing Widow-Maker."

swell rolled up against the *Bush*. She buckled amidships and, with bow and stern angling skyward, went down. It was a desperate time for the crewmen cast into the sea. The *Cassin Young* arrived, along with a gunboat and a fleet tug, and began picking up survivors. But some of the sailors, horribly burned and unable to endure their agony, slipped out of their life jackets and went under. Others exhausted themselves fighting the big seas and drowned. Still others were crushed against the hull of a rescue vessel or mangled by its propellers. Of the *Bush's* 333-man crew, 94 were lost.

The *Colhoun* was still half afloat, listing 23 degrees and awash to her after turret. By 9 p.m. Commander Wilson had ordered most of the crew to abandon ship, and a few hours later, when fires flared up again, he and his skeleton crew followed. All but 35 of Wilson's 330 men were saved. At his request, the *Cassin Young* sank his ship with gunfire.

The fatal assaults on the *Bush* and the *Colhoun* set a pattern for all the Kamikaze attacks that followed: Many pilots concentrated on the vulnerable picket ships—destroyers, destroyer escorts, gunboats and assorted support ships. But some planes did press on to attack ships of higher priority. On the first day of Kikusui No. 1, two U.S. carriers experienced trouble, though it was not serious. The *Bennington* was attacked around midday, but her planes, together with nearby light cruisers and destroyers, threw up a protective wall of fire. The only Kamikaze that got through was shot down 20 yards astern, briefly disabling the carrier's rudder. Elsewhere in the task group, the light carrier *Belleau Wood* was attacked and suffered minor damage.

In most respects, April 6 turned out to be a profitable day for the U.S. The pilots and ships' gunners of Task Force 58 claimed 249 kills, and the ships of Admiral Turner's inshore support force claimed 108. But the Navy paid a price. By nightfall the Kamikazes that got through had scored 33 hits on 17 American ships, killed at least 367 sailors, sunk four ships besides the *Bush* and the *Colhoun* and damaged seven heavily enough to knock them out of the War.

On the next morning, April 7, the seaborne elements of Kikusui No. 1—the mighty *Yamato* and her fleet—were steaming at full speed toward a fateful encounter with the planes of Task Force 58. The Americans had an excellent idea of where the Japanese ships were. When the ships emerged from Bungo Strait, they were shadowed by two American submarines, the *Threadfin* and the *Hackleback,* which immediately reported their position to Task Force 58. At 8:32 a.m., the Japanese ships were spotted by a flier from the carrier *Essex,* and a little later they were picked up and shadowed thereafter by PBM Martin Mariner flying boats.

In the meantime, a difference of opinion cropped up on the American side. The Fifth Fleet commander, Admiral Spruance, was determined to let the American heavy ships around Okinawa have a crack at the *Yamato;* U.S. battleship sailors had not seen much ship-to-ship combat in recent months, having been restricted to bombarding beaches and escorting carriers. But Admiral Mitscher, the commander of Task Force 58, wanted to prove that his carrier airmen could sink the most powerful ship afloat. He told his chief of staff, Commodore Arleigh Burke, to inform Spruance that "I propose to strike the *Yamato* sortie group at 12:00 unless otherwise directed." Burke sent the message in a simpler form: "Will you take them or shall I?" Spruance yielded, replying, "You take them."

At 10 o'clock Mitscher launched his first big strike—more than 350 planes—Curtiss SB2C Helldivers with 1,000-pound and 500-pound bombs, and TBM Avengers with Mark 13 torpedoes. The weather was overcast and getting worse. But the strike force was able to locate Admiral Ito's ships by homing on the American flying boats, which were orbiting under the clouds and just out of range of the Japanese antiaircraft weapons.

At 12:32, the *Yamato's* radar picked up the oncoming attack planes. "From the after radar room, the hoarse voice of the monitor could be heard reporting the distance and direction of the approaching planes," said a report written later by Ensign Yoshida, whose battle station was on the *Yamato's* bridge. "Alerts were flashed to the other ships at the same time as our loudspeakers announced the emergency. Tension mounted and every lookout strained in the direction of the oncoming planes."

The lookouts soon sighted the Americans. The *Yamato's* navigator shouted, "Over one hundred hostile planes are heading for us!"

The order came through, "Open fire!" The guns of the *Yamato* and her escorts erupted with a tremendous roar. Two Helldivers managed to penetrate the *Yamato's* umbrella of shellbursts and shrapnel, and at 12:41, each plane sent a bomb crashing on the battleship near her mainmast, destroying her after radar room and killing eight crewmen. Four minutes later, a torpedo from an Avenger hit the big ship in her port bow. Soon afterward, the attackers broke off and returned to the carriers.

The officers on the *Yamato's* bridge knew that a single torpedo could not inflict serious damage on the great ship. The navigator even smiled and said, "And so at last a torpedo got us, eh?" But Ito was not so casual. He watched grimly as three bodies, the victims of strafing, were carried from the bridge. He knew the worst was yet to come.

Ito's fears were confirmed minutes later, when the second American strike force attacked. At 1:37 p.m., a wave of Avengers sent five more torpedoes into the *Yamato*, all on the port side. "Even the invulnerable *Yamato* was unable to withstand such overwhelming attacks," said Ensign Yoshida. Sea water poured through the jagged holes, and the

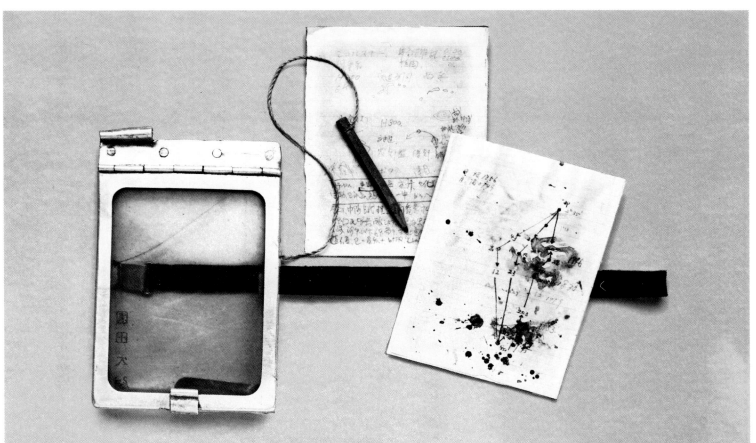

A JAPANESE PILOT'S LAST THOUGHTS

Among the pieces of equipment carried by Japanese fighter pilots assigned to escort Kamikazes to Okinawa were plexiglass writing boards, which they would strap to their thighs. The tablets were for noting combat information that would go into the pilot's report on his return to base. But the flier who carefully scratched his name "Sonoda" into the board above also recorded his tormented thoughts as he led his doomed formation to its destiny.

Amid a jumble of memos, Sonoda complained: "This company has not been put to best possible use. As acting commanding officer, I see the war situation become more desperate. All Japanese must become soldiers and die for the Emperor."

Noting that five of his pilots had begun their suicide dives, Sonoda wrote: "Circumstances are closing in. Even fresh laundry is infrequent. Defeated but not conquered, men of the 65th Fighter Squadron were born separately but die together."

A little later, Sonoda was shot down over Okinawa. He died in the crash, his blood spattering a navigation sheet.

ship started listing to port. "There were so many casualties among damage-control personnel," Yoshida said, "that it became impossible to maintain our watertight integrity."

The officers on the bridge now realized that it would take a radical step to right the ship and save her. Rear Admiral Kosaku Ariga, the skipper, did not hesitate. He ordered that the starboard engine and boiler rooms be flooded.

"I hastily phoned these rooms to warn the occupants of the flooding order, but it was too late," Yoshida recalled. "Water, both from the torpedo hits and the flood valves, rushed into these compartments and snuffed out the lives of men at their posts, several hundred in all. Caught between the cold sea water and the steam and boiling water from the damaged boilers, they simply melted away."

The measure was only partly successful. By then the ship was losing speed rapidly. Her steering gear was disabled; as she slowed down, she wandered aimlessly to port.

The American bombers kept coming, destroying the battleship's antiaircraft gun mounts one by one. Said Yoshida, "Here and there torpedoes pierced new holes in the port side, while more than ten bombs hit on the mizzenmast and quarter-deck. On the bridge casualties from machine-gun bullets were mounting, and shrapnel flew all over. We were completely at the mercy of the hot relentless steel." Under the steady pounding, the *Yamato's* topside was ripped into a jagged jumble of pock-marked steel. The blood of her crewmen ran down the tilting deck; gore and parts of bodies littered the heaving masses of metal. But the survivors fought on. When a strafer's bullet killed the gunner on a triple 25mm gun, Seaman Noboyuki Kobayashi shoved the body aside and took over. A moment later a fragment from a Helldiver's bomb knocked out his center gun and drove a splinter into his forehead. "I pulled it out, wrapped a towel around my head and kept shooting," he said.

The Americans returned to attack again and again. At 2:07 the *Yamato* took another torpedo on her starboard side. Within the next 10 minutes three more torpedoes punched into her ravaged port side. After that, the ship was little more than a broken derelict.

Meanwhile, the *Yahagi* had been stopped dead in the

water by a single torpedo, and the American planes were ganging up on the helpless cruiser. They finished her off with six more torpedoes and a dozen bombs. She went under at exactly 2:05. Admiral Komura, the destroyer squadron commander, who was flying his flag in the cruiser, knew the time because he looked at his watch just as he was sucked into the maelstrom of the ship's death. He thought he was drowning, but somehow he bobbed to the surface beside another man whose face was blackened with oil. He recognized the *Yahagi's* Captain Hara.

By then, the *Yamato's* list had gone past 30 degrees, and it kept increasing until she was nearly on her beam-ends. Her skipper, Admiral Ariga, prepared to go down with his ship and ordered a seaman to lash him to a compass pedestal. He called out to Admiral Ito: "Fleet Commander, your person is valuable. Please leave the ship with the crew." But Ito intended to die himself. Without answering, he entered his sea cabin and locked the door behind him.

Captain Jiro Nomura, the executive officer, thought of only one thing. He was afraid that the ship's sacred portraits of the Emperor and Empress might float free and that they would fall into the Americans' hands. The pictures were kept in the main gun command room. Nomura raised the gun post on an intercom and was reassured that he need not worry. He was told that the gunnery officer had already taken the paintings to his own cabin and locked himself in. He would personally take the holy totems down with him.

Seaman Kobayashi, his 25mm guns now useless, scrambled to the high starboard side and found a place to perch. He broke out his packet of imperial cigarettes, lighted one and passed the rest to men nearby. Kobayashi expected to die there, but somewhere deep inside the hull a magazine exploded. The force of the blast knocked him unconscious and propelled him 300 yards out to sea. When he came to, he was swimming and seeing visions of his mother.

At 2:23 p.m. the *Yamato* rolled over and exploded, spewing into the sky a towering pillar of flame that reportedly was seen at the southern tip of Kyushu 120 miles to the northeast. Then the mighty vessel went down.

Captain Nomura felt himself being sucked under by an irresistible force. The water was clear around him as he descended, and he could see other men "dancing about" in it. As he was pulled farther down, the sea darkened to an endless deep blue. Then, suddenly, red flashes of light shot through the depths; somewhere below, the rest of the *Yamato's* magazines were exploding. Although the concussions were agonizing and made him think "heaven and earth were blowing up," they saved Nomura's life. The great upsurge of water carried him to the surface. He rolled over on his back and floated.

Of the eight destroyers, four were sunk and one was limping home. The skippers of the remaining three conferred and decided that in spite of damage to their ships it was still their duty to carry on with Kikusui No. 1. Accordingly, boat crews put over the side to pick up survivors were instructed to save only able-bodied men who would be useful in a fight. The highest-ranking officer found alive was Admiral Komura, who was rescued near sunset. Preparing to resume the battle, he washed off the oil, climbed into a borrowed uniform and wrote out a dispatch to Combined Fleet headquarters: "We are now heading for Okinawa." But before the message could be transmitted, an order arrived from Tokyo aborting the mission.

And so, for the surface navy, Kikusui No. 1 ended some 210 miles short of its objective with the loss of six of the original 10 ships and more than 3,000 of the crew of the *Yamato* alone. The operation had cost the U.S. 12 airmen, plus three Hellcats, four Helldivers and three Avengers.

When Admiral Turner learned of the sinking of the *Yamato* and the destruction of five accompanying vessels, he sent a jubilant message to Admiral Nimitz in Guam. "I may be crazy," said Turner, "but it looks like the Japs have quit the war, at least in this section." To this appraisal, Nimitz coolly replied, "Delete all after 'crazy.'" He sensed, correctly, that the U.S. Navy's ordeal at Okinawa was far from over.

But the fleet did get a brief respite from the Kamikazes. Poor flying weather, the difficulties of replacing planes and the constant American strikes on airfields delayed the Japanese for a few days. It was not until April 11 that they launched Kikusui No. 2, a two-day assault by 185 suicide planes in the company of 150 escort fighters. This time the pilots found the U.S. carriers off Okinawa.

In the early afternoon, the carrier *Enterprise* had encounters with two "Judys." The first Kamikaze sideswiped the ship's port side and struck two 40mm gun mounts; the

A Kamikaze, skimming the water amid antiaircraft bursts and splashing shrapnel, makes a run at the battleship Texas off the northwestern coast of Okinawa. The plane, an old "Kate" bomber, evaded fire for a few hundred yards, then was blown to bits by a direct hit from the Texas.

plane's bomb exploded under the carrier, causing slight damage. An hour later the second Judy crashed under the *Enterprise's* starboard bow and started minor fires on the flight deck. As a result, the "Big E" was out of action for two days. The carrier *Essex* ran into trouble a few minutes after 3 o'clock that same afternoon, when a glancing blow by a Kamikaze's bomb caused extensive damage to the carrier's fuel tanks and steam lines. The *Essex* continued in operation, but 33 men were lost and 33 wounded in the attack.

On April 12, the Kamikaze pilots turned their attention to the battleship *Tennessee*. A single-engined Val, shielded from the ship's gunners by blinding smoke from a destroyer that had just been hit, bored in on the battlewagon, crashed into a 40mm gun mount and tumbled aft, spewing flaming gasoline. Aboard the ship, Commander Samuel Eliot Morison, the famed naval historian, watched a sailor "blown into the air, land on top of a 5-inch gun turret where he very calmly stripped off his burning, gasoline soaked clothes while awaiting a stream of water from the nearest fire hose." Twenty-three men were killed aboard the *Tennessee* and more than 100 were burned or wounded.

The same day, the first American ship was sunk by an *ohka*, Japan's piloted buzz bomb. The new destroyer *Mannert L. Abele* was on guard at picket station No. 3 northeast of Okinawa when her lookouts spotted two circling Mitsubishi "Bettys." Her gunners opened up on the twin-engined bombers at long range, but were diverted at 2:45 by other Kamikazes attacking close in. The gunners downed one plane, but the second, a Zeke, plunged into the starboard side, blowing out the after engine room and fracturing the keel and the propeller shafts. The *Abele* lost power and began to buckle amidships.

Suddenly one of the Bettys dropped an *ohka*. It fell lazily until the rockets cut in; then it came streaking toward the destroyer at a dazzling 600 miles per hour. The missile struck the ship's wounded starboard side and plunged into the forward fireroom, where its ton of explosive detonated. The explosion split the *Abele* in two, and within five minutes both the bow and stern sections went down at once. Other Japanese planes moved in to strafe and bomb the survivors struggling in the sea. Of her 345-man complement, the *Abele* lost 79 killed and missing and 35 wounded.

The punishment being taken by the picket ships com-

pelled Admiral Turner to modify his tactics. Instead of stationing a single destroyer and a companion gunboat at all picket stations, Turner assigned two tin cans and four gunboats at the most vulnerable ports, thus more than doubling the available antiaircraft firepower. Of course, the move also more than doubled the targets available to the "hell birds," as the Kamikazes were coming to be called.

When Kikusui No. 2 ended on April 12, the Kamikazes had sunk one destroyer and damaged 18 other ships—a smaller toll than the previous *kikusui* but still worrisome to Admiral Nimitz. Ever since the Kamikazes had first appeared, Nimitz had seen to it that no word of their attacks was released to the public; he had no desire to help the Japanese learn how successful their suicide campaign was. But pressure to release the story had been building up, and on April 12 (U.S. time), Nimitz' headquarters broke the news. If Nimitz expected the nation to be stunned, he was mistaken; Americans barely noticed the news, for they had just been dealt a more shocking blow. That day in Warm Springs, Georgia, President Franklin Roosevelt had died.

Kikusui No. 3 kicked off on April 15 and quickly produced a phenomenal story of seamanship and survival. In 80 minutes on April 16, one U.S. destroyer fought through 22 Kamikaze and bombing attacks, shot down nine planes and withstood hits by four bombs and eight Kamikazes.

The destroyer was the *Laffey* and April 16 was her third day at radar picket station No. 1, where the *Bush* and the *Colhoun* had gone down. At sunrise, following a relatively quiet night, the radar scopes aboard the *Laffey* were suddenly crowded with blips indicating 50 incoming bogeys. At 8:30 a.m. four Vals made the first pass, two coming in astern, two on the bow. The *Laffey's* 5-inch main battery and her antiaircraft guns managed to get all four.

But then in little more than five minutes the destroyer took aboard six Kamikazes. The first, a Val, tried for the bridge area, but because the *Laffey* was turning at high speed it came down on the after gun mount and spun off over the side. Two "Judy" dive bombers came from either side. The ship's guns got one, but the second crashed into the after deckhouse. Four more hit, two on the deckhouse, two on the after gun mount. Thus far, most of the damage had been confined to the after part of the ship. Amidships,

boilers and engine rooms were intact. The captain, Commander Frederick J. Becton, still had full power and maneuverability. Then a bomb fell and exploded just off the fantail. The blast jammed the rudders, which were hard over in a tight turn. Thereafter the *Laffey* plowed around in circles.

The last Kamikaze to connect was an "Oscar" fighter, closely pursued by an American Corsair. The Oscar came in over the port quarter, sliced into the mast and spun off into the sea. The Corsair nearly did the same; it knocked off the *Laffey's* port yardarm. But the pilot managed to control his damaged fighter long enough to climb and bail out.

The *Laffey* was still fighting. Her main battery could now fire only under manual control, but the gunners got two planes, one with a direct hit. "It was a pleasure to see the Oscar poised in space a few feet above the water," Commander Becton said later, "and then just disintegrate."

A little later, the destroyer took her last hit, a bomb on the forward 20mm batteries. The explosion tore the legs off a seaman, who kept firing until the plane passed over his position. "Please, please get me out of here," he muttered to his rescuers. But before they could get him out of the gun harness, he died—one of 31 crewmen killed or missing.

The *Laffey*, unable to steer a course, was towed to the fleet anchorage at Hagushi on the west coast of Okinawa. There she was patched up, and six days later went off to the repair base at Guam under her own steam.

By mid-April, the Kamikaze attacks were taking another kind of toll, even aboard ships that had so far escaped unscathed. Officers and men were near nervous exhaustion under the stress of permanent alert—of constantly anticipating the roar of diving Kamikazes and the seismic explosions that blew men into the sky like broken dolls.

To many sailors, the Kamikazes were inhuman instruments of terror, flown by incomprehensible fanatics whose minds had been twisted by their superiors. Other Americans watched in grudging admiration. Captain Charles R. Brown, chief of staff of one of Mitscher's task groups, later wrote: "I doubt if there is anyone who can depict with complete clarity our mixed emotions as we watched a man about to die, a man determined to die in order that he might destroy us in the process." Like other thoughtful men, he viewed Kamikazes with "a strange admixture of respect and pity—

respect for any person who offers the supreme sacrifice to the things he stands for, and pity for the utter frustration which was epitomized by the suicidal act."

Yet apparently many Kamikaze pilots found it quite easy to volunteer to die. Captain Rikihei Inoguchi, the senior staff officer in the Navy's suicide corps, said that most Kamikaze fliers welcomed the chance for patriotic suicide because they saw no chance of living out the War. Inoguchi considered their attitude an indispensable asset. "If the pilots had entertained a hope of survival," he said, "their determination and singleness of purpose would have been weakened. This would have lessened their chance of success." As men who felt doomed in any case, the volunteers much preferred to die gloriously, destroying great enemy ships, than to perish in some obscure engagement.

While they prepared for patriotic death, the Kamikaze pilots were treated by their countrymen with the same ritual respect accorded the heroes enshrined in Japan's war memorials. Yet to those who knew them intimately, they remained ordinary young men. "They were neither saints nor devils," Inoguchi wrote. "They were human beings, with all the motions and feelings, faults and virtues, strengths and weaknesses of other human beings. So they sang songs, laughed, cried and got drunk; did good things and bad."

Though all the Kamikaze pilots wrote wills and final letters home, they retained their normal interest in life to the very end. Lieutenant (jg.) Saburo Dohi, an *ohka* suicide pilot who was sent to await his last mission at a field near Kanoya in southern Kyushu, was annoyed on his arrival by the emergency quarters assigned to his unit. The building, a bombed-out schoolhouse, was filthy, windowless, bedless—a disgraceful place, not fit for even short-lived tenants. So Dohi organized his fellow pilots and cleaned out the barracks. Then he managed to requisition several bamboo beds and straw tatami sleeping mats. But at this point Dohi's housekeeping chores were interrupted by his final assignment—to die attacking Task Force 58.

On the way to the airstrip on April 12, Dohi made a detour and informed a senior officer that six more beds and 15 tatamis were due that day. "May I ask," Dohi said, "that you watch for them and make sure they go to the billet?"

Then Dohi went on to his mother plane. The old bomber was one of eight planes that carried *ohka* rockets into battle that day—and the only plane that managed to return to base. Its crewmen fully reported Dohi's last hours. The men said that after takeoff, Dohi fell asleep on a mat and had to be roused as the plane approached the target area. Dohi awakened smiling and said, "Time passes quickly, doesn't it?" Then he climbed down into his rocket and minutes later crashed to his death attacking a battleship.

On April 27, the Japanese launched Kikusui No. 4 with 115 aircraft. This time the operation disappointed Admiral Ugaki. The Kamikazes damaged five destroyers and five lesser ships but did not sink a single combat vessel.

It may have been the fliers' frustration that moved a suicide pilot to commit the most ignoble act of the Kamikaze campaign. On the night of the 28th the hospital ship *Comfort,* lighted up under Geneva Convention rules and riding under a full moon, was steaming toward Saipan with a load of wounded. A Kamikaze flew across the ship at masthead height, circled back and dived into the superstructure. Its bomb exploded in the surgery where medical teams were operating. Thirty men were killed, and six Army nurses. Thirty-four men and four nurses were wounded.

The next *kikusui,* mounted on May 3, was timed to support General Ushijima's banzai counteroffensive on Okinawa. As it happened, the Kamikazes did far more damage to the Navy offshore than Ushijima's troops inflicted on the Tenth Army on land. Again, the suicide planes concentrated on the picket ships. The two-day aerial attack cost the picket line three ships sunk and 450 sailors dead or missing.

Though the Kamikazes never let up on the picket destroyers, some of them were getting through to the top-priority targets, the big carriers. Shortly after 10 a.m. on May 11, two Kamikazes and their bombs hit Admiral Mitscher's flagship, the fast carrier *Bunker Hill (pages 164-175).*

Admiral Mitscher moved his flag to the carrier *Enterprise,* but three days later the Kamikazes forced him to move again. Soon after daybreak on the 14th of May, 26 Japanese planes appeared over Task Force 58. American carrier planes shot down 19, and antiaircraft fire took care of six. But at 6:56 a.m. the one survivor plunged into the Big E near her forward aircraft elevator, which was blown into the sky. The Kamikaze bomb plunged deep into the ship before it exploded, setting off wild fires on the hangar deck and in the elevator pit. It was the Big E's third wound by a Kamika-

ze and the sturdy veteran was finished for the War. Fortunately for the Americans, the attack on the *Enterprise* was the last successful Kamikaze strike on U.S. fast carriers.

The British aircraft carriers in action around Sakishimagunto also felt the lash of the Kamikazes. But to the astonishment of the Americans, the British carriers proved much less vulnerable to them. The reason was simple: The flight decks on British flattops were made of 3-inch-thick armor plate instead of teak. The steel made the British carriers hellishly hot in tropic seas, and the tremendous weight of additional metal made them slower and more cumbersome than the U.S. flattops. But there was no denying the superior resistance of the steel decks.

The difference was amply demonstrated on April 1 when a Zeke dived onto the flight deck of the carrier *Indefatigable.* Though 14 men were killed, the ship suffered no damage more serious than a three-inch dent in the armor plate. Planes were again landing on the *Indefatigable* within an hour. This prompted the American liaison officer aboard to make an invidious comparison: "When a Kamikaze hits a U.S. carrier, it's six months repair at Pearl. In a Limey carrier it's a case of 'Sweepers, man your brooms.'"

By the end of May, both the British and the American fleets noticed that the Kamikaze attacks were losing their punch. After each *kikusui,* Admiral Ugaki found it increasingly difficult to scrape together the large number of planes needed to make the next wave a smashing success. American bombing of the Kyushu and Shikoku airfields and British bombing of the airstrips in the Sakishimas became more intense and efficient, and Japanese aircraft production was steadily reduced by heavy bombers from U.S. bases in the Marianas. Ugaki fell far short of the 4,000-odd planes called for in the original *Ten Go* plan.

Still, Ugaki had mounted 10 *kikusui,* and in each one a number of pilots got through. By the end of the operation, no fewer than 1,465 Kamikaze fliers went to their deaths attacking Allied ships, and the American toll was appalling: some 120 ships hit, 29 sunk, 6,035 sailors wounded and 3,048 killed or missing. More than anything else, the sheer will of the Kamikaze pilots in the face of overwhelming Allied might prompted Commander Louis A. Gillies, the intelligence officer of the Fifth Fleet, to declare, "The Japanese are defeated, but we have not yet won the victory."

SUICIDE OF A BATTLESHIP

The mammoth battleship Yamato, pride of the Japanese Navy, sends up great sheets of spray as she thrusts through heavy seas at 27 knots during a 1941 trial run.

AERIAL ASSAULT ON THE MIGHTY YAMATO

"Pilots, man your planes!" ordered the ready-room intercoms on 12 U.S. carriers in Okinawan waters.

At 10 a.m. on April 7, 1945, the first strike forces of Navy aircraft—280 fighters, dive bombers and torpedo planes—swooped off the carriers' flight decks and headed north to seek and destroy a 10-ship Japanese force that had been sighted by U.S. submarines the day before. The pilots were in a state of high excitement, for their chief target was reportedly the mighty battleship Yamato.

The Yamato outstripped every other battleship afloat. A sixth of a mile long and displacing 72,800 tons under full load, she packed an awesome offensive punch, with nine 18.1-inch guns that could fire a 3,200-pound shell 22.5 miles. For defense, she mounted no fewer than 100 antiaircraft guns, ranging from 25mm to 155mm, and the heaviest armor plate of any battleship—16 inches thick in places.

But now this formidable monster had been dispatched on a suicide mission. She and her escorts—the light cruiser Yahagi and eight destroyers—were steaming south from Honshu under orders to lure the American carriers away from Okinawa, then to beach themselves on the island and die fighting the American forces there.

One group of pilots, flying through rain and heavy clouds, spotted the Yamato at 12:32 p.m. and was greeted by thunderous gunfire from the battleship. The fliers then discovered that their radios were jammed by high-powered transmitters on board the Yamato. Unable to coordinate their attacks, they began what pilot Thaddeus T. Coleman later called "the most confusing air-sea battle of all time. Bomber pilots pushed over in all sorts of crazy dives, fighter pilots used every maneuver in the book, torpedo pilots stuck out their necks all the way, dropped right down on the surface and delivered their parcels so near the ships that many of them missed the ships' superstructures by inches."

The first attacks sank one destroyer and severely damaged the cruiser. The Yamato took two bombs and a torpedo, and shifted course to the west, then south, hoping to escape in the stormy weather.

Lieut. Commander Herbert Houck (second from left) and fellow pilots from the carrier Yorktown swap stories after their attack on the Yamato.

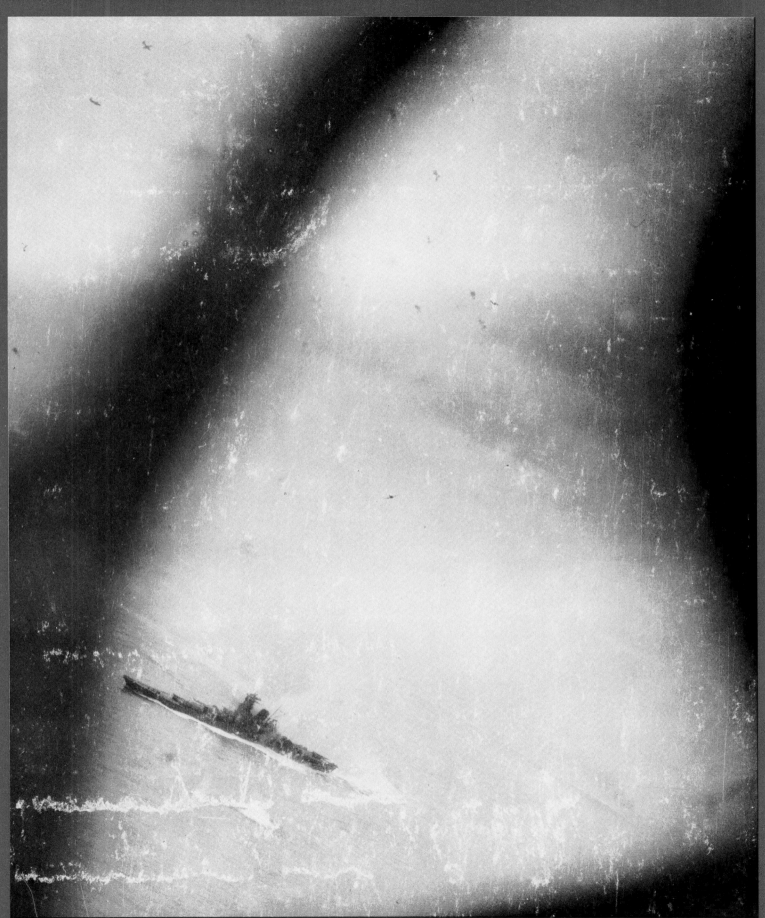

Diving from 3,000 feet, U.S. Navy planes attack the Yamato in a photograph taken from the cockpit of a Curtiss Helldiver carrying 1,500 pounds of bombs.

On fire from bomb hits, a Japanese destroyer (foreground) fires her after batteries at an attacking American plane. In the background, the crippled Yamato follows an erratic course after repeated hits by bombs and torpedoes.

DEATH-DEALING RUNS BY TORPEDO PLANES

At about 1 p.m., soon after the first U.S. strike force completed its helter-skelter attack, a second wave of 167 planes arrived over the Japanese ships. The pilots found that the *Yamato's* radio-jamming equipment had been silenced, and they were able to coordinate their attacks by voice communication. By 2 p.m., when their attacks ended, they had hit the *Yamato* with five torpedoes, leaving a battered wreck.

The assault was continued without interruption by a third carrier strike force of 106 planes. An air group from the *Intrepid* slammed at least eight bombs and one torpedo into the *Yamato*. As the torpedo bombers from the *Yorktown* started their run, the battleship was listing heavily to port, exposing her vulnerable underbelly.

"Hit her in the belly—now!" yelled the leader of the *Yorktown* planes. Four more torpedoes blasted the *Yamato's* bottom.

The great battleship was wracked by a series of internal explosions. She capsized and began to go under.

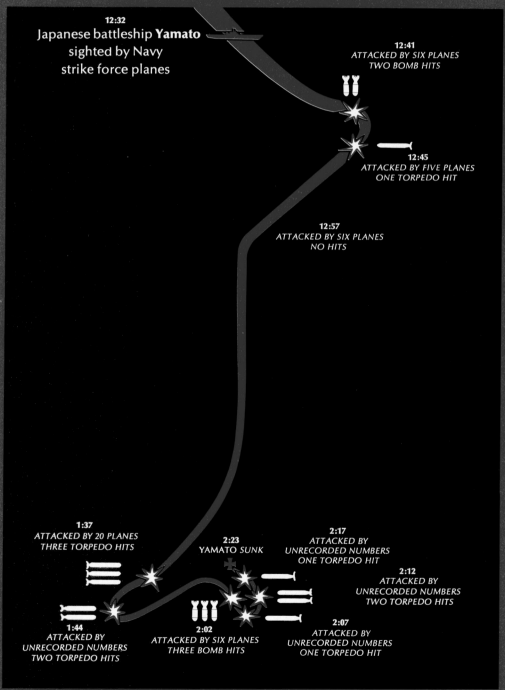

12:32
Japanese battleship **Yamato** sighted by Navy strike force planes

12:41
ATTACKED BY SIX PLANES
TWO BOMB HITS

12:45
ATTACKED BY FIVE PLANES
ONE TORPEDO HIT

12:57
ATTACKED BY SIX PLANES
NO HITS

1:37
ATTACKED BY 20 PLANES
THREE TORPEDO HITS

2:23
YAMATO SUNK

2:17
ATTACKED BY
UNRECORDED NUMBERS
ONE TORPEDO HIT

2:12
ATTACKED BY
UNRECORDED NUMBERS
TWO TORPEDO HITS

1:44
ATTACKED BY
UNRECORDED NUMBERS
TWO TORPEDO HITS

2:02
ATTACKED BY SIX PLANES
THREE BOMB HITS

2:07
ATTACKED BY
UNRECORDED NUMBERS
ONE TORPEDO HIT

The attacks on the Yamato by three U.S. strike forces are diagramed from entries in the battleship's log.

An American bomb hits the water near the

burning Yamato, raising a geyser of water off her port side. The battleship's zigzagging run came to an end 210 miles north of her destination, Okinawa.

Belching flame and smoke from exploding magazines, the Yamato goes under after 105 minutes of battle. Three Japanese destroyers stand by to pick up survivors.

163

THE BUNKER HILL'S AGONY

The U.S. carrier Bunker Hill erupts in flames and black smoke after being hit by suicide planes off Okinawa. The carrier Randolph (foreground) escaped damage.

SIX HOURS ABOARD A FLOATING INFERNO

On the morning of May 11, 1945, the fast carrier U.S.S. *Bunker Hill*—flagship of Vice Admiral Marc A. Mitscher's Task Force 58—was mounting air strikes on Okinawa from a position 76 miles to the east. At 10:05 a.m., 25 of her planes were flying sorties; 30 stood ready on the flight deck, and 48 more were being fueled and armed on the hangar deck below. The carrier had been resupplied at sea the day before, and her tanks were brimming with aviation gas and 1,873,000 gallons of fuel oil.

Suddenly, a Japanese "Zeke" fighter burst out of a cloud on the starboard beam. The pilot flew in low and crashed into the planes on the *Bunker Hill's* flight deck, igniting them like a string of firecrackers. Just 30 seconds later, another Kamikaze screamed down in a vertical dive and smashed amidships into the base of the carrier's island.

Three of the *Bunker Hill's* top decks were engulfed in a roaring inferno from amidships to the fantail, and the 3,000 men on board threw themselves into a frantic struggle to save the ship and their own lives. While damage-control teams broke out hoses, other crewmen raced to turn on sprinklers, jettison ammunition, and close hatches and vents to cut down drafts. Other vessels in the task force steamed to the carrier's aid. While some of them screened the stricken ship against further attack, the cruiser *Wilkes-Barre* and three destroyers trained their hoses on the fires, evacuated wounded and rescued men from the sea.

The *Bunker Hill's* commanding officer, Captain George A. Seitz, made two critical maneuvers. Shortly after his ship was hit, he swung her broadside to the wind so that smoke and flames would not be blown the length of the carrier. Later, when water, debris and gasoline from ruptured pipes had accumulated dangerously on the hangar deck, he made a sharp 70-degree turn that sloshed tons of fuel overboard through openings in the deck's siding. These moves, and six hours of courageous struggle by the crew, finally brought the fires under control. But 396 crewmen were dead or missing, another 264 were injured and the Kamikaze's devastating blows had knocked the *Bunker Hill* out of the War.

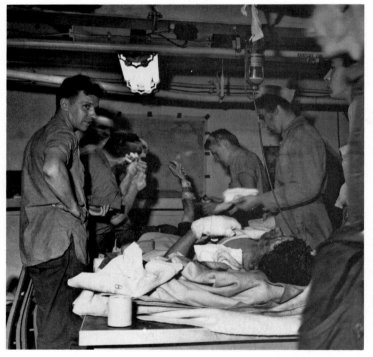

Two wounded survivors of the Kamikaze raid on the Bunker Hill are treated by corpsmen on the Wilkes-Barre, a sister ship in Task Force 58.

A second Kamikaze, a "Judy" dive bomber visible directly over the carrier, plunges past a towering smoke ball toward the Bunker Hill's blazing flight deck.

168

Aft of the island, fire fighters train hoses on the flames; fire consumed 30 planes loaded with 12,000 gallons of aviation fuel. The black smoke of burning gasoline is mixed with clouds of white steam released when the safety valves popped on the carrier's main steam line. At far left, gun crews man their battle stations; they later shot down a third Kamikaze.

As the fires on the flight deck wane, repair parties look over the wreckage of the still-smoldering hangar deck below. A hole 40 feet across was ripped open by a 550-pound bomb from the second Kamikaze. The force of the bomb's blast peeled back the one-and-a-half-inch armor plating, collapsed part of the gallery deck, which housed the ready rooms, and completely destroyed the nearby aircraft elevator.

Advancing behind a blanket of fine spray from a new and highly effective fog nozzle, five fire fighters battle the flames on the Bunker Hill's hangar deck.

FIGHTING THE FIRES ON THE DECKS BELOW

The fiercest battles for the *Bunker Hill's* survival were waged in the raging infernos below the flight deck.

On the hangar deck, fire fighters hurried toward the conflagration in the carrier's stern, but they found their way blocked by smoke, heat and parked aircraft. The men wrestled planes onto the one undamaged elevator and sent them topside, gradually clearing a path toward the flames. Sailors trapped in the stern also fought the blaze, playing their hoses against a wall of burning gasoline while molten metal dripped on them from overhead. Below the hangar deck, fire-fighting teams battled small but intense electrical fires and streams of burning gasoline that leaked down from the hangar deck. More than 100 men in this area were overcome by smoke and died in the murky passageways before rescuers could reach them.

Fortunately for the rescuers, the engine and boiler rooms were undamaged; their crews kept the *Bunker Hill* moving and maneuverable, and maintained pressure in water mains throughout the carrier. But they worked in 130° F. heat, amid suffocating smoke that poured in through open vents. Dozens of men might have been asphyxiated here had not a courageous sailor somehow managed to grope his way through the gloom with several armloads of breathing masks.

The flames subsided gradually. In two hours, the fires on the hangar deck were put out. But it took four more hours—until four in the afternoon—before the fires on the lower decks were declared to be under control. The *Bunker Hill* was a shambles. Gun galleries were demolished, more than 50 planes were destroyed and decks were buckled, and the flight deck was broken and twisted skyward.

A bomb hole yawns in the flight deck. The bomb actually did not explode inside the ship: it went through the side and burst in the air 100 feet away.

Salvage crews working near an elevator warped by the heat clear the wreckage of airplanes that had been fueled for takeoff when the Kamikazes struck.

Incinerated chairs stand in a ready room (left) where 30 pilots had been awaiting action. The fliers escaped into a passageway (right) but suffocated there.

Surrounded by broken airplane wings, dead crewmen clutch the hose they had used to fight the blaze on the hangar deck until they were felled by smoke.

A badly injured seaman is evacuated from the Bunker Hill to the cruiser Wilkes-Barre by means of a pulley system known as a transfer whip. The Bunker Hill's sick bay was knocked out, and injured crewmen, many horribly burned, were placed under the wings of undamaged aircraft to shield them from the sun until they could be moved to other ships.

Their bodies wrapped in canvas, four of the Bunker Hill's dead are buried at sea on the day after the attack. Funeral services for 352 men were begun at noon and ended at sunset. In the meantime, the Bunker Hill, escorted by destroyers, was zigzagging out of the combat zone toward the Ulithi atoll, 1,200 miles from the site of the Kamikaze attack.

175

6

"We will take our time and kill the Japanese gradually." With that grim remark to correspondents, General Buckner summed up his expectations for the May fighting in southern Okinawa. Buckner was doing all he could to comply with orders from Admiral Nimitz to speed up the campaign, thus shortening the fleet's exposure to deadly Kamikaze attacks. But the fighting to date had been brutal and slow, a bloody struggle to root out the Japanese hill by hill, cave by cave, and Buckner anticipated more of the same.

On May 9 Buckner ordered his army to prepare for a general offensive against the enemy's second major defense line, where the Japanese were concentrated after their calamitous counterattack on May 4 and 5. The line stretched across the island in an arc eight miles long that ran from the Yonabaru area on the east coast, through the ancient town of Shuri in the center, to the port of Naha on the west coast (map, page 179).

Buckner had available for the attack three Army divisions and two Marine divisions—around 85,000 men, backed by the Tenth Army's artillery and support troops, as well as the guns and planes of the fleet. He ordered the 1st Marine Division and the 77th Infantry Division to keep up heavy pressure on the center of the Japanese line in front of General Ushijima's Shuri headquarters. In the meantime, the 96th Infantry Division would try to turn the Japanese eastern flank at Yonabaru and the 6th Marine Division would attempt to crack through on the western flank near Naha. Buckner's remaining unit, the 7th Infantry Division, would be held in reserve just to the northeast. (A sixth division, the 27th, was engaged in occupation duty in the northern two thirds of the island.)

With luck, the battle might be decided quickly. If either of Buckner's flank divisions broke through as planned, it could roll across the island on a paved road behind the Japanese line, trapping Ushijima's army for piecemeal destruction by superior U.S. firepower.

On the other side of the line, Ushijima did not like his prospects any better than Buckner did. In his retreat to the Shuri defense line, he had left behind some 6,000 dead soldiers, and he had been forced to bring forward elements of the 44th Independent Mixed Brigade to bolster his crack 24th and 62nd Divisions, which had borne the brunt of the fighting. But Ushijima's forces, reduced though they were,

USHIJIMA'S SAVAGE RETREAT

had a tremendous asset. The Shuri defense line had been constructed with meticulous care to take full advantage of the difficult terrain: rows of hills and ridges, riddled with caves and studded with coral outcroppings, all made to order for mortar pits and machine-gun nests, with an umbrella of protection from heavy guns in the rear. Ushijima's brilliant use of nature's jumble had produced the toughest defense line the Americans had faced in the Pacific war— tougher than even Iwo Jima and Tarawa. And it would claim far more casualties than Buckner feared.

On the morning of May 10, the 6th Marine Division prepared to launch Buckner's offensive along the west coast. The Marines were fresh after light duty mopping up in northern Okinawa, and the Japanese considered them a bellwether unit. Said a Japanese newspaper printed in Naha: "Among the badly mauled enemy, it is a tiger's cub and their morale is high. If we can deal the 6th Marine Division a mortal blow, we will probably be able to control the enemy's destiny."

The Marines soon sampled the kind of opposition they would face. While spearhead groups were crossing the Asa River on a footbridge, two Japanese soldiers carrying explosive charges suddenly appeared and hurled themselves at the bridge, destroying it and themselves. Marine engineers, working through the night under enemy shelling, threw a Bailey bridge over the river, and tanks as well as infantry crossed to the far bank.

The Marines found themselves fully engaged on May 11. Their infantry and tanks ran into heavy fire from artillery, mortars, machine guns and snipers. They pushed forward, but only slowly. At dusk, the 6th Division had advanced scarcely 1,000 yards.

Then on May 12, the leathernecks encountered an insignificant hillock that would dominate their lives for the next week. It rose 200 feet, and because of its shape they named it Sugar Loaf Hill. Captain Owen T. Stebbins led his company of the 22nd Regiment in a tank and infantry frontal assault on Sugar Loaf. Japanese machine gunners soon pinned down two of Stebbins' three platoons, and 47mm antitank guns pounded the supporting Shermans with deadly accuracy.

Stebbins saw only one way to eliminate the machine-gun nests. He led a headlong charge, followed by his executive officer, Lieutenant Dale W. Bair, and the 40 men of his third platoon. It was a slaughter. Within 100 yards, 28 Marines were killed or wounded. One of the casualties was Stebbins, his legs shattered by machine-gun fire.

Lieutenant Bair took over command—and was immediately hit in the left arm. With the arm dangling by his side, the lieutenant assembled the 14 remaining leathernecks of the third platoon, rounded up 11 replacements and led a new assault that carried the Marines all the way to the top of Sugar Loaf Hill. Only a handful of men reached the crest, and they barely managed to hold off the Japanese defenders long enough to evacuate their wounded comrades from the slope of Sugar Loaf.

By nightfall on May 12, after three more assaults were driven back by Japanese mortars and hand grenades, Stebbins' original company of around 200 men was reduced to 75, and the blackened hulks of three supporting Sherman tanks lay smoking in front of the hill.

Although the Marines did not know it, their 22nd Regiment had attacked the nerve center of the Japanese western flank defenses. Sugar Loaf was the northern point of a triangular defense system designed to halt any American breakthrough between Naha and Shuri. Directly south of Sugar Loaf lay another hillock called Horseshoe, and to the southeast was a crescent-shaped ridge called Half Moon. The slopes and interiors of all three hills were laced with interconnected trenches, mortar pits, machine-gun nests and pillboxes, all expertly camouflaged and impervious to anything but a direct hit. Manning this maze were some 5,000 fresh troops of the 44th Brigade, which Ushijima had brought up from the south.

As always, the defenses were ingeniously designed to support one another. Marines could win the northern slope and the crest of one hill, but the Japanese on the reverse slope and in the interior would then pop out of their hidden positions, and lob grenades and shower the Marines with high-angled mortar fire. On reaching the crest of a hill, the leathernecks would be exposed to fire from each of the other two hills, and tanks attempting to outflank a position by working their way around to the reverse slope would find themselves under fire from three directions. And all three hills were within easy range of the enemy's heavy mortars and field artillery on the Shuri heights, only 1,500 yards to the east.

The Marines attacked again and again on May 13, and each time they met with the same disastrous results. Then, on May 14, two depleted companies of the 22nd Regiment's 2nd Battalion, and a large part of the division's 29th Regiment were thrown against Sugar Loaf, supported by artillery, standard and flame-throwing tanks and 4.2-inch mortars. By 3 o'clock in the afternoon, men of the 2nd Battalion had secured a foothold on the hill—only to be thrown back by Japanese fire.

At 7:30 p.m. the executive officer of the 2nd Battalion, Major Henry A. Courtney Jr., found himself at the base of Sugar Loaf with only 43 survivors of the two companies that had been battling all day.

"Men, if we don't take the top of this hill tonight," Courtney told his troops, "the Japs will be down here to drive us away in the morning. When we go up there, some of us are never going to come down again. You all know what hell it is on the top, but that hill's got to be taken, and we're going to do it."

Courtney started up and his men followed, lugging their weapons and all the grenades they could carry. By 11 p.m. they were on the top, digging in under steady Japanese mortar and machine-gun fire. A mortar fragment ripped into Courtney's neck, mortally wounding him. Throughout the night, enemy mortars and snipers whittled away at Courtney's group. By dawn, only 15 Marines were left to hold the hilltop, and daylight made the position even more precarious. Enemy gunners on Half Moon and Horseshoe zeroed in on the survivors and at last forced them to withdraw.

The 22nd Regiment had suffered a bloody defeat; Major Courtney's battalion alone had lost 400 men dead or wounded in just three days—almost half its normal complement. From now on, the 29th Regiment would do the lion's share of the fighting.

Sugar Loaf was no easier for the 29th than it had been for the 22nd. Nothing worked until May 18, when Captain Howard L. Mabie came up with the winning strategy for Sugar Loaf. While other elements of the 29th pressured the enemy gunners on Half Moon and Horseshoe, Mabie sent a tank-infantry team around one flank of Sugar Loaf. With the Japanese distracted by this move, Mabie dispatched another team around the opposite flank. The tanks began blasting the enemy positions on Sugar Loaf's reverse slope from two directions. Meanwhile, First Lieutenant Francis X. Smith took 80 men up Sugar Loaf's forward slope. Smith's men dug in and held the hill, raining hand grenades down on the Japanese positions from the crest.

By nightfall on May 18, Sugar Loaf was in American hands. The next day, the 4th Regiment relieved the 29th and nailed down the victory. Mike Goracoff, a gunnery sergeant of the 4th, summed up the 10-day battle for Sugar Loaf. "We made eleven thrusts at that hill and fell back each time with most of our boys dead or missing," he said. "It wasn't uncommon to see a PFC commanding the platoon as it fell back from a push at the hill. It seemed that the lieutenants fell first, then the sergeants." To help take up the slack, a cook volunteered for frontline duty, and two shoemakers from the divisional quartermaster unit went forward as mortarmen. "They knew no more about mortars than I did about the shoe business," said Goracoff. "But they learned, and quickly. Had to, with over 100 per cent casualties."

However, General Ushijima had no intention of abandoning the most important of his three positions, without which the Japanese on Half Moon and Horseshoe would find it hard to hold out. On the night of May 20, Ushijima sent a battalion to counterattack the 4th Regiment on Sugar Loaf. After a night of fierce fire fights and grenade-tossing duels, the few Japanese survivors withdrew. The Marines counted 494 enemy dead.

Sugar Loaf had been taken, but at a terrible price. The 6th Division had lost 2,662 men killed or wounded between May 10 and 19. And that was not all. An additional 1,289 men had succumbed to what the doctors and corpsmen called combat fatigue. Under the terrific stress of battle, they had suffered nervous breakdowns. Some of the Marines cracked after a single traumatic experience, such as seeing a buddy disintegrate in the blast of a mortar shell. But for many leathernecks and GIs, combat fatigue was a slow, cumulative debilitation, the result of the long, bitter and apparently hopeless fighting, from which there was no relief but sudden death.

Combat-fatigue cases had begun to crowd divisional hospitals as early as mid-April, and by the end of the month the

Tenth Army had opened a special field hospital to accommodate an influx of more than 3,000 victims. Before the fighting was over, Okinawa would produce the most and the worst cases of combat fatigue in the Pacific war.

Doctors soon discovered that the greatest single cause was the weight and accuracy of the Japanese artillery. To the 6th Marine Division attacking Sugar Loaf, it seemed uncanny when an enemy shell landed precisely in the middle of a battalion headquarters where U.S. officers were planning an attack. The battalion commander, two tank officers and three radio operators were killed, and all three of the battalion's company commanders were wounded. Some men refused to believe that the Japanese artillery was this good, and they even speculated that German officers were directing the Japanese fire.

But General Ushijima had no need for outside help. His heavy weapons were in the hands of Major General Kosuke Wada's 5th Artillery Command. And Wada's 3,200 men, most of whom had at least three years of experience, were among the best artillerymen in the Japanese Army. They had many more 75mm, 120mm and 150mm guns and howitzers, and many more 81mm and 320mm mortars, than any other Japanese artillery unit in the Pacific.

Many of these big guns were solidly dug in on the heights surrounding Shuri Castle. Their deadly fire now prevented any further advance to the southeast by the 6th Marine Division. The brutal task of neutralizing these gun positions fell to the 1st Marine Division and the 77th Division, attacking the center of Ushijima's defense line.

On the 11th of May, the 1st Marine Division moved against a succession of craggy hills and narrow clefts that made up General Ushijima's line of defense north of Shuri. This proud and professional outfit, under the command of Major General Pedro A. Del Valle, disdained the other divisions' practice of giving descriptive American names to the terrain features in their sector and used instead the names of the Okinawan villages that lay between the hills. Thus the three main obstacles between the 1st Marine Division and Ushijima's headquarters were known, in turn, as Dakeshi Ridge, Wana Ridge and Wana Draw.

The division's 7th Regiment jumped off early on May 10

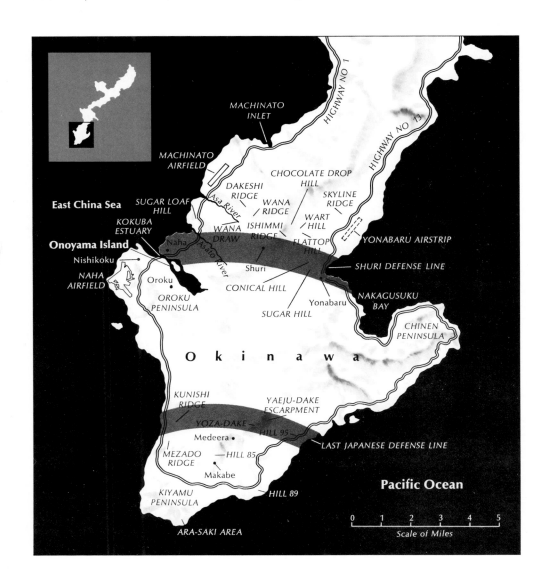

For three weeks in May of 1945, the Japanese Thirty-second Army halted the U.S. Tenth Army along the rugged natural ramparts of the Shuri defense line (top), which ran west from Yonabaru, past General Ushijima's headquarters in Shuri Castle, to the port of Naha. Then, still in control, the Japanese slipped away to the southern tip of Okinawa for their last stand along another line of fortified hills.

with a brave and foolhardy attempt to take Dakeshi Ridge by storm. By nightfall the Marines had reached only the two points of the U-shaped ridge. "We did damned little attacking," said one Marine. "Every time a man raised his head he was hit." It was another Sugar Loaf Hill: the Japanese were solidly dug in on both the forward and reverse slopes of Dakeshi, and were covered by the fire of machine guns, mortars and artillery from the high ground to their rear. Again, as at Sugar Loaf, it was up to the tanks to make the breakthrough at Dakeshi.

On May 12, a platoon leader led three Sherman tanks, one armed with a cannon and two with flamethrowers, around the flank of the ridge. The cannon-armed tank blast-ed the cave openings on the reverse side with direct fire from its 75mm gun. The flamethrowers then seared the slope while all three tanks raked the area with .30-caliber machine-gun fire. The Marine infantrymen were then able to storm the ridge and clear out the surviving Japanese with grenades, portable flamethrowers and demolition charges.

By now, the Japanese as well as the American commanders fully appreciated the critical role played by the U.S. tanks in reducing the Japanese cave defenses. In a battle order issued before the attack on Dakeshi Ridge, General Ushijima had warned his field commanders that "the enemy's power lies in his tanks. It has become obvious that our battle against the Americans is a battle against their

tanks." The fighting for Wana Ridge and Wana Draw would prove him right.

As the Marines and tankers of the 1st Division pushed on toward Wana Draw on May 13, they were functioning smoothly as mutually supporting elements of a deadly fire team. The tanks blasted and burned out the Japanese positions on either side of Wana Draw, opening a corridor for the infantry while at the same time protecting them from small-arms fire. The infantry, moving close behind or alongside the tanks, scouted out their routes and protected them from the Japanese suicide squads that popped suddenly from spider holes in the draw or came charging out of cliffside caves to hurl themselves and their satchel charges under the tanks. On one day alone, the 1st Division's tanks fired 5,000 rounds of 75mm shells and 175,000 rounds of .30-caliber ammunition in Wana Draw, while flamethrowers spewed 600 gallons of liquid fire on targets in the draw and on the ridge.

The artillery's job of grinding down each enemy cave and gun position on the surrounding ridges went on from morning to nightfall, when the Marines pulled back to consolidate their positions against enemy attack. The conventional artillery got powerful assists from the Navy and Marine fighter-bombers and from the big guns of the offshore Navy warships, which were especially effective against the enemy's 47mm antitank guns. On May 16, when two 1st Division tanks were knocked out by antitank fire in Wana Draw, alert Marines spotted the muzzle flashes of a pair of 47mm guns. The coordinates were quickly relayed to the battleship *Colorado,* standing by for fire support off the west coast. The *Colorado's* main 16-inch batteries made short work of both positions.

But in the end, the troops and tanks had to root out an enemy that never quit. "It was always hot up there on Wana," recalled Lieut. Colonel Arthur J. "Jeb" Stuart, the commander of the division's 1st Tank Battalion. "Every day something happened that wasn't in the book. Only one thing was always the same; those men, the tank-infantry teams, stuck with each other, went in the draw together, came out of the draw together—alive, wounded, dead, maimed, crying in anguish, limping, bleeding—no matter how, they came out together."

Casualties had mounted steadily as the Marines moved closer to the Shuri heights that formed the southern boundary of Wana Draw. By May 17, one battalion of the 7th Regiment was so depleted that its survivors barely formed a single company, and when the regiment was finally relieved on May 19 its total casualty count was more than 1,000 dead, wounded or missing. Navy medical corpsmen tending to the wounded suffered such heavy casualties that the division had to replace them with hastily trained Marines.

The battered 7th Regiment was relieved by the 1st Regiment, which had been strengthened with some 500 replacements while in division reserve. With this rested and rebuilt regiment setting the pace, the 1st Marine Division made substantial progress in reducing enemy positions on May 20. The 5th Regiment, which had been hammering enemy defenses in Wana Draw for almost a week, had finally captured a hill commanding the western entrance to the valley. And yet for all their firepower and teamwork, the Marines of the 1st Division could not make a breakthrough. For the time being, the determined Japanese stalemated them one ridgeline short of Shuri.

On the eastern flank of the two Marine divisions, the GIs were absorbing heavy punishment, too. Two regiments of the 77th Division were struggling to advance toward Shuri from the northeast but could make little headway against the remnants of the tough Japanese 24th Division. By May 15, one regiment had been reduced to a quarter of its original strength. The other regiment had suffered so many casualties that its survivors barely made up a single full-strength battalion; this outfit was relieved by the division's third regiment, the 307th, on May 15.

In an attempt to get the line moving, the division took a leaf from the Japanese tactical notebook and launched the Americans' first large-scale night assault of the Okinawan Campaign. Before dawn on May 17, the attack group—204 men of Company E, 2nd Battalion, 307th Regiment, led by First Lieutenant Theodore S. Bell—quietly climbed to the crest of Ishimmi Ridge, a coral escarpment 350 feet high and 500 yards long barring the way to Shuri, just a third of a mile beyond. A signal victory seemed to be within easy reach. But there on that ridge the GIs would stay for three days, unable to escape their suffering.

At the top of the ridge in the darkness, Bell and his men

Shell-pocked Conical Hill, the eastern anchor of the Naha-Shuri-Yonabaru defense line across southern Okinawa, overlooks the remains of the town of Yonabaru, where a scattering of pup tents reveals the presence of U.S. infantry. When the GIs took the eastern slope on May 21, 1945, after a bloody 10-day struggle, they had come through mortar barrages so heavy that nearly every yard they covered had been hit at least once.

paused to make sure that they had not been detected. Their next step was to rout the Japanese defenders, who occupied a network of tunnels and trenches on the reverse slope. In a quick, vicious flurry, the GIs bayoneted or shot a dozen sleeping Japanese and mowed down an officer and his aide as they strolled out of their trench, talking and laughing. Bell's men, unwilling to risk using the interconnected Japanese defense positions, began carving foxholes of their own out of the coral and rock that formed the flat crest of Ishimmi Ridge.

Twenty minutes later, the surrounding Japanese awakened to the surprise attack, and they began hitting the exposed American positions with their deadly 50mm knee mortars, with rifle and machine-gun fire, and with heavy artillery from the Shuri heights to the southwest. "As daylight came," recalled platoon leader Second Lieutenant Robert F. Meiser, "we finally realized that we were in a spot and that the enemy controlled the position from every direction, including the rear."

By 7 a.m. enemy gunners had knocked out both of the GIs' light .30-caliber machine guns. By 10 a.m. they had destroyed all but one of the 60mm mortars and killed or wounded most of the crewmen. They blew up the GIs' two .50-caliber heavy machine guns. They picked off the American radios, which they readily spotted by their whiplike aerials. Of six radios that Bell's men had carried to the top of the ridge, only two survived the first day, and one of these was blown apart early the following morning.

The Americans were helpless. With fire pouring in on them from both flanks and from the Shuri heights, they lay prone in their shallow, uncompleted foxholes, certain they would be killed if they raised up to resume digging. Four knee mortars fired from tunnel mouths on both sides of the ridge, systematically raking the U.S. positions. "Riflemen were blown to bits by these mortars," said Lieutenant Meiser, "and many men were struck in the head by machine-gun fire. The blood from wounded was everywhere; in the weapons, on the living, splattered all around. The dead lay where they fell, in pools of their own blood."

By nightfall, all medical supplies, rations and water were exhausted, and the remnants of Company E pulled back into a tight perimeter around the company command post. A call came through on the one remaining radio, promising relief. The GIs strained their eyes, hoping to see friends coming toward them before an enemy counterattack overran their position. Shells from Japanese mortars and field guns continued to burst among them. Answering shells from U.S. guns whined overhead; some of them landed so close that they showered the men with rock fragments. American star-shell flares, floating lazily to earth on miniature parachutes, kept the ridgeline illuminated and enabled the GIs to pick off enemy infiltrators with rifle fire or grenades. But at daybreak the relief force was still nowhere in sight. The Japanese had ambushed it, forcing the survivors to turn back.

On the morning of the second day, May 18, Lieutenant Bell received a radioed order to hold the ridge "at all costs." In a quiet but firm voice, Bell passed along the word to his men: "We stay." They fought off repeated Japanese forays, using up all of their grenades in the process. They were also short of ammunition and had to search their dead comrades for cartridges and clips. They carefully laid their bayonets within easy reach for the hand-to-hand struggle they felt sure would come.

One by one, the GIs were hit. As the day wore on, the bodies of the dead began to putrefy in the broiling heat. The wounded moaned with pain, but morphine supplies had long since been exhausted. Men with serious wounds insisted that their buddies prop them up and put their rifles in their hands so that they could fight when the Japanese attacked again.

In the late afternoon, help came. An officer and five men—the only remnants of a sizable relief force—crawled into Company E's perimeter. As the officer reached the edge of Lieutenant Bell's foxhole, he slumped dead with a sniper's bullet in his head. The men abandoned all hope of being rescued.

But they dared to hope again when a radio message informed Bell that a rescue party of 80 men was on the way to evacuate the wounded. On hearing this news, said Lieutenant Meiser, "the men took on new life. After enduring two days of this hell, anything was looked upon as a Godsend." As enemy fire slackened slightly toward 10 p.m., the litter carriers arrived. By 1 a.m. they had evacuated several walking wounded and 18 stretcher cases. Meiser remem-

Clambering cautiously down a slope with explosive charges in hand, a couple of GIs prepare to close the yawning maws of three caves on Okinawa. The dangerous undertaking of sealing shut a single system of interconnected caves frequently took a few days and usually required what Lieut. General Simon Bolivar Buckner Jr. called "blowtorch and corkscrew" tactics: Flame-throwing tanks provided the blowtorch, while dynamite charges and grenades served as the corkscrews.

bered that "a great worry was lifted off our minds and those remaining felt better, even though their predicament still seemed hopeless." The litter party had brought a small quantity of ammunition and water, but no reinforcements had yet arrived.

The GIs spent a second sleepless night. The next morning, May 19, enemy attacks and artillery fire resumed at full strength. Mortar fire cut down more men, and only accurate U.S. artillery support prevented the Japanese from forming ranks for an all-out attack. Before noon, a radio message came through informing Bell that a relief force would attempt to break through that night. Shortly afterward, the radio conked out, cutting all communication with supporting units. Bell's remaining men held on through that afternoon and that evening. But still no one came.

Then the impossible happened. At 10 p.m. on the third day, troops of a relief company from the 306th Regiment began to trickle in. As each replacement arrived, he was led through the darkness to a foxhole, and the weary, grime-caked occupant was given permission to withdraw.

By 3 a.m. on May 20, after Lieutenant Bell had briefed the new commander, the last group of Company E left Ishimmi

Ridge, carrying two newly wounded members of the relief force. The ordeal of Company E was finally over.

Back in American lines, the survivors gulped hot coffee and crawled into deep foxholes to catch their first sleep in 70 hours. "Shells might fall on us that night," said Meiser, "but anything over 25 yards distant would be considered miles away compared to previous experience." Of the 204 men who took Ishimmi Ridge on May 17, only 48 had come out unscathed on May 20; most of the rest were dead.

While Company E was making its gallant stand on Ishimmi Ridge, other elements of the 307th Regiment had assaulted an ugly pair of interlocking hill positions that the Americans had named Chocolate Drop and Flattop. By the 20th of May, both had fallen, and with them some of the artillery responsible for so many American casualties. In a spacious cave on the reverse slope of Chocolate Drop, GIs had captured four antitank guns, a field artillery piece, four heavy mortars and two light mortars.

To the east of the 77th Division's sector, Major General James L. Bradley's 96th Infantry Division came up against the eastern anchor of Ushijima's defense line: a 476-foot

peak that was known as Conical Hill. None of the American commanders expected an easy breakthrough here. They knew that Conical was defended by Ushijima's best troops, who were deeply dug in, and heavily armed with mortars and 75mm artillery pieces.

The burden of taking this bastion fell to Colonel Edwin May's 383rd Regiment. The most promising avenue of attack seemed to be from the west. But after two days of bitter fighting from this direction, May's 1st Battalion had hardly advanced. The 2nd Battalion, however, made unexpected progress from the north and by May 12 it had gained a foothold on Conical's forward slope. Elated at the possibility of a breakthrough by Bradley's 96th Division, the corps commander, General Hodge, told his staff: "We'll have the key to the Shuri Line if he can make it."

General Hodge had a tactical plan in mind. If the 96th Division could take and hold not only Conical but also Sugar Hill—a lesser hill only 800 yards to the south—Hodge could slip a division through the 800-yard corridor between the Conical defense system and Nakagusuku Bay to the east. Only 1,000 yards to the south lay the town of Yonabaru and the road leading west to Naha along which the Ameri-

cans could complete the encirclement of the Japanese positions from the rear.

The third day of Colonel May's attack on Conical Hill, May 13, was the turning point in the battle for Shuri. At 11 a.m., with General Buckner at his side, May sent two companies of his 2nd Battalion straight up Conical's steep northern face. Company F, followed by Company E, found the initial going so easy that the men did not stop until they had reached the shelter of some rocks halfway up the incline. There, two platoon sergeants decided to seize the initiative and drive all the way to the top. A few minutes later, without suffering a single casualty, they were digging in only 50 feet below Conical's crest.

While Company F was blazing a trail to the top, supporting tanks completed a two-day bombardment of Japanese positions on the north slope, forcing the defenders to seek shelter inside the deep caves on the reverse slope. The Japanese, emerging from their holes when the shelling ceased, mounted counterattacks over the crest of Conical and around the hill from the American left. The GIs of Company F checked both attacks. Then an American artillery observer, circling overhead in a "grasshopper," spotted

the enemy movements and called for fire support. A barrage of 4.2-inch mortar fire and artillery airbursts again drove the Japanese back to the shelter of their reverse-slope defenses. By early evening on May 13, Company F had been reinforced by Companies E and G. Colonel May now had a strong, battalion-size force holding a perimeter just below Conical's pointed peak.

For the next three days the three companies held off one counterattack after another. Each attack thinned their ranks and wore them down. Finally on May 17, they were relieved. The battalion that replaced them promptly pushed its way down a hogback ridge and after stiff fighting captured Sugar Hill on May 21.

With the eastern slopes of Conical and Sugar Hills cleared of enemy guns, the coastal corridor to Yonabaru now lay wide open. A vital chink had been cut in the enemy's armor. But the 10-day offensive against the eastern half of the Japanese defense line had cost the 96th Division 138 killed, 1,059 wounded and nine missing; the 77th Division had lost 239 dead, 1,212 wounded and 16 missing.

It was a high price, and in a propaganda broadcast Tokyo reminded the GIs of their losses with heavy irony. "Sugar Loaf Hill . . . Chocolate Drop . . . Strawberry Hill. Gee, these places sound wonderful! You can just see the candy houses with the white picket fences around them and the candy canes hanging from the trees, their red and white stripes glistening in the sun. But the only thing red about those places is the blood of Americans. Yes sir, those are the names of hills in southern Okinawa where the fighting's so close that you get down to bayonets and sometimes your bare fists. I guess it's natural to idealize the worst places with pretty names to make them seem less awful. They sound good, don't they? Only those who've been there know what they're really like."

General Hodge, with Buckner looking on, moved quickly to exploit the 96th Division's success at Conical Hill. On May 21 he brought down the 7th Infantry Division, which had been rested and resupplied since its battles at Hill 178 and Kochi Ridge. On the rainy night of May 22, one regiment of poncho-clad GIs, the 184th, marched south toward Yonabaru. According to plan, that regiment would secure the eastern end of the road to Naha, and then another regiment, the 32nd, would swing westward on the road and complete the encirclement of Shuri—a move that the planners called Checkmate.

The drive promised to be a speedy thrust. The division commander, Major General Archibald V. Arnold, had surveyed the terrain from a scout plane and decided that it was ideal tank country. For the first time on Okinawa, the tanks—standard and flamethrowers alike—would be able to blast and burn out the reverse slopes of Japanese ridges at the beginning of a battle rather than at the end.

But the tanks never left their assembly area near Skyline Ridge, one and a half miles in the rear. Okinawa's rainy season had swallowed up the front; the rains would continue with only brief breaks for almost two weeks, until June 5. In a single day, May 26, three and a half inches of rain soaked the ground, and by the end of the month the total rainfall measured nearly 12 inches.

Okinawa's roads were transformed into quagmires. The Shermans bogged down like so many steel dinosaurs, and trucks, jeeps and ambulances piled up in mile-long traffic jams. Wana Draw in the 1st Marine Division's sector turned into a lake of slime. Nothing moved but sodden, desultory patrols, and the American troops were completely at the mercy of the deep mud.

To make matters worse, the rain and the clouds curtailed aerial operations. Only rarely could planes take off from the Fifth Fleet's escort carriers and from the two airfields that had been reopened at Kadena and Yontan. The lack of aerial reconnaissance reports hurt the Americans on the very first day of heavy rainfall, May 22. General Buckner, forced to guess at what Ushijima and his Thirty-second Army were doing, told his staff that evening: "I think all Jap first-line troops are in the Shuri position. They don't appear to be falling back."

Buckner was wrong. That day, 150 conscripted Okinawan laborers had loaded ammunition and rations on 80 trucks at Japanese storage depots in Shuri. After dark, the column—light trucks with skillful daredevils driving—had pulled out onto the muddy roads and headed south, in the van of a massive Japanese withdrawal from the Shuri defense line.

Ushijima's grim decision to withdraw had been made the night before in the Japanese command bunker deep under Shuri Castle. The general and his staff realized that their

In an early-May rain signaling the start of the monsoon season, a truckload of Marines clad in ponchos plows toward the front through a morass of gooey mud. By the 21st of May, torrential downpours had transformed the roads into wheel-deep bogs and drowned all hope that any kind of dramatic advance could be made by the U.S. Tenth Army.

Shuri line could not hold out much longer, and though retreat was anathema according to their code, they hoped that the remaining 50,000 combat-effective troops would be better able to defend a smaller perimeter. "It was recognized that to stay would result in a quicker defeat," said Ushijima's planning officer, Colonel Yahara. "Consequently it was decided to retreat in accord with the Army policy of protracting the struggle as long as possible." The Army would pull back to the southern tip of the island and organize a new battle line behind another set of imposing ridges and escarpments.

The retreat was a brilliant feat of planning and logistics, executed under the most difficult conditions imaginable. The trucks carrying supplies and the wounded churned precariously along the inundated roads between Shuri and the Kiyamu peninsula to the south. Behind them came the walking wounded, tended by Okinawan nurses and clinging to guide ropes in the darkness. Next, the communications personnel moved out, followed by the armored forces and artillery units. The main combat formations and the Thirty-second Army headquarters staff brought up the rear.

Ushijima did not abandon his Shuri line all at once. To slow down the Americans and protect the rear, he left behind about one tenth of his army, 5,000 men. These troops fought hard against probing attacks around Shuri Castle, convincing U.S. intelligence officers that the Japanese still held the Shuri line in strength.

General Buckner did not get his first solid evidence of the evacuation until four days after it had begun. On May 26, during a brief break in the weather, carrier-based planes spotted and strafed heavy traffic on the roads south of Shuri, and the pilots reported that some of the individuals appeared to explode when hit, indicating that they were carrying ammunition.

Clearly the Japanese were on the move. The pilots' reports also contained the disturbing news that many of the people on the roads were dressed in white, not the dark uniforms of Japanese soldiers. Presumably the people in white were civilians, even though American psychological-warfare teams had showered southern Okinawa with leaflets urging civilians to stay clear of the soldiers so they would not be attacked by mistake. Or was it possible that the people in white were soldiers masquerading as civilians?

The American commanders decided reluctantly that it was a military necessity to shell the roads, and they so ordered. Within 13 minutes of the first sighting of heavy road traffic, the 8-inch main batteries of the cruiser *New Orleans* were blasting the slow-moving enemy column.

To the white-clad civilians, the bombardment proved that the Japanese propagandists were right when they said the Americans came bent on murder. The propaganda had initially served Japanese interests well: Many Okinawan men, fearing the American troops, had willingly labored for the Japanese. But now that the civilians were of little use to Ushijima, he ordered them to move to the relative safety of the Chinen peninsula on the east coast. Tragically, most civilians disobeyed Ushijima's instructions and clung to the Japanese for protection from the Americans. By the time the withdrawal ended, an estimated 15,000 civilians lay dead by the roadsides.

Ushijima's troops suffered as severely as the unfortunate civilians. Only 30,000 soldiers—two thirds of the troops who evacuated the Shuri line—reached the new line in the south. Nevertheless, Ushijima had been twice blessed by the monsoon-like rains. But for the muddy roads, the Americans might well have surrounded and wiped out Ushijima's army on the Shuri heights. But for the miserable flying weather, U.S. planes would have come close to destroying the army on the road.

On May 28 the rains abated just long enough for some revealing action on the drowned front. Tanks of the 6th Marine Division had entered the port of Naha against light resistance. A few Marines of the 1st Division, searching for a way out of Wana Draw, reported that the Shuri heights appeared less strongly defended than before. Early the next morning, a battalion of the 5th Regiment scaled the heights unopposed, and the amazed Marines found themselves only 800 yards from the enemy headquarters, which seemed to be quite empty.

Although the castle lay in the 77th Division's sector, it was captured by Captain Julian D. Dusenbury's Company A of the 5th Marine Regiment. Stealing a march on the soldiers, the leathernecks crossed the divisional boundary and pushed right into the castle at 10:15 a.m. on May 29. The occasion clearly called for a flag raising, but the only

Caught between the sea and the oncoming Marines on June 4, Japanese Navy men on the Oroku peninsula surrender to Lieutenant Glen Slaughter. Moments after this picture was taken, a Marine sergeant knocked Slaughter aside and threw away the live grenade that a Japanese was about to hand the lieutenant. The prisoner was attempting to take the whole group with him in what one observer called "poor man's hara-kiri."

flag that could be found was a Confederate banner that Dusenbury, a South Carolinian, carried in his helmet liner. So the stars and bars of the Confederacy went up to proclaim the fall of the Japanese Thirty-second Army headquarters. This irregular display caused a certain amount of uneasiness at Tenth Army headquarters, and the staff was relieved two days later when the commander of the 1st Division sent forward a proper flag—the one that his Marines had raised on Peleliu Island.

General Buckner now realized that the enemy was in full withdrawal, but not that he was too late to stop it. Still hoping to trap a large part of the Thirty-second Army on the roads south of Shuri, Buckner jubilantly told his staff on May 31, "Ushijima missed the boat on his withdrawal. It's all over now but clearing out pockets of resistance. This doesn't mean there won't still be stiff fighting, but the Japanese won't be able to organize another line."

By then, the Japanese had already organized their defense line on the Kiyamu peninsula. Ushijima, along with his staff chief, General Cho, and planning chief, Colonel Yahara, had set up the new Thirty-second Army headquarters in a roomy cave inside Hill 89, about 10 miles due south of Shuri. The line stretched about four miles across the Kiyamu peninsula, passing Hill 89 two miles to the north. On the east coast, the line was anchored on Hill 95, and on the west coast it terminated at Kunishi Ridge. Along Ushijima's new defense line rose two steep and forbidding escarpments, Yoza-dake and Yaeju-dake.

Ushijima prepared to make his last stand along this line; behind it, there were no more unbroken ranges of hills to defend. He issued a final general order to the remnants of his army: "The present position will be defended to the death, even to the last man."

American patrols continued to probe the thinned-out Japanese defenses around Shuri, and by June 1 their reports made it painfully clear to General Buckner that the main Japanese force had escaped. Hastily he revised his plans. The 77th Division would remain behind to mop up enemy rear guards at Shuri. Three other units—the 7th Infantry Division on the east coast, the 96th Infantry Division in the center and the 1st Marine Division on the west coast—would launch a hot pursuit of the retreating Japanese.

Even as Buckner drafted his new orders, the light rainfall of the past two days swelled once more into a torrential

downpour. The American tanks, still waiting for the swollen streams to recede enough to be bridged by the engineers, would have to wait longer. Nevertheless, Buckner put his infantrymen into motion, closing in as best they could on Ushijima's final defense line.

For the time being, there was only one objective that the Americans could attack with reasonable speed, unimpeded by the weather. The 6th Marine Division, which had been mopping up in the west-coast port of Naha, could make an amphibious landing on the Oroku peninsula, which lay just across the Kokuba estuary from Naha. The little peninsula, only three miles long and two miles wide, possessed one of Okinawa's biggest prizes, the Naha airfield. By taking Oroku, the Americans would also prevent Japanese raiding parties from harassing their operations farther south, and they would secure Naha harbor for incoming supplies needed in the forthcoming battles. On June 1, General Buckner ordered the III Amphibious Corps to invade the peninsula, and the corps ordered its 6th Division to mount the assault.

The Oroku peninsula was held by a hard-luck Japanese Naval unit whose commander, Admiral Minoru Ota, had no love for the Army. Part of his force, originally numbering 10,000 men and made up mostly of hastily trained Okinawan laborers, had been sent north to man torpedo boats and midget submarines. General Ushijima had thrown many of these men into the abortive May 4 counteroffensive, and they had suffered heavy casualties. Ota and his staff were thoroughly disenchanted with Army strategy.

Most of Ota's troops had withdrawn from the Shuri line with Ushijima's army in late May. But when they arrived at their designated southern position, many men found the terrain unfavorable and asked Admiral Ota to take them back north; they wanted to fight and die on their own base, including Naha airfield. Without consulting General Ushijima, Ota ordered his troops—now reduced to fewer than 5,000 men—to steal back north to Oroku even as the rest of the Japanese were finishing their retreat southward. On reaching Oroku on May 28, Ota's troops laid broad minefields and manned their large arsenal of light cannon and 8-inch coastal batteries. They trained the guns eastward toward the neck of the peninsula, where they were sure the 6th Marine Division would attack.

Their preparations played into the hands of the com-mander of the III Amphibious Corps, General Geiger, who planned to mount the invasion of Oroku by sea. Marines of the 6th Division would board amtracs at Naha, make a sweep toward the sea and then loop onto the northeast beaches near the town of Nishikoku—a journey of two miles intended to take the Japanese by surprise from the rear. In order to ensure a steady flow of reinforcements and provisions to the assault force on Oroku, the division commander, Major General Lemuel C. Shepherd, planned to capture the small island of Onoyama in the Kokuba estuary and to connect it by bridges to both shores.

Early on the morning of June 4, after enjoying their first cooked meal in weeks and a radio show rebroadcast from the States, Marines of the 4th and 29th Regiments gathered at the beacon lights that marked the line of departure. Only 72 amtracs could be mustered for the two regiments of troops; the rest of the corps's 400 landing vehicles were damaged or disabled by missing parts. At 6 a.m., after 4,300 shells had been fired by warships offshore and by the Marines' self-propelled assault guns at Naha, seven waves of assault landing craft churned toward their 600-yard stretch of invasion beach. The regiments met with only scattered sniping from the startled Japanese. By nightfall, the Marines were 1,500 yards inland and held a large part of the Naha airfield, now swampy and overgrown—and, they reported, "bombed and strafed to a mess of useless wreckage." The next day, Marine engineers threw two Bailey bridges across the estuary, one of them 340 feet long, the biggest ever built by Marines. Supplies immediately began flowing to Oroku.

For the next nine days, the 4th and 29th Marines, helped by the division's 22nd Regiment pinching in overland from the east, fought through terrain as rugged as on the Motobu peninsula in the north. They gradually realized that there were far more Japanese on Oroku than the 1,200 to 1,500 given in original intelligence estimates.

As usual, many Japanese fought from the mouths of fortified caves, and the Marines had to drive them back with flamethrowers, then seal the caves with satchel charges. Other defenders made devastating use of the big guns at their disposal, scoring hits on many tanks with their powerful naval guns and numerous light cannon. Improvising effectively, Japanese troops ripped cannon and machine guns out of the carcasses of wrecked planes and turned them on the advancing Americans. "Every Jap seemed to be armed with a machine gun," a Marine later said.

But the gallant Japanese fight stood no chance of success against the well-trained and aggressive Marines. On June 10, Ota sent a final message to the Army commander he had disobeyed. "Enemy tank groups are now attacking our cave headquarters," he told Ushijima. "The Naval Base Force is dying gloriously at this moment. We are grateful for your past kindnesses and pray for the success of the Army." Except for 200 men who surrendered, the 4,000 Japanese fought to the death, killing or wounding 1,608 U.S. Marines.

The Marines spent two days combing the cave labyrinth that had been Ota's headquarters. Among the piles of dead and dying Japanese they finally came upon the admiral and his five top aides. Their bodies were neatly lined up on blood-soaked mattresses. At their command, their throats had been neatly cut.

On June 5, the second day of the Oroku invasion, the heavy rains that had bogged down General Buckner's main force suddenly came to an end. With the flooded roads draining and drying, Army and Marine units—infantry and tanks together—slogged into position facing the last Japanese line of defense across the southern tip of Okinawa. By June 8, the lines were formed for a general attack.

The eastern anchor of the Japanese line was the target assigned to General Arnold's 7th Division. Arnold had little choice but to launch a frontal attack on the key Japanese position there, a long fortified rise that had been designated Hill 95; the strong point could not be outflanked, for its seaward side was a cliff that dropped 300 feet into the water, and its landward side sloped sharply into a valley interdicted by Japanese guns on the formidable Yaeju-dake escarpment to the west. After two days of hard fighting, the 7th Division had made scant progress toward the base of Hill 95. Heavy gunfire from caves on the rocky slope prevented a frontal assault.

Colonel John Finn, commander of the 32nd Regiment, looked for another way up the hill. Studying a steep 170-foot-high section of the hill, Finn saw the distant figures of surrendering Okinawans descending the slope on a narrow, zigzagging path. Concluding that Americans could just as easily climb that path, he sent for Captain Tony Niemeyer, commander of the 713th Armored Flamethrower Battalion's Company C. Niemeyer had been working over otherwise inaccessible areas with a new device, a long hose attached to the flame nozzle of a tank. Finn said that the flexible flamethrower had to be the answer to Hill 95.

On the morning of June 11, Niemeyer parked a flame tank at the foot of the hill in plain view of the enemy. With the help of an infantry platoon under Lieutenant Frank Davis, he began snaking a 200-foot length of hose up the slope along the zigzag path. The task took 45 long minutes, during much of which time the GIs were exposed to enemy fire from positions on the front slope. But heavy American fire from machine guns, mortars and tanks kept the Japanese in their holes and not a single GI was hit. Climbing to the crest in the midst of the enemy positions, Niemeyer lighted his elongated flamethrower and incinerated the Japanese below. By nightfall, infantrymen held a secure perimeter on the eastern rim of Hill 95, and the next day American tanks completed the job.

The capture of Hill 95 eased the work of the 17th Regiment, which for two days had been edging toward the 1,200-yard-long Yaeju-dake escarpment. The GIs had to cross a wet, exposed valley before they could get at the Japanese in the heights. Only a few men made it to the foot of the escarpment, crawling on their bellies through the waters of rice paddies.

General Arnold approved a regimental plan for a surprise night attack. Three companies began moving out at 3:30 a.m. on June 12 through a providential fog that reduced visibility to 10 feet. It took them two hours to reach the top of the escarpment. They found it undefended; the Japanese had evacuated the ridge, just for the night, to escape American artillery fire. The GIs prepared a warm welcome for the Japanese when they returned in the morning.

At daybreak, a platoon leader on the edge of the perimeter looked up and saw about 50 Japanese marching toward him two abreast. Immediately his men poured rifle fire into the column. It was a complete rout. Thirty-seven of the Japanese were mowed down on the spot, and the remainder ran for their lives. The eastern flank of Ushijima's line had collapsed.

West of the 7th Division, in the middle of the American

line, the 96th Division faced the most imposing terrain features in Ushijima's final wall. These were the main mass of Yaeju-dake, a series of cliffs and steep slopes 290 feet high, and the lower ridges of Yoza-dake to the southwest. For two days, two regiments of the 96th had tried to scale the face of Yaeju-dake's cliffs, sometimes under a smoke screen. They made some progress. One battalion got to the foot of the cliffs but was halted by small-arms fire coming down from some 500 cave openings in the face of the escarpment. In the end, the 7th Division's capture of the eastern end of the defense line furnished a solution.

On June 12, a company of the 96th circled eastward through the 7th Division's zone and on up to the crest of the escarpment. From there the GIs were able to fight westward until they were directly above their comrades at the foot of the cliffs. Working from above and from below, they began the dangerous drudgery of clearing the cliff face so that tanks and men could climb a road and an ancient stone stairway carved in the face of the cliff.

In addition to their usual arsenal of grenades, satchel charges and flamethrowers, the Americans employed a new weapon to clear the enemy caves and tunnels. It was a recoilless rifle—a lightweight, portable artillery piece that fired a shell somewhat in the manner of a bazooka, without the usual heavy bucking recoil. A number of the weapons—both 57mm and 75mm—had just arrived from Guam for test-firing under combat conditions. The rifles could be lugged into firing positions that tanks could not reach, and their flat-trajectory fire was much more effective against caves than high-angled mortar fire. The recoilless-rifle gunners were rapidly clearing the cliff's caves when they ran out of ammunition. It took the 96th Division through June 13 to complete the job by conventional means.

To the right of the 96th, the 1st Marine Division was then beginning a five-day operation aimed at taking Kunishi Ridge, the western anchor of Ushijima's last defense line. To reach the 2,000-yard-long coral barrier, the Marines first had to cross a flat, treeless valley that left men and tanks exposed to enemy machine-gun, mortar and antitank fire. Colonel Edward W. Snedeker, commander of the division's 7th Regiment, opted for a night attack, and by dawn on June 12, two companies reached the crest of Kunishi, surprising groups of Japanese as they cooked breakfast.

The Marines quickly dug in, and a fierce Japanese coun-

terattack soon hit the isolated companies on the top of the ridge. Responding to their calls for help, Snedeker sent reinforcements across the valley, but these troops were thrown back three times by withering machine-gun fire. So Snedeker improvised. He crammed reinforcements into nine tanks—six men to a tank. By late afternoon the tanks had crossed the valley and climbed the slope to the crest of Kunishi Ridge. There the 54 reinforcements scurried out escape hatches in the tank bottoms, while the tankers loaded 22 wounded Marines for the return trip.

Thus began a bitter, cave-by-cave battle to root the Japanese from their last major ridgeline on Okinawa. By the time it was over five days later, Snedeker's tanks had made dozens of daylight dashes to the ridge, feeding some 90 tons of supplies and 550 reinforcements into the fight. In the course of these missions, 21 tanks were damaged or destroyed by enemy artillery fire. But many Marines owed their lives to the tankers' courageous taxi service. When the 7th Regiment was finally relieved on June 18, the tanks had evacuated 1,150 casualties.

The unit that took over the battle was the 8th Regiment of the 2nd Marine Division, which had been in the original invasion force but had been optimistically returned to its Saipan base without landing. The 8th had been brought back to speed up the interminable, grinding land campaign. The newcomers went into action on June 18, and General Buckner himself climbed to an observation post on Mezado Ridge to watch.

Buckner had come a long, hard way to the threshold of success. But as he gazed out over the battlefield, the blind chance of war denied him his victory. Five enemy shells landed nearby in quick succession. Buckner fell mortally wounded and died before he could be evacuated to a hospital. Not one of the officers surrounding Buckner was even scratched.

The battle ground on. General Geiger, boss of the III Amphibious Corps, took over command, and by the end of the day, Ushijima's surviving men were bottled up in less than eight square miles of the Kiyamu peninsula. Only a few isolated pockets of resistance remained: Hill 89, the site of Ushijima's headquarters; the Medeera-Makabe area, where remnants of the 24th Division were clinging to Hill 85; and the Ara-saki area at Okinawa's southernmost tip, where

Exhausted after 30 days at the front, grimy GIs from the 96th Division catch a few winks on June 10 behind a protective embankment in southern Okinawa. Before them lay another 10 days of grueling combat for Yoza-dake, a coral peak in the last Japanese defense system.

At the southwestern tip of Okinawa, General Buckner (right) witnesses an attack by the 8th Marine Regiment on June 18. Moments later, an enemy shell splintered the rock near Buckner and drove a sharp fragment into his chest. He died within minutes—the highest ranking officer killed in combat in the Pacific.

motley units were desperately holding on. The Japanese fought on for two days more, with the Americans steadily squeezing them into smaller and smaller perimeters.

On June 20, a regiment of the U.S. 7th Division reached the flat top of Hill 89. Resistance was still strong, and flame-throwing tanks used nearly 5,000 gallons of napalm to burn snipers and mortarmen out of the coral crevices of the seaside hill. Now all that remained to be conquered was the command cave, which had entrances on the landward and seaward sides of the hill. A Japanese officer taken prisoner by the 7th Division volunteered to approach the cave and to offer Ushijima one last chance to surrender. The prisoner went forward to the landward cave mouth. But as he called his message into the entrance, a Japanese demolition crew inside blew the cave shut.

Inside the cave, Ushijima was not surprised by the Americans' invitation to surrender. It was the second such suggestion he had received. An air-dropped letter from General Buckner had reached him a few days before, on June 17. "The forces under your command have fought bravely and well," Buckner had said, "and your infantry tactics have merited the respect of your opponents. Like myself, you are an infantry general long schooled and practiced in infantry warfare. I believe, therefore, that you understand as clearly as I that the destruction of all Japanese resistance on the island is merely a matter of days."

Ushijima had read the letter and passed it to his chief of staff, General Cho. Then, recalled Cho's secretary Akira Shimada, "Cho and Ushijima both laughed and declared that, as samurai, it would not be consonant with their honor to entertain such a proposal."

On his last night, Ushijima ordered his cook to prepare a special dinner, then radioed a final message to Imperial Headquarters in Tokyo. Colonel Yahara, the cool, solemn strategist, asked his superior for permission to join in his final act. Ushijima refused, saying, "If you die there will be no one left who knows the truth about the battle of Okinawa. Bear the temporary shame but endure it. This is an order from your Army commander." Yahara would obey and fall prisoner to the Americans.

At 10 p.m. Ushijima and Cho sat down to an elaborate meal of rice, salmon, canned meats, potatoes, fried fish cakes, bean-curd soup, fresh cabbage, pineapples, tea and sake. After dinner, the generals and their staff exchanged

numerous toasts with Scotch whisky, which Cho had carried from Shuri Castle.

Then, at 4 a.m. on June 22, both Ushijima and Cho began preparations for their suicide. A Japanese prisoner, who learned the details of their deaths from witnesses, wrote an account of the generals' last moments: "Four o'clock, the final hour of hara-kiri: the commanding general, dressed in full field uniform, and the chief of staff, in a white kimono, appeared. The chief of staff says as he leaves the cave first, 'Well, Commanding General Ushijima, as the way may be dark, I, Cho, will lead the way.' The commanding general replies, 'Please do so, and I'll take along my fan since it is getting warm.' Saying this, he picked up an Okinawan-made Kuba fan and walked out quietly fanning himself.

"These are calm minds that face death. The generals passing before the row of their subordinates give the air of immortals walking by.

"The moon, which had been shining until now, sinks below the waves of the western sea. Dawn has not yet arrived, and at 4:10 a.m. the generals appeared at the mouth of the cave. Four meters from the mouth, a sheet of white cloth is placed on a quilt. This is the ritual place for the two generals to commit hara-kiri.

"The commanding general and the chief of staff sit down on the quilt, bow in reverence toward the eastern sky, and Adjutant J respectfully presents the sword. At this time several grenades were hurled near this solemn scene by the enemy troops who observed movements taking place beneath them."

Unperturbed by these explosions, the two generals calmly proceeded with the prescribed ritual. Each man bared his stomach for disembowelment by a ceremonial knife, at the same time bowing his head for decapitation by the adjutant's drawn saber. According to the Japanese prisoner's account, the end came quickly. "A simultaneous shout and a flash of a sword, then another repeated shout and a flash, and both generals had nobly accomplished their last duty to their Emperor."

The day of Ushijima's death, June 22, marked the end of organized Japanese resistance on Okinawa. The two remaining pockets, Hill 85 and the Ara-saki area, had fallen to regiments of the 77th Infantry and 6th Marine Divisions. To solemnize the official end of the campaign, General Geiger raised the American flag over his headquarters near the Kadena airfield.

There still remained 10 days of mopping up—the perilous task of rounding up Japanese stragglers, thwarting prisoners who tried to blow up themselves and their captors with grenades, checking out overlooked caves and tunnels, killing bypassed soldiers who refused to surrender.

When Graves Registration teams had finally completed counting all the bodies, the figures told a story that came as no surprise to the fighting men: Okinawa had been the bloodiest land battle of the Pacific war. The Japanese had lost approximately 110,000 killed and 10,755 taken prisoner during the 83-day land struggle for the island. The victory on Okinawa had cost the Army and Marines 7,613 killed and missing, 31,807 wounded and 26,211 other casualties, most of them victims of combat fatigue. Added to these losses were heavy casualties among sailors and Naval aviators who had provided more than three months of supply, air and artillery support for the land operations. Kamikaze attacks and conventional air strikes had killed 4,320 and wounded 7,312 Naval personnel.

The terrible cost of the Okinawa campaign—coming on top of the 26,000 casualties on Iwo Jima—provoked cries of outrage from influential American journalists, who laid the blame on "ultraconservative tactics." General Douglas MacArthur, who had conducted most of his Pacific campaigns with remarkably little loss of life, joined the controversy, accusing Admiral Nimitz' command of "sacrificing thousands of American soldiers because they insisted on driving the Japanese off the island" instead of cordoning off southern Okinawa and letting the enemy troops there wither on the vine.

But whatever the cost of Okinawa to the Americans, the loss of the island was a savage blow to the Japanese. In Tokyo, the recently formed government of Prime Minister Kantaro Suzuki was stunned by the defeat. "The Prime Minister now admitted that the war situation was far worse than he thought," reported veteran diplomat Mamoru Shigemitsu. "Okinawa left little room for doubt as to the outcome of the war." In fact, Okinawa had made it possible for the Japanese officials to seriously contemplate what had once been the unthinkable: the possibility of sending out peace feelers.

Great mounds of brass artillery shell casings await salvage at Yonabaru on June 27, 1945, five days after the battle for Okinawa ended. During the campaign, U.S. field guns fired 1,766,352 rounds in support of the troops—more than were fired by Americans in any other Pacific campaign.

HARD-WON HAVEN FOR B-29s

With Mount Suribachi in the background, a B-24 Liberator takes off from Iwo Jima past a crippled B-29 Superfort that crash-landed after bombing Japan.

"ROCKY'S WAYSIDE SERVICE STATION"

Almost every day during the spring and summer of 1945, the B-29 Superforts returning from night raids on Japan met the dawn over Iwo Jima, the halfway mark on the 1,300-mile journey back to their bases in the Marianas. And there, on the main runway of Iwo's Airfield No. 2, Major Charles A. "Rocky" Stone was always waiting to meet B-29s coming in for refueling or emergency landings. "In a jeep, Rocky rides herd on these monsters that come piling out of the dawn sky," wrote a reporter for *Impact,* a classified Army Air Forces journal. "There is the feeling of haste and strain. The big boys have dropped out of the race and everyone on Iwo Jima is hurrying to get them back in it again."

Major Stone, a crusty, tobacco-chewing taskmaster, was chief of B-29 maintenance of what *Impact* called "Rocky's Wayside Service Station" and the "busiest little air base in the world." Like "sparrows pecking at eagles," Stone's men swarmed over wounded B-29s and decided their fate: quick repairs for those that could make it home; thorough overhauls for some; the spare-parts heap for others. Rocky's crews rebuilt hundreds of shot-up Superforts and patched up hundreds more.

The B-29s' need for emergency landing strips had been the primary reason for the U.S. invasion of Iwo Jima on February 19. Even before the fighting ended, some 7,000 Seabees were at work expanding the three battle-scarred Japanese airfields, and by early July they had built a 9,800-foot main runway at Airfield No. 2 and a 6,000-foot airstrip at Airfield No. 1. Besides serving as an invaluable refuge for crippled B-29s, these installations were home base for an air-sea rescue team and for the fighter squadrons that escorted the Superforts.

Aircrews in trouble came to rely on Iwo, knowing they could find help there for the wounded—men and machines alike. And the high price paid to capture the island—the lives of some 7,000 American fighting men—brought a return with compound interest. More than 24,000 B-29 crewmen who might have been lost in the Pacific were saved by Rocky's Wayside Service Station.

Boss mechanic Rocky Stone (right) confers with an aide. Stone reportedly got his job by telling a superior, "Your maintenance section stinks."

With a joyful wave, Sergeant John Gander, a tail gunner, signals that all's well after his severely flak-damaged B-29 managed to land safely on Iwo Jima.

Prevented by heavy fog from landing on Iwo Jima, a B-29 lies in shallow water off the beach after the crew was forced to ditch and swim to the shore.

An airman peers into a B-29 ripped open in flight by a shattered propeller.

As two ground crewmen take shelter behind a jeep, a crash-landing B-29 is

Repair crews inspect a Superfort that missed its landing, rammed a truck, killed a Seabee and injured two men before being halted by an embankment.

consumed by flames. Before sluing to a halt, the bomber demolished four parked P-51s, one of which can be seen crumpled up against the starboard engines.

The tail fin of a B-29 wreck is hauled off for use on a bomber whose own tail was cut off by a Kamikaze.

INGENIOUS SALVAGERS AND QUICK-CHANGE ARTISTS

Nothing went to waste on Iwo. Rocky's 286 overworked mechanics, unable to rely on supply shipments from the States, ransacked each wrecked B-29 and salvaged any of its 55,000 parts that could be used in the rehabilitation of other Superforts for the continuing bombing raids on the Japanese home islands.

When one of the four huge 18-cylinder Wright Cyclone engines on a crashed B-29 was in working order, it was reconditioned and stockpiled. If an engine and its housing were too badly broken up to be rebuilt, the sound parts were cannibalized to replace the twisted propellers, flak-riddled nacelles and punctured fuel lines of otherwise airworthy engines.

Iwo's resourceful mechanics worked furiously to repair the battle-damaged B-29s and get the bombers back into the air. A top crew could replace an engine in less than a day. "The good engines scarcely jerk to a halt," said one astonished witness, "before mechanics begin tearing out the bad one, and a new engine is already on its way from the shop."

A ground crewman guides a crane to one of

hundreds of battle-damaged B-29 engines stacked up at Airfield No. 2 to be dismantled for spare parts. Rocky's mechanics often had to fashion parts and tools.

Wing tip to wing tip, Superforts crowd the flight line at Iwo's Airfield No. 2 after a night raid on Japan. "It was profoundly inspiring," wrote one of the men

who helped to build the field, "to see hundreds of these mighty bombers coming in to land or to see two-mile-long columns of them lined up for refueling."

BIBLIOGRAPHY

Adams, Henry H., *Years to Victory*. David McKay Co., 1973.

Aurthur, Robert A., and Kenneth Cohlmia, *The Third Marine Division*. Ed. by Robert T. Vance. Infantry Journal Press, 1948.

Bartley, Whitman S., *Iwo Jima: Amphibious Epic*. Historical Branch, U.S. Marine Corps, 1954.

Belote, James and William, *Typhoon of Steel: The Battle for Okinawa*. Harper & Row, 1970.

Bergamini, David, *Japan's Imperial Conspiracy*, Vol. 2. William Morrow and Co., 1971.

Bishop, Jim, *FDR's Last Year, April 1944-April 1945*. William Morrow and Co., 1974.

Brown, David Tucker, Jr., *Marine from Virginia*. University of North Carolina Press, 1947.

Buell, Thomas B., *The Quiet Warrior: A Biography of Admiral Raymond A. Spruance*. Little, Brown, 1974.

Building the Navy's Bases in World War II (History of the Bureau of Yards and Docks and the Civil Engineer Corps 1940-1946), Vol. 2. U.S. Government Printing Office, 1947.

Burns, James MacGregor, *Roosevelt: The Soldier of Freedom*. Harcourt Brace Jovanovich, 1970.

The Campaigns of the Pacific War: United States Strategic Bombing Survey (Pacific). Naval Analysis Division, 1946.

Carter, Worrall Reed, *Beans, Bullets and Black Oil: The Story of Fleet Logistics Afloat in the Pacific during World War II*. Division of Naval Records and History, U.S. Navy, 1952.

Cass, Bevan G., ed., *History of the Sixth Marine Division*. Infantry Journal Press, 1948.

Chapin, John C., *The Fifth Marine Division in World War II*. Historical Division, U.S. Marine Corps, 1945.

Churchill, Winston S., *Triumph and Tragedy*. Bantam Books, 1953.

Craven, Wesley Frank, and James Lea Cate, eds., *The Army Air Forces in World War II*, Vol. 5, *The Pacific: Matterhorn to Nagasaki, June 1944 to August 1945*. University of Chicago Press, 1953.

"Cult of the Kamikazes." *Purnell's History of the Second World War*, No. 89. B.P.C. Publishing Ltd. (London), 1976.

Davidson, Orlando R., J. Carl Willems and Joseph A. Kahl, *The Deadeyes: The Story of the 96th Infantry Division*. Infantry Journal Press, 1947.

Dull, Paul S., *A Battle History of the Imperial Japanese Navy (1941-1945)*. Naval Institute Press, 1978.

The 81st Wildcat Division Historical Committee, *The 81st Infantry Wildcat Division in World War II*. Infantry Journal Press, 1948.

Fane, Francis Douglas, and Don Moore, *The Naked Warriors*. Appleton-Century-Crofts, 1956.

Forrestel, Emmet P., *Admiral Raymond A. Spruance, USN: A Study in Command*. Government Printing Office, 1966.

Frank, Benis M., *Okinawa: Capstone to Victory*. Ballantine Books, 1969.

Greenfield, Kent Roberts, ed., *Command Decisions*. Office of the Chief of Military History, Department of the Army, 1960.

Halsey, William F., and J. Bryan III, *Admiral Halsey's Story*. McGraw-Hill Book Co., 1947.

Henri, Raymond:
  Iwo Jima: Springboard to Final Victory. U.S. Camera (World Publishing Co.) 1945.
  The U.S. Marines on Iwo Jima. Dial Press, 1945.

Higgins, Edward T., *Webfooted Warriors*. Exposition Press, 1955.

History of the U.S. Marine Corps Operations in World War II, Historical Division, U.S. Marine Corps:
  Frank, Benis M., and Henry I. Shaw Jr., *Victory and Occupation*, 1968.
  Garand, George W., and Truman R. Strobridge, *Western Pacific Operations*, 1971.

Hough, Frank O., *The Island War*. J. B. Lippincott Co., 1947.

Hoyt, Edwin P., *How They Won the War in the Pacific: Nimitz and His Admirals*. Weybright and Talley, 1970.

The Imperial Japanese Navy in World War II. Military History Section, Special Staff, General Headquarters, Far East Command, 1952.

Inoguchi, Rikihei, and Tadashi Nakajima, *The Divine Wind: Japan's Kamikaze Force in World War II*. U.S. Naval Institute, 1958.

Isely, Jeter A., and Philip A. Crowl, *The U.S. Marines and Amphibious War*. Princeton University Press, 1951.

Ito, Masanori, *The End of the Imperial Japanese Navy*. Transl. by Andrew Y. Kuroda and Roger Pineau. W. W. Norton & Co., 1956.

The Japanese Navy in World War II. U.S. Naval Institute Proceedings, 1969.

Karig, Walter, Russell L. Harris and Frank A. Manson, *Battle Report: Victory in the Pacific*. Rinehart and Co., 1949.

Kirby, S. Woodburn, *The War against Japan*, Vol. 5, *The Surrender of Japan*. Her Majesty's Stationery Office (London), 1969.

Leahy, William D., *I Was There*. McGraw-Hill Book Co., 1950.

Liddell Hart, B. H., *History of the Second World War*. G. P. Putnam's Sons, 1971.

Love, Edmund G.:
  The Hourglass: A History of the 7th Infantry Division in World War II. Infantry Journal Press, 1950.
  The 27th Infantry Division in World War II. Infantry Journal Press, 1949.

McMillan, George, *The Old Breed: A History of the First Marine Division in World War II*. Infantry Journal Press, 1949.

Martin, Ralph G., *The GI War: 1941-1945*. Little, Brown, 1967.

Matthews, Allen, R., *The Assault*. Simon and Schuster, 1947.

Merrill, James M., *A Sailor's Admiral: A Biography of William F. Halsey*. Thomas Y. Crowell Co., 1976.

Millot, Bernard, *Divine Thunder: The Life and Death of the Kamikazes*. Transl. by Lowell Bair. McCall Publishing Co., 1970.

Moran, Lord, *Churchill: Taken from the Diaries of Lord Moran*. Norman S. Berg, 1976.

Morehouse, Clifford P., *The Iwo Jima Operation*. Historical Division, U.S. Marine Corps, no date.

Morison, Samuel Eliot:
  History of United States Naval Operations in World War II, Vol. 12, *Leyte, June 1944-January 1945*. Little, Brown, 1970.
  History of United States Naval Operations in World War II, Vol. 14, *Victory in the Pacific, 1945*. Little, Brown, 1975.
  The Two-Ocean War. Little, Brown, 1963.

Naval Chronology, World War II. U.S. Government Printing Office, 1955.

Newcomb, Richard F., *Iwo Jima*. Holt, Rinehart and Winston, 1965.

Nichols, Charles S., Jr., *Okinawa: Victory in the Pacific*. Charles E. Tuttle Co., 1955.

O'Callahan, Joseph Timothy, *I Was Chaplain on the Franklin*. Macmillan, 1956.

Ours to Hold It High: The History of the 77th Infantry Division in World War II. Infantry Journal Press, 1947.

Pater, Alan F., ed., *United States Battleships: The History of America's Greatest Fighting Fleet*. Monitor Book Co., 1968.

Pogue, Forrest C., *George C. Marshall: Organizer of Victory*. Viking Press, 1973.

Potter, E. B., *Nimitz*. Naval Institute Press, 1976.

Potter, E. B., ed., *Sea Power*. Prentice-Hall, 1960.

Pyle, Ernie, *Last Chapter*. Henry Holt and Co., 1946.

Reynolds, Clark G., *The Fast Carriers: The Forging of an Air Navy*. McGraw-Hill Book Co., 1968.

Roscoe, Theodore, *United States Destroyer Operations in World War II*. U.S. Naval Institute, 1953.

Roskill, S. W., *The War at Sea, 1939-1945*, Vol. 3, *The Offensive, Part II, 1st June 1944—14th August 1945*. Her Majesty's Stationery Office (London), 1961.

Sambito, William J., *A History of Marine Fighter Attack Squadron 312*. History and Museums Division, U.S. Marine Corps, 1978.

Shaw, Henry I., Jr., and Ralph W. Donnelly, *Blacks in the Marine Corps*. History and Museums Division, U.S. Marine Corps, 1975.

Sherrod, Robert:
  History of Marine Corps Aviation in World War II. Combat Forces Press, 1952.
  On to Westward: War in the Central Pacific. Duell, Sloan and Pearce, 1945.

Shigemitsu, Mamoru, *Japan and Her Destiny: My Struggle for Peace*. Ed. by F. S. G. Piggott and transl. by Oswald White. E. P. Dutton & Co., 1958.

Smith, Holland M., and Percy Finch, *Coral and Brass*. Charles Scribner's Sons, 1949.

Taylor, Theodore, *The Magnificent Mitscher*. W. W. Norton and Co., 1954.

Toland, John, *The Rising Sun: The Decline and Fall of the Japanese Empire, 1936-1945*. Random House, 1970.

United States Army in World War II, Office of the Chief of Military History, U.S. Army:
  Appleman, Roy E., James M. Burns, Russell A. Gugeler and John Stevens, *Okinawa: The Last Battle*, 1948.
  Bykofsky, Joseph, and Harold Larson, *The Transportation Corps: Operations Overseas*, 1957.
  Cline, Ray S., *Washington Command Post: The Operations Division*, 1951.
  Coakley, Robert W., and Richard M. Leighton, *Global Logistics and Strategy: 1943-1945*, 1968.
  Dod, Karl C., *The Corps of Engineers: The War against Japan*, 1966.
  Lee, Ulysses, *The Employment of Negro Troops*, 1966.

The U.S.S. Bunker Hill, November 1943-November 1944. Published by and for the personnel of the U.S.S. Bunker Hill at sea, 1944.

Vian, Sir Philip, *Action This Day: A War Memoir*. Frederick Muller Ltd. (London), 1960.

Wheeler, Keith, *We Are the Wounded*. E. P. Dutton & Co., 1945.

Wheeler, Richard, *The Bloody Battle for Suribachi*. Thomas Y. Crowell Co., 1965.

Winton, John, *The Forgotten Fleet: The British Navy in the Pacific, 1944-1945*. Coward-McCann, 1970.

Yank—the GI Story of the War. Yank magazine. Duell, Sloan & Pearce, 1947.

ACKNOWLEDGMENTS

For help given in the preparation of this book the editors wish to express their gratitude to Dr. Dean C. Allard Jr., Director, Operational Archives Branch, Naval History Division, Washington Navy Yard, Washington, D.C.; Dr. Fred Beck, Deputy Chief, Corps of Engineers, Historical Division, Washington, D.C.; Dana Bell, Archives Technician, U.S. Air Force Still Photo Depository, Arlington, Va.; Master Sergeant Thaddeus E. Bugay, Historian, Research Branch, Albert F. Simpson Historical Research Center, USAF, Maxwell Air Force Base, Montgomery, Ala.; Admiral Arleigh A. Burke, USN (Ret.), Bethesda, Md.; George Chalou, Assistant Branch Chief, Washington National Records Center, Suitland, Md.; George W. Craig, Supervisory Archives Technician, Photographic Archives, Marine Corps History and Museums Division, Washington Navy Yard, Washington, D.C.; Dan Crawford, History and Museums Division, Headquarters, U.S. Marine Corps, Washington, D.C.; Robert Cressman, Naval Historical Center, Washington Navy Yard, Washington, D.C.; Colonel T. M. D'Andrea, Marine Corps Aviation Museum, U.S. Marine Corps Base, Quantico, Va.; V. M. Destefano, Chief of Research Library, U.S. Army Audio-Visual Activity, Pentagon, Arlington, Va.; James N. Eastman Jr., Chief, Research Branch, Albert F. Simpson Historical Research Center, USAF, Maxwell Air Force Base, Montgomery, Ala.; Benis Frank, History and Museums Division, Headquarters, U.S. Marine Corps, Washington, D.C.; Hiroshi Funasaka, Tokyo; Charles R. Haberlein Jr., Photographic Section, Curator Branch, Naval History Division, Department of the Navy, Washington Navy Yard, Washington, D.C.; William Heindahl, Archivist, Office of Air Force History, Bolling Air Force Base, Washington, D.C.; Christopher Henderson, Indian Head, Md.; Dr. Kiro Honjo, Yokosuka, Japan; Agnes F. Hoover, Photographic Section, Curator Branch, Naval History Division, Department of the Navy, Washington Navy Yard, Washington, D.C.; Colonel Mikio Kuga, Embassy of Japan, Washington, D.C.; William H. Leary, Archivist, National Archives, Still Photo Branch, Washington, D.C.; Louis R. Lowery, *Leatherneck* magazine, Quantico, Va.; Raymond Mann, Naval Historical Center, Washington Navy Yard, Washington, D.C.; Vice Admiral William Martin, USN (Ret.), Alexandria, Va.; Satoshi Mizoguchi, Musashino, Japan; Toshio Morimatsu, Tokyo; Richard Newcomb, South Yarmouth, Mass.; Colonel F. B. Nihart, USMC Historical Center, Washington Navy Yard, Washington, D.C.; Frederick Pernell, Archivist, Reference Branch, General Archives Division, National Archives, Washington, D.C.; Captain Roger Pineau, USN (Ret.), Bethesda, Md.; John C. Reilly, Ships' Histories Branch, Naval History Division, Department of the Navy, Washington Navy Yard, Washington, D.C.; Joseph J. Rosenthal, *San Francisco Chronicle*, San Francisco, Calif.; Hiroshi Sekine, Ibaragi, Japan; Henry Shaw, Chief Historian, Marine Corps History and Museums Division, Washington Navy Yard, Washington, D.C.; Lieut. Colonel Roy M. Stanley, USAF, Fairfax, Va.; Regina Strothers, Film Library Assistant, Photographic Archives, Marine Corps History and Museums Division, Washington Navy Yard, Washington, D.C.; Kengo Tominaga, Tokyo; Dr. Vincent A. Transano, Historical Information Bureau, Naval Construction Battalion Center, Port Hueneme, Calif.; James H. Trimble, Archivist, National Archives, Still Photo Branch, Washington, D.C.; Lieut. Colonel Kenneth Walsh, USMC (Ret.), Santa Ana, Calif.; Lieutenant Miles Wiley, Deputy Chief, Magazines and Books Division, Air Force Service Information and News Center, San Antonio, Tex.; Edmund T. Wooldridge Jr., Associate Curator, Aeronautics, National Air and Space Museum, Smithsonian Institution, Washington, D.C.

The index for this book was prepared by Nicholas J. Anthony.

PICTURE CREDITS   *Credits from left to right are separated by semicolons, from top to bottom by dashes.*

COVER and page 1: U.S. Marine Corps.

THE FLEET'S ATTACK BASE—6, 7: U.S. Navy, National Archives. 8: Map by Elie Sabban. 9-17: U.S. Navy, National Archives.

MASTER PLAN FOR INVASION—20: United Press International. 22: Map by Elie Sabban. 25: U.S. Navy, National Archives. 26: Library of Congress—courtesy Mr. & Mrs. W. John Kenney. 28: Defense Intelligence Agency.

TARGET FOR THE LIBERATORS—30-32: U.S. Air Force. 33: Defense Intelligence Agency. 34-39: U.S. Air Force.

BRUTAL BATTLE FOR IWO JIMA—42: Military History Institute of Japan Defense Agency. 43: Drawing by Yasuo Kato, Yokohama—drawing by Mr. Hiroshi Funasaka and Mr. Hiroshi Sekine, Japan. 44: U.S. Marine Corps. 45: Map by Elie Sabban. 47: U.S. Coast Guard, National Archives. 48: U.S. Navy, National Archives. 51: U.S. Marine Corps. 52: W. Eugene Smith for *Life*. 54: United Press International.

TO THE TOP OF SURIBACHI—58, 59: U.S. Navy, National Archives. 60, 61: U.S. Marine Corps. 62, 63: Lou Lowery. 64, 65: U.S. Marine Corps. 66-69: Lou Lowery. 70-71: Lou Lowery; U.S. Marine Corps. 72, 73: Wide World.

BOLD FORAYS BY THE FLEET—76-81: U.S. Navy, National Archives. 82, 83: U.S. Navy.

PLAYGROUND IN THE PACIFIC—86-95: U.S. Navy, National Archives.

ASSAULT ON OKINAWA—98: U.S. Navy, National Archives. 99: Map by Elie Sabban. 100: U.S. Navy, National Archives. 101: Map by Elie Sabban. 102: Military History Institute of Japan Defense Agency. 104, 105: J. R. Eyerman for *Life*. 106: U.S. Marine Corps—U.S. Army. 108: U.S. Navy, National Archives—Defense Intelligence Agency. 111: U.S. Army.

SLUGFEST ON A RUGGED RIDGE—114-125: W. Eugene Smith for *Life*.

THE HOMELESS ISLANDERS—126, 127: U.S. Marine Corps. 128: U.S. Navy, National Archives. 129: U.S. Marine Corps. 130: U.S. Navy, National Archives—U.S. Marine Corps. 131: J. R. Eyerman for *Life*. 132: U.S. Navy, National Archives. 133: J. R. Eyerman for *Life*; W. Eugene Smith for *Life*—U.S. Navy, National Archives. 134, 135: U.S. Marine Corps; U.S. Navy, National Archives. 136: J. R. Eyerman for *Life*—W. Eugene Smith for *Life*. 137: J. R. Eyerman for *Life*—U.S. Navy, National Archives. 138, 139: U.S. Army.

ORDEAL BY KAMIKAZE—143: U.S. Navy, National Archives. 144, 145: Art by John Batchelor, London. 147: Courtesy Lieut. Colonel Kenneth A. Walsh, USMC (Ret.), copied by Fil Hunter. 148: U.S. Navy, National Archives. 151: U.S. Navy, National Archives.

SUICIDE OF A BATTLESHIP—154, 155: Imperial War Museum, London. 156: U.S. Navy, National Archives. 157: Defense Intelligence Agency. 158, 159: U.S. Navy, National Archives. 160, 161: Map by Elie Sabban; U.S. Navy, National Archives. 162, 163: U.S. Navy, National Archives.

THE BUNKER HILL'S AGONY—164-175: U.S. Navy, National Archives.

USHIJIMA'S SAVAGE RETREAT—179: Map by Elie Sabban. 180: U.S. Air Force. 183: Wide World. 184, 187: U.S. Marine Corps. 190: Wide World. 191: U.S. Marine Corps. 192: U.S. Army.

HARD-WON HAVEN FOR B-29s—194, 195: W. Eugene Smith for *Life*. 196-203: U.S. Air Force.